# Quilting

# Dress, Body, Culture

Series Editor: **Joanne B. Eicher**, *Regents' Professor, University of Minnesota*

Advisory Board:
**Ruth Barnes**, *Ashmolean Museum, University of Oxford*
**James Hall**, *University of Illinois at Chicago*
**Ted Polhemus**, *Curator, "Street Style" Exhibition, Victoria and Albert Museum*
**Griselda Pollock**, *University of Leeds*
**Valerie Steele**, *The Museum at the Fashion Institute of Technology*
**Lou Taylor**, *University of Brighton*
**John Wright**, *University of Minnesota*

Books in this provocative series seek to articulate the connections between culture and dress, which is defined here in its broadest possible sense as any modification or supplement to the body. Interdisciplinary in approach, the series highlights the dialogue between identity and dress, cosmetics, coiffure, and body alternations as manifested in practices as varied as plastic surgery, tattooing, and ritual scarification. The series aims, in particular, to analyze the meaning of dress in relation to popular culture and gender issues and includes works grounded in anthropology, sociology, history, art history, literature, and folklore.

ISSN: 1360-466X

Previously published in the series

Helen Bradley Foster, *"New Raiments of Self": African American Clothing in the Antebellum South*
Claudine Griggs, *S/he: Changing Sex and Changing Clothes*
**Michaele Thurgood Haynes**, *Dressing Up Debutantes: Pageantry and Glitz in Texas*
**Anne Brydon and Sandra Niessen**, *Consuming Fashion: Adorning the Transnational Body*
Dani Cavallaro and Alexandra Warwick, **Fashioning the Frame: Boundaries, Dress and the Body**
Judith Perani and Norma H. Wolff, **Cloth, Dress and Art Patronage in Africa**
Linda B. Arthur, **Religion, Dress and the Body**
**Paul Jobling**, *Fashion Spreads: Word and Image in Fashion Photography*
Fadwa El Guindi, **Veil: Modesty, Privacy and Resistance**
**Thomas S. Abler**, *Hinterland Warriors and Military Dress: European Empires and Exotic Uniforms*
Linda Welters, **Folk Dress in Europe and Anatolia: Beliefs about Protection and Fertility**
Kim K.P. Johnson and Sharron J. Lennon, **Appearance and Power**
Barbara Burman, **The Culture of Sewing**
Annette Lynch, **Dress, Gender and Cultural Change**
Antonia Young, **Women Who Become Men**
**David Muggleton**, *Inside Subculture: The Postmodern Meaning of Style*
**Nicola White**, *Reconstructing Italian Fashion: America and the Development of the Italian Fashion Industry*
**Brian J. McVeigh**, *Wearing Ideology: The Uniformity of Self-Presentation in Japan*
**Shaun Cole**, *Don We Now Our Gay Apparel: Gay Men's Dress in the Twentieth Century*
**Kate Ince**, *Orlan: Millennial Female*
**Nicola White and Ian Griffiths**, *The Fashion Business: Theory, Practice, Image*
Ali Guy, Eileen Green, and Maura Banim, **Through the Wardrobe: Women's Relationships with their Clothes**
Linda B. Arthur, *Undressing Religion: Commitment and Conversion from a Cross-Cultural Perspective*
**William J.F. Keenan**, *Dressed to Impress: Looking the Part*
Joanne Entwistle and Elizabeth Wilson, *Body Dressing*
Leigh Summers, *Bound to Please: A History of the Victorian Corset*
Paul Hodkinson, *Goth: Identity, Style and Subculture*
Michael Carter, *Fashion Classics from Carlyle to Barthes*
Sandra Niessen, Ann Marie Leshkowich, and Carla Jones, *Re-Orienting Fashion: The Globalization of Asian Dress*
Kim K.P. Johnson, Susan J. Torntore, and Joanne B. Eicher, *Fashion Foundations: Early Writings on Fashion and Dress*
Helen Bradley Foster and Donald Clay Johnson, *Wedding Dress Across Cultures*
Eugenia Paulicelli, *Fashion under Fascism: Beyond the Black Shirt*
Charlotte Suthrell, *Unzipping Gender: Sex, Cross-Dressing and Culture*
Yuniya Kawamura, *The Japanese Revolution in Paris Fashion*
Ruth Barcan, *Nudity: A Cultural Anatomy*
Samantha Holland, *Alternative Femininities: Body, Age and Identity*
Alexandra Palmer and Hazel Clark, *Old Clothes, New Looks: Second Hand Fashion*
Yuniya Kawamura, *Fashion-ology: An Introduction to Fashion Studies*
Regina A. Root, *The Latin American Fashion Reader*
Linda Welters and Patricia A. Cunningham, *Twentieth-Century American Fashion*
Jennifer Craik, *Uniforms Exposed: From Conformity to Transgression*
Alison L. Goodrum, *The National Fabric: Fashion, Britishness, Globalization*
Annette Lynch and Mitchell D. Strauss, *Changing Fashion: A Critical Introduction to Trend Analysis and Meaning*

# Quilting

*The*
*Fabric*
*of*
*Everyday*
*Life*

## Marybeth C. Stalp

Oxford • New York

English edition
First published in 2007 by
**Berg**
Editorial offices:
First Floor, Angel Court, 81 St Clements Street, Oxford OX4 1AW, UK
175 Fifth Avenue, New York, NY 10010, USA

Berg is the imprint of Oxford International Publishers Ltd.

**Library of Congress Cataloging-in-Publication Data**
Stalp, Marybeth C.
   Quilting: the fabric of everyday life/Marybeth C. Stalp. —
English ed.
      p.  cm.
   Includes bibliographical references and index.
   ISBN-13: 978-1-84520-654-3 (cloth)
   ISBN-10: 1-84520-654-1 (cloth)
   ISBN-13: 978-1-84520-655-0 (pbk.)
   ISBN-10: 1-84520-655-X (pbk.)
   1. Quilting—Anecdotes. 2. Quilting—Psychological aspects. I.
Title.

   TT835.S6852 2007
   746.46—dc22                                     2007039259

**British Library Cataloguing-in-Publication Data**
A catalogue record for this book is available from the British Library.

ISBN   978 1 84520 654 3 (Cloth)
       978 1 84520 655 0 (Paper)

Typeset by Avocet Typeset, Chilton, Aylesbury, Bucks
Printed in the United Kingdom by Biddles Ltd, King's Lynn

**www.bergpublishers.com**

# CONTENTS

Acknowledgments    vii

List of Illustrations    xi

1. Introduction: Why Quilting?    1

2. Tripping through the Tulips: Doing Research Close to Home    27

3. It's Not Just for Grannies Anymore: Learning to Quilt at Midlife    49

4. The Guilty Pleasures of the Fabric Stash    77

5. Quilt Rhymes with Guilt: Finding the Time and Space to Quilt    95

6. Coming Out of the Closet: Quilting is for Self and for Others    111

7. Piecing it All Together    129

References    141

Index    153

# ACKNOWLEDGMENTS

Like I tell my students, most individual accomplishments are actually shared endeavors, and this book is no exception – I had lots of help and support along the way, although I take sole credit for any and all errors. I am first indebted greatly to the women quilters who participated in the study, for without them, this research would never have happened. Not only did these women agree to talk with me about their quilting experiences, but they also let me into their lives, their kitchens, their living rooms, and their quilting spaces. Through their generosity, they helped me to understand how and why quilting is an important and meaningful activity in their lives. I am thankful to all the quilters that I encountered during this research, both those who participated officially in the study as well as those women I met in more casual encounters: quilt shows, fabric shops, museum exhibits, and quilting groups. Thanks also to the quilters and knitters I spent time with in the last few places I have lived while working on this project. This includes Stitch 'n Bitch in Athens, GA, Tuesday Night Strippers and Saturday Knitters in Gunnison, CO, and Stitch 'n Bitch in Cedar Falls, IA.

My dissertation committee at the University of Georgia guided me through the research and writing process. Thanks especially to Linda Grant and Barry Schwartz who collectively co-chaired my committee and provided wisdom, guidance, and support. Committee members Jim Dowd, Reuben May, Patricia Bell-Scott, and Janice Simon contributed greatly to the dissertation. Their marked experience and insightful questions kept me focused, yet open to the range of interdisciplinary applicability to which this work speaks.

There are a select few people who when you meet them, they change your life in immense and positive ways – this was my immediate experience in meeting Joanne Eicher in September 2005. Joanne saw the potential of my quilting research immediately, and her support and encouragement have been invaluable. Working with Joanne, the editor of the Dress, Body, Culture series at Berg Publishers, has been fabulous. Additionally, working with Berg has allowed me to meet some incredible people. Assistant Editor Hannah Shakespeare continually provided me with encouraging feedback throughout the entire writing and editing process, and models well what an editor can be. I was also able to work with Emily Medcalf, the Sales and Marketing Assistant, who, along with Hannah, helped with the book cover. My experience with Berg Publishers has been entirely positive.

I benefited from much needed and appreciated financial assistance in the writing of this book. In 2006 I received the University of Northern Iowa's College of Social and Behavioral Sciences Summer Research Grant, which allowed me to devote my summer months to composing and editing book chapters. Christine Twait and the Office of Sponsored Programs at the University of Northern Iowa assisted with grant writing to subsidize the color plates in the book. To produce the color plates, I received financial assistance from both the Quilter's Guild of Dallas and Dean Julia Wallace of the College of Social and Behavioral Sciences at the University of Northern Iowa. My thanks also go to Yvonne Duggan, the College of Social and Behavioral Sciences' office manager. I owe a huge thanks to my uber-talented quilting friend, Pattiy Torno, for making the beautiful quilt that dons the cover of this book and for granting permission for use of the image, which was photographed by Michael Mauney, and assembled as a cover by Berg.

I have been privileged to have an incredible local and global support system, not just for this project, but throughout my academic career. Martie Reineke encouraged me to draft the book proposal and start the book before I felt ready to do so, and Theresa Winge has been a constant support and fabulous friend, and also introduced me to Joanne Eicher and Berg Publishers. Thanks also to Phyllis Baker, Kim Knesting, Kristin Mack, Susan Hill, Susan Allbee, Gayle Rhineberger-Dunn, Cyndi Dunn, Ana Kogl, Gowri Betrabet-Guwaldi, Elise Radina, Annette Lynch, Maria Tapias, Xavier Escandell, Jen Gaukler, Thomas Bilstad, Courtney Fullmer, and Heather Thiessen-Reily for encouragement on the project and reading drafts when needed. Denise Copelton, Gayle Sulik, Beth Tracton-Bishop, and Stephanie Nawyn have read more drafts of the book than they ever deserved to, and thanks to Tracy Thibodeau, Kerri Smith, Cherise Harris, Kelly Manley, Michallene McDaniel, Sigrid Ballanfonte, Jane Wilson, Nicole Ortmeier, and Pattiy Torno for being supportive and always having a listening ear, and/or shoulder upon which to cry. The summer of 2006 was quite a successful writing period for me, with special thanks to Theresa, Bill, and Kim for our precious summer writing sessions, and thanks to Brian at Cottonwood Canyon for a quiet space to hide out and write all summer. Thanks also to Department Head Kent Sandstrom who provided support for this project, to Betty Heine, the Sociology, Anthropology, and Criminology department office manager, and the graduate and undergraduate students who assisted with various tasks related to assembling the manuscript, including Rachel Williams, Catherine Fruehling-Wall, Kate Niman, Micaela Ring, and Mari Longoria. Thanks to Mark Dobie, computer technician extraordinaire in the College of Social and Behavioral Sciences, and to Barb Weeg and Rosemary Meany at Rod Library for locating hard to find but necessary items and granting regularly my odd interlibrary loan requests.

Chapters 3, 4, and 5 are based on journal articles published previously. For permission to include this material I would like to thank the respective journals. Chapter 3 is an expansion of, "Creating an Artistic Self: Amateur Quilters and Subjective Careers," which appeared in 2006 in *Sociological Focus* 39(3): 193–216. Chapter 4 stems from the 2006 article, "Hiding the (Fabric) Stash: Fabric Collecting, Hoarding, and Hiding Strategies of Contemporary U.S. Quilters," which appeared in *Textile: The Journal of Cloth & Culture* 4(1): 100–121. Finally, Chapter 5 originally derived from the 2006 article, "Negotiating Time and Space for Serious Leisure: Quilting in the Modern U.S. Home" in the *Journal of Leisure Research* 38(1): 104–132. Thanks to Leslie for the use of the poem in Chapter 6.

As always, I am forever grateful to my parents, Paul and Mary Clare Stalp, for continually prioritizing and supporting my professional pursuits. I am thankful to my sisters and to their respective spouses for giving me the space I need to work, and specifically to my siblings' spouses for every once in a while offering our family's gaggle of drama queens some much needed perspective. I am also ever grateful to my late and youngest sister, Stacey, who is typically present in the back of my mind, pushing me daily to find importance in what I do. I hope to be part of the passing down of sewing, quilting, and knitting skills to my nieces so that they too can benefit from growing up in a supportive and creative community.

I dedicate this book to the women and men who have kept the art of quilting alive and well in the world. Specifically, I include those quilters in my life who have passed on and who have shaped my thinking about quilting and its importance in women's lives: Genevieve Meiergerd (my Aunt Jenny), who taught me how to quilt, Sharon Kreikemeier, who was an expert machine quilter, fabulous hairdresser and friend, and my youngest sister, Stacey Lynn Stalp, who not only accomplished a great deal of quilting in her young life cut tragically short, but who had more than her share of a dry and wicked sense of humor, which I continue to appreciate to this day.

Marybeth C. Stalp
*Cedar Falls, IA*

# LIST OF ILLUSTRATIONS

## PLATES

| | |
|---|---|
| 1 | My first quilt, 1991. |
| 2 | "The Last Straw," down position, 1999. |
| 3 | "The Last Straw," up position, 1999. |
| 4 | "Sue Does Hoops," 2001. |
| 5 | "Sue Does Music," 2001. |
| 6 | "Oh Shit!" |
| 7 | Kelly's sewing space. |
| 8 | Loretta's design wall. |
| 9 | Judy's brother's quilt. |
| 10 | "You've got a bug on you." |
| 11 | Traditional craft learning. |
| 12 | "Dissertation Quilt: Vampire Quilt," 2001. |
| 13 | "Red 9/11 quilt," 2001. |
| 14 | "Black 9/11 quilt," 2001. |
| 15 | "Theresa's fabric stash by color." |
| 16 | Quilt shop sign. |
| 17 | Bumper sticker. |
| 18 | Storefront of Ginny's Fine Fabrics and Support Group, 2006. |
| 19 | Karen's quilt room. |
| 20 | Angela's quilt room. |
| 21 | Sewing room, 2006. |
| 22 | Sarah's frog quilt. |
| 23 | Sarah's frog quilt, close-up 1. |
| 24 | Sarah's frog quilt, close-up 2. |
| 25 | Emma's anger quilt. |
| 26 | Leslie's divorce quilt. |
| 27 | Henry on his baby quilt. |
| 28 | Deven and Derek enjoying their new quilts. |
| 29 | A weekend quilting retreat. |
| 30 | Caleb and his quilt. |

## FIGURES

| | | |
|---|---|---|
| 1.1 | Quilt used as furniture pad 1. | 2 |
| 1.2 | Quilt used as furniture pad 2. | 3 |
| 1.3 | Quilt as furniture pad, close-up. | 4 |
| 1.4 | Quilt show (quilts hung vertically as art). | 11 |
| 1.5 | Fabric sandwich. | 15 |
| 1.6 | Agricultural worker quilting in the sewing room, 1942. | 15 |
| 1.7 | Making a quilt in a Scranton, IA, home, 1940. | 16 |
| 1.8 | Members of the women's club making quilt. Granger Homesteads, IA, 1940. | 16 |
| 1.9 | Sarah's quilts on the clothesline. | 17 |
| 1.10 | Barn Quilt Project, Grundy County, IA: Bakker "Eight Pointed Star." | 18 |
| 1.11 | Barn Quilt Project, Grundy County, IA: Kitzman "County Fair." | 19 |
| 1.12 | Barn Quilt Project, Grundy County, IA: Nason "Windmill." | 19 |
| 2.1 | Church group, quilting in the rectory basement. | 34 |
| 2.2 | First quilting experience. | 38 |
| 2.3 | Kim's quilt frame in the kitchen. | 39 |
| 4.1 | Eileen's fabric stash hidden away. | 79 |
| 4.2 | "Feed your addictions," The Sow's Ear. | 81 |
| 4.3 | "The Quiltmaker's Will." | 85 |
| 6.1 | Mom's embroidery clock. | 112 |
| 6.2 | Mom's embroidery clock, close-up. | 113 |

# 1 INTRODUCTION: WHY QUILTING?

## WHY QUILTING (AND QUILTS) MATTER...

I was having lunch with a good friend, downtown during spring break in 2006. Coincidentally enough, we had just left the post office where I had mailed off the contract for this book and we were celebrating by treating ourselves to lunch downtown. We were in a local delicatessen where the second floor was being renovated, so it was not very busy. While we were lunching leisurely and chatting, I was surprised to see a quilt above my friend's head. The quilt was hanging from the outside window upstairs, and was being used to cover/protect the awning from renovation debris. It was a traditional quilt with a white background and a flying geese pattern on the border. Other than that, I could not see much of the quilt. I found myself a bit annoyed that the quilt was being misused as a furniture pad, covered with debris, instead of being used on a bed – but I reminded myself that this was not my quilt or how I would have used it. I had learned through my research how quilts can be political/cultural objects with multiple meanings – here was the evidence in front of me – in this case specifically, one person's art was another person's furniture pad. And, knowing that quilters often have great sentimentality attached to the quilts that they make and also often take great offense when their gifted quilts are not used as they intended, I wondered what the quilter might think if s/he saw how this quilt was being used, as I imagine that most quilters do not envision during the time- and labor-intensive quilting process, that their quilts will eventually be used as furniture pads. I wanted to get a picture of the quilt for the book to show how quilts can be political/cultural objects with multiple meanings. But, I did not have my camera with me, what to do? As my friend and I were paying our lunch bills, I asked our server if I could take a picture of the quilt for my book. She said yes, and off we went to buy a disposable camera from the local camera shop.

On the way, my friend and I talked about quilts and how they sometimes get (mis)used in everyday ways like this, and how it is kind of unusual to see evidence of it in public. I usually see quilts being "mistreated" at home by myself or other family members, but not this badly and not in public, and I could not believe that this quilt had not yet been rescued by someone, as this restaurant is on the main street of the downtown shopping district. I do know of people, mostly avid quilt collectors, who regularly "rescue" quilts from situations like these. They keep a pile of cheap blankets and/or quilts made in global sweatshops and sold at discount stores in their car trunks, and whenever they see a quilt that they feel is being "mistreated" they try to buy the quilt from the owner or trade them a blanket to mis/use instead. Note that

FIG. 1.1. Quilt used as furniture pad 1. Personal photograph.

store-bought quilts from discount stores created in global sweatshops are not considered by quilt collectors or quilt rescuers (or much of the global quilt world) to be the
equivalent of a handmade quilt, yet both are given the same name of "quilt" – it gets
quite complicated once you really start to think about it. Anyway, to my surprise, this
type of quilt rescue had not yet happened to this traditional quilt being used as a
furniture pad, and I wondered why.

As my friend and I walked back to the delicatessen I began to take pictures of the
quilt from a variety of angles. I was under the awning taking a picture amidst falling
debris, when out of the corner of my eye I saw a young man walking by. I could only
see the bright blue of his shirt and a dust mask on his face – my first thought was,
"what is a surgeon doing here?" I walked around the truck and met up with a young
Amish man, dressed in a blue shirt and black vest and pants, a black brimmed hat,
and a dust mask pulled down, which was resting on his chin. He was standing in the
flatbed of the truck. We said hello and I asked him if he knew anything about the
quilt and if it would be alright to take pictures of it. He said that the quilt was there
when he arrived, and that someone else must have put it there, and that we could
come back later and ask about the quilt. At first, I think he took me to be a quilt
collector wanting to buy Amish quilts – but I explained that I was writing a book and
just wanted a picture. Also, this quilt did not look traditionally Amish, as it had a
light background and included a variety of print fabrics, so the quilt most likely was
not Amish, and belonged to the construction company or the building owner.

FIG. I.2. Quilt used as furniture pad 2. Personal photograph.

After taking pictures, I asked this young Amish man if he would take a picture of the quilt, as he was closer to the quilt than I was. Although I was pretty sure that I could get in and out of the truck just fine, I thought that I might not be allowed to do that. So he agreed to take the pictures and to prevent me from entering the truck. However, I was conflicted about asking him to take the pictures. I really wanted images of this quilt/furniture pad for the book, but here I was asking a young Amish man to disregard his precarious relationship to technology just to get these images for me. I resolved the issue when I recalled that I was in a part of the U.S. where there were numerous Amish construction companies that regularly used electronic equipment. Apparently this is fine as long as they do not themselves own the equipment. My frenzied actions to get images of the quilt were not entirely absolved though, as it was clear that he did not know how to use the camera. But, with some basic instruction from me, he eventually figured it out and took some great pictures of the quilt. I said thanks, and we left, though I was concerned about how my excitement about the quilt overtook my judgment, which I choose to believe is typically sound.

FIG. 1.3. Quilt as furniture pad, close-up. Personal photograph.

My overexcitement about how this quilt was being mis/used during a spring break lunch, among many other reasons, is why I wrote this book. But, seriously, what does asking a young Amish man to take a picture of a quilt being mis/used as a furniture pad have to do with this book? Well, nothing, really, but this story illustrates how quilts are complicated, have multiple meanings, and can be political. When I stop to think about it, it is fine that the quilt was being used to protect an awning, that it was covered in debris, that I photographed it (with the help of the young Amish man), that I did not rescue it, and that it may never be rescued. Additionally, it is fine if it does get rescued and preserved and is used on a bed or hung up on a wall in a home or in a museum if that is the owner's wish.

Quilts are complicated cultural objects, embedded with many meanings for many people. They can inspire confusion and potentially bad judgment (as was my reaction to this situation); celebration and joy in quilts made for newborn babies, weddings, and wedding anniversaries; excitement and fascination at newly found quilts as is the case with the Gee's Bend quilts of rural Alabama; anger and sorrow in quilt panels made for the AIDS quilt, and the like. And, quilts are just the finished cultural objects. The *process* of quilting is even more complicated, as it involves the creation, reception, and use of these complex cultural objects.

I also wrote this book because I have been talking for years with women quilters who shared their experiences with me about the process of producing quilts for personal enjoyment and for gift giving. According to them, quilting has unexpectedly changed their adult lives, for it has allowed them to make creative space and time for themselves. Quilting has revealed to many women the complicated and sometimes problematic gender dynamics within their households, which some women are not at all happy about, and are certainly not happy when I point this out through my research findings.

In the social sciences, we know that women and men in the U.S. are socialized from childhood to "do gender" (West and Zimmerman 1987) appropriately (e.g., in accordance with gender expectations) throughout the life course (Adler et al. 1992; Goffman 1976; Lucal 1999; Thorne 1997). This means that families are gendered institutions, requiring at times different behavior from women and men. Midlife women (aged forty to sixty years) within traditionally gendered families choose to take care of others instead of themselves – this is sort of a taken for granted assumption about our societal expectations for wives and moms, and multitasking for the family has simply become a way of life for many women. It is no surprise, then, that some midlife women finding that as their children leave home, they have more time for themselves, choose to learn how to quilt. Women learn to quilt in gendered ways – they negotiate their quilting interests as ways to take care of their family members and friends, rather than the more controversial reason of women finally allowing themselves to express their personal creativity at midlife, *after* the needs of the family have been met.

Midlife women in the U.S. take up quilting for individual reasons, such as personal enjoyment, gift giving, and creating family heirlooms. As women quilt more intensely and more consistently on their own time, they develop personally derived standards for setting goals and measuring their success, independent of the judgments of friends, family, or the economy. Quilting becomes an important means of autonomy and identity development for midlife women, even as they practice a somewhat old-fashioned process of cultural production traditionally defined (often pejoratively) as "women's work." As these women engage in quilting, they are caring for others in making gifts, and preserving family traditions, also known as women's work. Women's work can then be understood as unpaid carework for others.

I present quilting in this study as a form of gendered cultural production. This statement might not seem at all alarming, except when considering the research traditions this study is built upon. With this research, I suggest a rethinking of culture and gender research and make two important contributions to sociological knowledge and theoretical development. First, most culture research is not examined through a gender lens but instead is considered universal, and not gender-laden. Second, most of women's activities, when examined by gender scholars, are considered relevant because they are important to the economic sphere. My research combines both of these research traditions. Within this study quilting is done by women outside the economic sphere, and is viewed conscious of how women "do quilting" as *women*. That is, women quilt in gendered ways, by incorporating quilting into their family activities, and make quilts as gifts for others, indicative of how they care for others often before themselves. Thus, quilting is affected by gender, and by being a private and non-economic activity.

The development of this theoretical frame includes research in identity development, subjective measures of success in quilting, family, leisure, and carework. Women gain a complex understanding of themselves as cultural producers through quilting, and they turn to quilting to escape other family carework duties that are expected but often unappreciated. Other forms of attending to the emotional needs of others (e.g., cooking family meals, driving children to leisure activities) leave little evidence of women's regular carework for themselves and for others. Even other gendered leisure escapes for women, like reading romance novels and participating in book clubs, do not leave tangible evidence of their activities. Quilting instead leaves a finished product – a quilt which can link the maker with the recipient in sentimental ways. In addition to producing a tangible object and often gifting the finished product to a friend or family member, the creative process of quilting is personally fulfilling. The quilting process provides women the opportunity to engage in leisure, produce something tangible, and document physically and visually the carework that they engage in for others. Through this creative carework process, quilters strengthen their identities as women and as cultural producers, and make connections with other women in their local and global quilting communities. They also have created cultural products that document the process of quilting over time, which is rich in both personal and social history. Together, these arguments build to understanding quilting as a form of gendered cultural production.

*Quilting: The Fabric of Everyday Life* focuses on the recent global phenomenon of quilting (also known as patchwork). As a form of women's leisure, quilting reveals much about the modern U.S. family and the modern midlife woman's everyday struggles in finding time and space for herself. Within the past generation (thirty years or so), quilting has become an international multibillion-dollar industry. I examine one of the main audiences that made the current proliferation of quilting possible – U.S. women who learned to quilt at midlife. These women have been driving the current development of the quilting industry, and have used their checkbooks to nod approval to advances in quilting equipment, fabric development, shows/contests, quilt-related tours and cruises, extensive classes, and books and magazines that began in the mid 1970s. This book is based on seventy in-depth interviews with U.S. midlife quilters and four years of ethnographic fieldwork in the U.S.

## THE (RECENT) GLOBAL QUILTING PHENOMENON

Although currently enjoying a global resurgence in interest, quilting techniques and their everyday use are anything but new. In fact, the first image of quilting dates back to the thirty-fifth century B.C., in an Egyptian ivory carving depicting "the king of the Egyptian First Dynasty wearing a mantle/cloak that appears to be quilted" (Colby 1971). Quilting techniques have been used widely over time, including Chinese silk bedcovers from the Eastern Zhou dynasty from 770–221 B.C. (Liddell and Watanabe 1991), Mongolian carpets in the first century (Colby 1971), European bedcovers in the fourteenth and fifteenth centuries (Berenson 1996; Colby 1971; Von Gwinner 1988), quilted clothing for Japanese royalty (Liddell and Watanabe

1991), and Irish military clothing (Colby 1971), both in the sixteenth century. The actual quilted bedcovers with which we are familiar survive in oldest physical form in Britain, with a seventeenth-century "dated, crewel embroidered quilt" (*Quilt Treasures of Great Britain* 1995), whereas the first "North American-made patchwork quilt" was made in the eighteenth century and is housed in Montreal (Beaudoin-Ross 1979–1980) and the earliest surviving American-made quilt, also in the eighteenth century, was made in Maine (Bassett and Larkin 1998). The eighteenth century also produced a Swedish wedding quilt with "embroidered silk patches" (Wettre 1995), as well as Norwegian (Foster 2002) and German quilts (Von Gwinner 1988). Clearly, from this abridged list of uses, quilting has been part of our global history for much longer than we may realize (International Quilt Study Center 2006).

Specifically, Euro-American quilting traditions and techniques reached the U.S. from European nations by way of immigration patterns. As white ethnics "settled" the U.S., women used European patchwork techniques to make a variety of quilts in commemoration of their experiences in the New World. In the 1800s, women constructed friendship quilts and gave them as gifts to friends who were leaving the northeast for western territories (Lipsett 1985). The friendship quilt is one of many examples of quilting patterns developing specific meanings, and the friendship quilt is still used in contemporary times to connect wedding guests to a newly married couple, when guests sign fabric at the reception, and a quilt is made including all the guests' names.

Traditional quilting patterns in U.S. history have been constructed to carry with them specific and sometimes mythical meaning, and some quilt patterns carry multiple names as they were carried across the country during western expansion (Brackman 1997). For example, one of the most well-known, oft cited, and contro-versial quilting myths is that the color schemes of the quilt patterns known both as Log Cabin and Underground Railroad were carefully manipulated for easier identifi-cation of safehouses of the Underground Railroad, or implicit political support for abolition in the American South (Brackman 1997; Freeman 1996; Von Gwinner 1988). In contrast, the Drunkard's Path quilt pattern was created by and associated with supporters of the Temperance Movement, and was constructed purposefully with the Women's Christian Temperance Union's organizational colors of blue and white (Jenkins and Seward 1991). Quilting traditions have become rooted in U.S. heritage, and can be seen as independent of their European patchwork beginnings in terms of social meaning.

Although African American, Native American, and Latina women were part of the passing down of quilting, the industry's publishing and advertising markets do not usually consider them explicitly as foremothers of quilting (for exceptions see Freeman 1996; Fry 1990). Additionally, the history of African American quilting does not necessarily fall into the artistic categories of many of the current quilt competitions and shows nationwide. Collins (1991:89) discusses the differing approaches to quilting from the African American and European American artistic perspectives:

the symmetry in African-American quilts does not come from uniformity as it does in Euro-American quilts. Rather, symmetry comes from diversity [and] individual uniqueness that enhances the overall "beauty" of the group. Using such criteria, no individual is inherently beautiful because beauty is not a state of being. Instead beauty is always being defined in a context as a state of becoming.

The quilting of African American women and other women of color is not presented as central to U.S. quilt history in comparison to white ethnic women's historical and contemporary quilting efforts. The absence of women of color as cultural producers in quilting history results in the systematic neglect of the audience of women of color in the quilting industry, as well as in historical analysis of quilting. Quilt history is complicated, many historical and contemporary quilts are anonymously credited, and women's quilting efforts have not been thoroughly documented. Fry (1990) has documented numerous instances in which quilts were passed off as being made entirely by white plantation owners' wives in the southern U.S.; in actuality, former women house slaves made quilts, and taught quilting techniques to both women of color and white women. Research on African American quilting traditions as well as women of color is beneficial as it brings to light a more inclusive albeit somewhat controversial history of U.S. quilting practices (Benberry 1993; Freeman 1996; Fry 1990). Quilting literature deviating from the white ethnic norm is often written on a more academic level, such as the analysis of slave quilts (Fry 1990), or the political impetus behind the construction of specific quilts (Friedlich 1991; Williams 1990, 1994). And, as many of these books are written at an academic level rather than an instructive level for quilters, they are not as likely to reach or have an impact on a general quilting audience as industry magazines and books.

Women have been quilting steadily through the nation's history, and a renewed interest in quilting surfaced in the U.S. during preparations for the Bicentennial anniversary in 1976 (Gunn 1992). This was the nation's bicentennial as well as a pivotal crossroads in determining women's roles in the context of the second wave of the women's movement begun in the 1960s. Scholars consider the post-Bicentennial interest in quilting as controversial (Cerny 1991; Crothers 1993; Gunn 1984, 1992). Some see the resurgence of "feminine" or "domestic" activities such as quilting, knitting, and embroidery as a pastoral attempt to recapture the trappings of femininity, and as complying with the politically conservative backlash against women. Others argue that quilting and other feminine activities are the base construct of women's social networks, and are actually spaces of agency and empowerment, for these networks "provide mutual support within a context of 'warmth and emotional openness'" (Cerny 1991: 35; also see Stalp and Winge 2006). Furthermore, they posit that feminine activities such as quilting are not compliant with patriarchal domination, but constitute a separate sphere of existence outside the male-dominated mainstream.

Popular sentiment constructs current quilters as sharing characteristics with their colonial-era ancestors. According to our social memory regarding quilting, women dutifully and resourcefully sewed together clothing fabric scraps to keep families warm. Despite this idealized notion of quilting as purely functional and resourceful, women took great pride in sewing beautiful quilts for their families, even purchasing new fabric specifically to make clothes and quilts. Sewing for the family during earlier times certainly was much more of a necessity than it is today, and regardless of whether or not women enjoyed sewing, their efforts contributed to fulfilling the family's needs. Pleasure and pride in producing items of aesthetic worth have typically been part of sewing and quilting. These women-centered activities were likely accorded more status and prestige when deemed essential for family survival.

During wartime in the U.S. (e.g., Civil War, First and Second World Wars), the state taught and encouraged sewing and other handcrafts such as knitting. Specifically during the World Wars, educational institutions taught children (both boys and girls) to knit and repair soldiers' wool socks, scheduling a daily knitting period during the school day to support the war (Macdonald 1988). Burman (1999) found this also to be the case in England during wartime, while Kelly (1987) and Nelson, LaBat, and Williams (2002, 2005) note state-supported handcrafts in Ireland even outside of wartime. During wartime, learning a handcraft such as knitting was seen as contributing something vital to the nation.

In the U.S., during the Great Depression, farm women recycled cloth sacks formerly holding livestock feed and food staples (e.g., flour, sugar) into clothes and household items for the family (e.g., curtains, dishcloths, towels). Companies constructed cloth sacks from pre-printed fabric to meet women's clothing-construction needs, and to increase the appeal of their product: "The reuse of the cotton-sack fabric became more desirable when feed-sack manufacturers offered a wide variety of attractive sack prints by the end of the 1930s" (Rhoades 1997: 122). Two sacks, apparently, provided enough yardage for a woman's dress. Women sent their husbands and sons back to town if they bought feed sacks with mismatching fabric (fieldnotes 1999). Handcrafts were once again viewed as essential for the well-being of families during difficult economic times.

Americans living through the Great Depression and the Second World War associated homemade goods with memories of economic suffering. Once the U.S. began its post-war economic upswing, the availability of ready-made goods increased, including pre-made blankets and clothing. Families soon replaced homemade goods with store-bought goods. In this era, many quilts were simply thrown away in exchange for manufactured blankets, and, soon after, electric blankets (Brackman 1997). As Sarah told me, "There are a couple of family quilts in my family but my aunt told me that when they were able to buy blankets that they threw the quilts away because they were moving up, they didn't have to have that handmade stuff anymore." Quilting has transformed from a necessity during colonial times to a contemporary form of serious leisure (Stalp 1998; Stebbins 1996, 1979). Valentine (2000: 1) elaborates upon the changing meaning surrounding quilts and quilting: "At one time, quilts provided necessary protection from cold weather, piled high on the bed to provide wintertime warmth when the household fires were banked low for the night. With today's heated bedrooms and insulated dwellings, patchwork quilts often fulfill a more symbolic than utilitarian role, adding a homey atmosphere to the modern environment." Sewing and similar handcrafts (e.g., knitting, crocheting, embroidery, lace-making) have also been influenced by modernization and technology (see Channer and Buck 1991; Macdonald 1988; Palliser 1984). With changes in technology, these goods formerly made by individual women have become more available as they are produced in mass quantities in factory and sweatshop settings. As a result, women (and men) no longer needed to possess handcraft skills to ensure the survival of their families, because sewn, knitted, and crocheted goods (e.g., sweaters, clothes, linens, and other everyday household items) can be readily purchased on the market. In economic terms, producing a handmade item can be more costly than buying its equivalent in the marketplace.

Preserving and maintaining handcraft skills has definitely decreased as modernization has progressed. For example, teaching children (usually girls) to sew in the home and in schools has diminished sharply: "By the mid-1970s, sewing education had already been dropped from many school curriculums, and great numbers of women were entering the workforce and were neither sewing themselves nor teaching their daughters to sew. They simply did not have the time" (The American Sewing Guild 2000: 1). National organizations such as the American Sewing Guild, 4-H, the American Knitting Guild, and others are currently working to reverse this trend (The American Sewing Guild 2000). To highlight women's creative contributions and to keep handcraft techniques alive, many of these organizations have learning campaigns during which they urge those with such knowledge to teach others, sometimes with a recognized day. For example, September is National Sewing Month, and National Quilting Day is the third Saturday in March, when many quilt guilds espouse educating others about quilting as one of their purposes.

Currently, there are approximately 1,000 registered guilds/quilt groups with the National Quilting Association and the American Quilter's Society (American Quilter's Society 2006; National Quilting Association 2006). This, I would argue, is a conservative estimate of the actual numbers of quilt guilds and groups, for many are not registered with national organizations, but rather meet informally in women's homes, church basements, and city buildings with only local affiliation/recognition.

Quilting is a gendered activity, with 99 percent of roughly twenty-seven million U.S. quilters being women (Leman Publications 2003, 2006), which also shapes the values and attitudes surrounding quilting. Quilting is especially popular among midlife women (Leman Publications 2003). Quilting increased by 50 percent from 1997 to 2003, with more than 17 percent of U.S. households participating (Leman Publications 2006), and it is a multibillion-dollar, international industry (Quilter's News Network 2006).

At the national level, annual and biennial shows, contests, and festivals feature both traditional and contemporary quilts. Beginning in 1979 and occurring biennially, Quilt National hosts an international juried show featuring "contemporary innovative" quilts (Quilt National 2006), while the American Quilt Society has hosted an annual show in Paducah, KY, since 1984, with both traditional and contemporary quilts. On an international level, quilting festivals have increased. For example, one can attend the International Quilt Festivals in Houston, TX, and Chicago, IL, the Quilt Expo in Europe, and the Tokyo Great Quilt Festival in Japan (Ruyak 2002; Tokyo Great International Quilt Festival 2006).

For those who cannot travel to these national and international venues, media venues are an option. *Quilter's Newsletter Magazine* has been in circulation since 1969, and Fons & Porter's *Love of Quilting* since 1981. Television programs include

FIG. I.4. Quilt show (quilts hung vertically as art). Personal photograph.

*Sewing with Nancy, Simply Quilts* on HGTV, and Fons & Porter's *Love of Quilting.* Additionally, June 2006 marked the launch of the Quilter's News Network, "the first and only broadband channel dedicated to around-the-clock media content for quilters (Quilter's News Network 2006). For a more thorough discussion of contemporary quilting practices, see *The Quilter's Catalog: A Comprehensive Resource Guide* (Cox 2007).

Research focused on historical and existing quilts began in the early 1980s in the U.S. with state quilt projects. The first state quilt project was in 1981, in Kentucky, and led by quilt collector and aficionado, Shelly Zeman. Typically, state quilt projects held "quilt documentation days" where the focus was on locating and documenting existing quilts in the state, recording known information about and photographing each quilt, and sometimes preserving quilts for families. These efforts resulted successfully in raising awareness about quilts and quilting, and in highlighting current quilting efforts and quilters within each state. Since then, additional U.S. states and other countries (e.g., Canada, Britain, New Zealand, and Australia) have followed suit, assessing the types and numbers of quilts in existence and increasing visibility for quilts, quilting, and the care of quilts (The Quilt Index 2006). Books with a state's quilts featured in them soon appeared, as did the development of research-based organizations interested in documenting quilt history.

At the same time as state quilt projects were documenting existing quilts, a group of interdisciplinary academics also became interested in quilts and quilting. The American Quilt Study Group (AQSG) was founded in 1980 as a "non-profit quilt research organization" that publishes *Uncoverings*, a journal devoted entirely to quilt-based research (AQSG 2006). In 1992, the Alliance for American Quilts was founded to link together the "world of quilts, scholarship, and the general public" (The Alliance 2006), and in 1998, the British Quilt Study Group (BQSG) was founded with similar goals, publishing both *Quilt Treasures of Great Britain* and the journal *Quilt Studies* (BQSG 2006).

Quilt scholarship has since spread to the larger academic community, and scholars in anthropology, communications, English literature, folklore, history, sociology, textiles, dress, and the like conduct research and publish within their disciplines. In 1997, the International Quilt Study Center was founded at the University of Nebraska and it houses the world's largest collection of quilts. It is also the only place worldwide where one can pursue a graduate degree in textile history with an emphasis in quilt studies (International Quilt Study Center 2006).

The general public has also become noticeably more aware of quilts. Museum-goers, art connoisseurs, and art collectors have focused attention on historical quilts and contemporary art quilts. Appreciation for quilts as art can be attributed to two American quilt enthusiasts with art backgrounds (Peterson 2003). In the 1960s, Jonathan Holstein and Gail van der Hoof began collecting quilts. Somewhere in the process of collecting, they began to appreciate the design elements present in quilts. They noticed, with their art backgrounds, that quilts were quite capable of displaying artistic design: "At first, we simply noted and discussed them [quilts] casually, as we did other areas of the decorative arts. They were there, many were painstakingly made, I was aware of their supposed history, that they were an indigenous American phenomenon … it was perhaps inevitable that one day the two files, American quilts and modern painting would cross" (Holstein 1991: 15). In 1971, Holstein and Van der Hoof convinced the Whitney Museum of American Art in New York City to house a quilt exhibit and to hang quilts as art, on the wall instead of laid flat, which would be reminiscent of a bedcovering. The Whitney Museum exhibit was a success, and it is now regarded as the moment when quilts were first considered "art" (McMorris and Kile 1996; Peterson 2003; Proeller 1998). This museum-centered appreciation for quilts further highlights the finished product of the quilt, rather than the quilter, or the quilting process necessary to produce a quilt. Currently, there are a handful of U.S. museums devoted specifically to collecting and displaying quilts in both contemporary (art) and traditional (craft) forms, favoring art over craft in many cases.

The hierarchical division between art and craft has been debated for some time within the art world and within sociology of art, and quilts have been considered along these binaries as well (Becker 1982; Peterson 2003). Politically, and incorrectly, in my opinion, high art has almost a blind preference for Euro-American styling in quilts over any other style, and disregards other rich historical quilting traditions in the U.S., including African American, Latina, and Native American. One must keep in mind that historical quilts still in existence might have been quilts for special or little use in wealthy families. Established quilt collections thus are not necessarily an accurate representation of all quilts ever made, but instead represent some quilts that have been preserved. Since fabric disintegrates rather quickly in comparison to other mediums, everyday quilts most likely are not preserved for us to study or to enjoy.

A recent discovery of a group of quilters has certainly showcased quilting on an international level. The Gee's Bend quilts were produced by African American women in an economically destitute and remote region of Alabama where there was little exposure to formal schooling and even less exposure to the fine arts (Beardsley, Arnett, Arnett, and Livingston 2002; Becker 1982; Peterson 2003). These quilts were recently discovered as forms of "outsider art" when an authority in this area came across their work and brought it into the formal art community (Zolberg and Cherbo 1997). Thus Gee's Bend quilts are considered high art (Art with a capital A), are displayed regularly in prominent museums, and, most importantly, their makers are now considered to be Artists, although the quilters do not necessarily define or label themselves in those ways ("The Quiltmakers of Gee's Bend" 2004). The Gee's Bend quilts are described here as contributing to our understanding of women's everyday lives:

> Quilts were always (even if unintentionally) self-portraits. Indeed, all of the imperatives of womanhood, quiltmaking (and sometimes sacred music) provided the most creative experience. Tending to a home, procreation (often a pregnancy a year) and child rearing, working in the fields – all were expected of

women but were forums for limited self-expression. In piecing a quilt, everything could be controlled, simplified, magnified, miniaturized, and rearranged –
a genuine and culturally sanctioned occurrence of artmaking as an emancipatory
act. (Beardsley et al. 2002: 39)

The Gee's Bend quilters (and their supporters) have helped bring international attention to quilting (e.g., the 39 cent U.S. postage stamp, numerous books, a national
museum tour, an Emmy-winning PBS documentary, and miscellaneous products
available at museum gift shops), and are described as creating beautiful quilts in less-
than-beautiful life circumstances. Although very visible on an international level,
these quilters are not driving the current quilting industry in the same ways that
middle class, midlife quilters are. The Gee's Bend quilters represent a very different
population from the women in my study, as they learned as young girls from family
members, worked together on quilts in the evenings after working at the textile mill,
and needed the quilts for warmth rather than making them for fun.

When discussing quilts, one must also consider with care the impact of the
NAMES quilt, which honors the lives tragically lost to the AIDS epidemic.
Intentionally, the panels in the quilt are coffin-sized, and when laid out for display
end to end, it is hauntingly easy to imagine the numbers of people who have died at
the hands of AIDS complications. This quilt project is also different from my study,
as the focus is not on the quilt maker, but on the person for whom the panel is made.
The AIDS quilt is a collective effort by numerous people, probably some of whom
are not quilters, working to raise awareness, and it demonstrates most clearly that
quilts are complicated material objects with profound meanings.

## WHAT IS A QUILT, ANYWAY?

In its most basic, traditional, and familiar form, a quilt is a three-layered fabric sandwich with a top, a filling, and a back. People are most familiar with the quilt top that
displays the design. A quilt top consists of patchwork or piecing (sewing pieces of
fabric together), appliqué (sewing pieces of fabric on top of larger pieces of fabric), or
wholecloth (a single, large piece of fabric). The filling, which falls between the top and
back, varies in thickness and texture, often by region (e.g., in warmer regions quilters
use less or no batting, and in colder regions, thicker batting is used). The usually
nondescript backing encases the filling and provides support to the entire unit.

These layers, piled atop each other, make up the landscape upon which quilting
takes place. Stitches placed in consideration of the quilt top penetrate through each
layer of the sandwich to add additional design aspects to the quilt and functionally
keep the three layers secure. There are both hand and machine quilting techniques,
sometimes with political ramifications for either choice within the quilting world (for
example, there is a "hand quilting stitch" available on some high end sewing
machines, complicating the authenticity of hand quilting). A final strip of fabric as
binding is sewn around all edges, containing the filling edges and the unfinished
edges of the top and back.

FIG. 1.5. Fabric sandwich. Personal photograph.

Historical quilters are often credited with being thrifty and making quilts only out of old clothing and household scraps. This is indeed somewhat the case, especially with feed-sack quilts and scrap quilts, yet both kinds of quilts were made with great care and can be strikingly beautiful. Additionally, we now know that quilters in the past also bought new fabric to make beautiful quilts when they were financially able to do so. Thus, U.S. women have historically bought new fabric for the purposes of quilting.

FIG. 1.6. Woodville, CA. FSA (Farm Security Administration) farm workers' community. Agricultural worker quilting in the sewing room, 1942. Russell Lee, photographer. Historical Photograph (Library of Congress, Prints & Photographs Division, FSA/OWI Collection [LC-USF34-071797-D]).

FIG. 1.7. Making a quilt in a Scranton, IA, home. The ladies will give the quilt to a needy family, 1940. John Vachon, photographer. Historical Photograph (Library of Congress, Prints & Photographs Division, FSA/OWI Collection [LC-USF34-060704-D]).

FIG. 1.8. Members of the women's club making quilt. Granger Homesteads, IA, 1940. John Vachon, photographer. Historical Photograph (Library of Congress, Prints & Photographs Division, FSA/OWI Collection [LC-USF34-060921-D]).

In the past, a quilt was often considered an item of utility, although women took great efforts to make aesthetically pleasing quilts. Most quilts made in the past also had personal or hidden meaning attached to them, similar to quilts produced today. Contemporary women often use new, 100-percent cotton fabric manufactured specifically for quilting. Quilts have multiple meanings and purposes, both utilitarian and sentimental, and the general public has been developing a sentimental and an artistic appreciation for quilts.

Quilting is currently enjoying a revival due in part to the 1976 U.S. Bicentennial (Gunn 1992), celebrating 200 years of existence as a country. Women constructed quilts in the mid 1970s to commemorate their foremothers and the household work that supported the revolutionary movements toward freedom from England. Rather than purchase ready-made textiles from England, revolutionaries learned to make their own textiles, in efforts to renounce the support of England's economy. In addition to being warm and cuddly, and reminding us of our grandmothers and great-grandmothers, quilts are mementos of obvious things and events. Historical events like the 1976 U.S. Bicentennial, the AIDS epidemic (Jones and Dawson 2000), and 9/11 have been marked in our personal and collective memory through the intentional and public construction of commemorative and memorial quilts (Cerny 1997b). Other well-known quilts marking history include former slave Harriet Power's Bible Quilt (Lyons 1993), the controversial oral history of one African American family's quilts carrying messages concerning the Underground Railroad

FIG. 1.9. Sarah's quilts on the clothesline. Personal photograph.

(Tobin and Dobard 1999), friendship quilts bonding women together during white ethnics' western expansion of the United States (Lipsett 1985), the Freedom Quilting Bee in Alabama, which allowed African American women in the area to make a living from their quilting efforts (Callahan 1987), and, more recently, the internationally renowned quilts of Gee's Bend (Beardsley et al. 2002). Some quilts commemorate natural disasters such as the 1997 Red River Valley flood in North Dakota (Enarson 2000), the terrorist attacks on the World Trade Center and the Pentagon on 9/11/2001 ("United in Memory" 2003), and quilting organizations continue to raise money and collect and make quilts for victims of Hurricane Katrina in the southern U.S. (The Quilter Community 2007).

Quilts are also used to promote public tourism and economic development. Adams County, Ohio, in 2001, launched the first "barn quilt" project, which celebrates two local cultural products – barns and quilts. Volunteers painted quilt blocks on the sides of barns, both preserving quilting traditions and preventing old barns from being torn down. Barn quilts appeared in other areas of Ohio as well (Adams County Ohio Quilt Sampler Project 2006; Not Barn Yesterday: A Clothesline of Quilts in Appalachia 2006; Ohio Quilt Barns 2006; Patchwork Jewels of Monroe County 2006). The initial Ohio project was adopted by economic developers in Iowa in 2003. The Barn Quilts of Grundy County began in 2003, with quilt blocks painted on century barns (barns that are over 100 years old), and a driving tour (Barn Quilts of Grundy County IA 2006), with other Iowa counties following (Barn Quilts of Pocahontas County, IA 2006; Barn Quilts of Sac County, IA 2006).

FIG. 1.10. Barn Quilt Project, Grundy County, IA. Bakker "Eight Pointed Star," copyright 2006 Ruth Ratliff.

FIG. 1.11. Barn Quilt Project, Grundy County, IA. Kitzman "County Fair," copyright 2004 Ruth Ratliff.

FIG. 1.12. Barn Quilt Project, Grundy County, IA. Nason "Windmill," copyright 2006 Ruth Ratliff.

Additionally, the marriage of industry and technology in the quilting products arena has continued since the 1976 quilt revival. At no other time in history have quilters enjoyed the variety of quilt fabric available, helpful tools designed specifically for quilting which introduce time-saving techniques, and sewing machines with extraordinary technological advancements available for individual use (Brackman 1997). With more women involved in the paid workforce since the 1970s, the expendable income of working women has a logical, gendered outlet in the quilting industry; this is especially so when considering many midlife women of the baby boom generation in the U.S., nearing retirement and an empty nest, return to or engage in new activities for which they did not have time while tending to their families and to their paid-work lives. At this time in history, we can see a full generation of women in the paid workforce who are now entering midlife, and choosing how to spend their retirement years. Many of these midlife women are deciding to learn how to quilt and are quilting with a passion, becoming cultural producers that exist outside the economic sphere.

## CULTURAL PRODUCTION OUTSIDE THE ECONOMIC SPHERE

Cultural production research explores the processes within creating cultural objects – the *how* of producing cultural objects, or, as Fine (1996) states, the culture of production. Most research on cultural production focuses on the economic sphere, noting how successful artists become so. Examples of this type of scholarship include art and artistic careers (Ardery 1998; Becker 1982; Mishler 1999; Peterson 2003), and musicians and the music industry (Curran 1996; Krenske and McKay 2000; Peterson 1997; Stebbins 1996). These studies are based within the economic or commercial sphere, and artistic success is dependent upon reputation, status, and, most importantly, economic success, usually focused on public events and activities. Missing from much of the cultural production literature are everyday contributions to cultural production, those that exist beyond the structures of outsider art (Zolberg and Cherbo 1997), more specifically, non-economic cultural production.

Women are not often thought to be cultural creators and are rarely studied as such. Despite some research on women's writing as a form of women's cultural production, scholarly attention to how gender affects cultural production is rare. In existing research, women writers recount their difficulties in gaining time, support, and legitimacy to write (See Aptheker 1989; Bateson 1990; Ferriss 1999; Kallet and Cofer 1999; Olsen 1978; Romero and Stewart 1999). Women have particular challenges setting aside time to write in the face of familial duties. Additionally, scholars note that normative modes of expression in several forms of writing, such as absence of the author's voice, and writing in the third person further constrain women's expression (DeVault 1999; Reinharz 1992; Richardson 1997). These writing conventions are limiting for women writers, since they are often incompatible with the content of women's concerns.

Olsen (1978: 13) documents the centuries of loss in cultural production by women writers, what she terms the *silences* resulting from the missed opportunities to write. Women called to write often could pursue their passion only part-time:

> But what if there is not that fullness of time, let alone totality of self? What if the writers, as in some of these silences, must work regularly at something besides their own work – as do nearly all in the arts in the United States today … But the actuality testifies: substantial creative work demands time, and with rare exceptions only full-time workers have achieved it. Where the claims of creation cannot be primary, the results are atrophy; unfinished work; minor effort and accomplishment; silences.

Ferriss (1999: 55) supports this position, observing, "I have no time! It is the writer's – especially the women writers' – most frequent complaint." Women writers' reflections lend insight to other forms of women's cultural production. The constraints faced by women who write are also felt by women who engage in other forms of cultural production, like quilting. Most face the divided consciousness brought about by frequent interruptions within the home and the struggle to find time and other resources needed for their creative work.

## THE SOCIOLOGY OF CULTURE AND THE CULTURE OF NON-ECONOMIC CULTURAL PRODUCTION

A small number of culture scholars do document the everyday importance embedded in non-economic forms of cultural production. Fine examines the complex cultures of U.S. mushrooming (1998) and kitchen workers (1996). Sinha (1979) documents the relatively unknown complexity of the social organization of pottery production. Neapolitan (1985a, 1985b, 1986), and Ethridge and Neapolitan (1985) discuss the expansion of craft worlds in the latter half of the twentieth century, focusing on the economic developments crafts are undergoing, and how an economic focus will change the culture of pottery production, not always for the better. Butsch (1984) documents the changes happening in model airplanes, from a hobby to an ever-growing, commodified industry. These scholars suggest that craft worlds and art worlds rely too much upon economics to determine one's status (amateur or professional) as well as artistic success.

Sociologists of culture emphasize the study of the cultural product and how it is measured as economically and reputationally successful, over the creative process of the production of culture. Such culture research usually examines public events and activities, those occurring in an economic or commercial sphere, and those that are also male dominated. In this way, culture research overlooks meaning-making processes, private and everyday cultural acts, as well as gendered differences between men and women as cultural producers. Thus, missing in much culture research is the recognition of women as legitimate cultural producers, and an understanding of the non-economic meaning-making process of the production of culture.

Culture research highlights men's contributions to cultural production, claiming gender neutrality by default. By this I mean that culture research does focus on men and men's experiences as cultural producers, but this research is not explicitly conscious of how gender might influence men's lives – notably missing from culture research are the theoretical gains from men's studies and the sociology of masculinity. Culture scholars thus continue to imply that the production of culture is gender-neutral, rather than gender-laden. Acker (1992: 249) critiques this thinking, stating: "The view that all social relations are gendered ... opens up the possibility that many apparently gender-neutral processes are sites of gender production." Two exceptions to this line of research are Lang and Lang (1988, 1990, 1993), who focus on differences between men's and women's experiences in building and maintaining successful artistic reputations, and Tuchman (1984) and Tuchman and Fortin (1980), who explore the gendered patterns present historically in opportunities provided to men and women in the novel-publishing industry. These works are cognizant of gender, and of the economy as a defining factor in artistic success, yet these works have had little effect on contemporary cultural production research. Thus, culture research continues to rely upon economic measures to determine artistic success, privileges men's experiences over women's, and highlights cultural objects typically produced by men over those made by women, mostly by overlooking the importance of both gender and non-economic forms of cultural production.

Where privatized domains or leisure activities have been studied as sites of non-economic cultural production, the emphasis has been on male-dominated activities that are less routine and more tangible (e.g., building a deck for the house), with women viewed as supporters of their families' sports and leisure interests (Chafetz and Kotarba 1995; Thompson 1999). Yet, women's non-economic cultural production typically takes place in the private sphere, through routine, everyday activities often in service of the family: cleaning, cooking, caring for children, and the like (Beoku-Betts 1994; DeVault 1991; Di Leonardo 1987; Hochschild 1989; Long 2003; Oakley 1974a, 1974b; Olsen 1978; Radway 1991). While women's work is a key site for studying (Burman 1999; Harris 1997), little research has been centered on women as artists or cultural producers in their own right. As a result, women's cultural contributions through everyday life activities remain invisible within the sociology of culture research.

Gender scholars have similar blind spots in researching women's everyday lives. When gender scholars analyze feminized culture production sites, they are not necessarily inclusive of everyday cultural production. For example, women's everyday home-based and unpaid tasks that are rich in cultural meaning include food preparation, caretaking, housework and childcare, and communication within families. Beoku-Betts (1994) found that Gullah coastal women use food-making traditions to transmit important cultural norms, primarily to their daughters. DeVault's (1991) account of mothers as family caretakers shows that women perform daily cooking with great care, attempting to make the family members feel like honored individuals. Oakley (1974a, 1974b) discusses women's emotional investments in childcare and housework, as these often-devalued home-work tasks have significant long-range implications for women as they consider their children's lives beyond the home. Di Leonardo (1987) shows how the routine, yet thoughtful, act of sending greeting cards, done much more by women than men but directed toward the kin of women as well as their spouses' kin, helps maintain familial and kin relationships within families and helps establish family traditions.

Because culture production research has for so long had an economic focus, everyday meaning-making activities that occur in private spaces such as the home are also overlooked as relevant culture production sites. Therefore, I examine the "underside" of the traditional gender dichotomy, where it is more easily evident that the feminized world of quilting is also a gendered one. Delineating the tenets of a gendered world within an under-researched population makes clearer how gender permeates all aspects of our lives, including women's culture-producing processes. From this perspective, when sociologists study quilting, they generally emphasize quilts as cultural and political artifacts. Quilts are important in how they are used and viewed by non-quilting outsiders (e.g., political activists, museum-goers, art connoisseurs, and consumers). For example, Krouse (1993), Lewis and Fraser (1996), and Mueller (1995) focus on the important and global political aspects of AIDS awareness and prevention through the NAMES quilt.

Other scholars investigate quilting in a variety of ways, and from a multitude of disciplines. Collectively, they examine the social and organizational aspects of quilts, with attention to U.S. quilts (Elsley 1995). Forrest and Blincoe (1995) document the natural history of the traditional quilt, Todd (1997) notes quilters' levels of involvement and competition in quilting activities, while Cerny et al. (1993) and Schofield-Tomschin and Littrell (2001) explore the positive role that artistic guilds play in women's lives. Rake (2000) notes that quilting is an important gendered activity among Mennonite women, because it serves as an income-generating activity for many women, elevating women's status in their communities, while Ice (1984) discusses women's identity development in a quilting group within a small community in the U.S. Barkley Brown (1988), Benberry (1993), Freeman (1996), and Fry (1990) discuss African American quilts and quilting traditions in the U.S., with Dunn and Morris (1992) researching Faith Ringgold's narrative quilts in particular. Przybysz (1987) and Langellier (1992) examine the performance aspects of U.S. quilt exhibitions, and the "show and tell" portions of quilt guild meetings, respectively; while Pryzbysz (1989) and Cerny (1997a) explore the role of quilted garments in quilters' lives, again in the U.S. Hanson and Smucker (2003) and Hawley (2005) explore the changes in meaning of U.S. Amish quilts over time.

Reaching outside the U.S., Weidlich (1986) studies Canadian quilting, Rolfe (1988) and Herda (2000) examine quilting traditions in Australia and Tonga respectively, while Eikmeier (2001) documents Korean quilting styles. Importantly, Doyle (1998) and Nelson et al. (2002, 2005) come closest to examining the gendered creative process of quilting. Doyle (1998) studies Australian leisure quilters who struggle to find the time and space to quilt amidst family responsibilities. Nelson, LaBat, and Williams (2002, 2005) highlight the gendered culture facing twenty-five Irish textile artists. In Nelson et al. (2002, 2005), they note that not only were their learning processes gendered as they learned to sew as young girls, but these textile artists also continue to face misunderstanding regarding their creative work. Interestingly, these studies inform my work a great deal, for although both include quilters as research participants, one study focuses on leisure quilters, and the other on professional textile artists. That they are both involved in gendered creative work is clear, with both groups of women facing difficulties in engaging in their chosen creative work of quilting.

The majority of quilt research is centered on finished quilts, and not quilters. Research that does center on quilters often highlights professional or artistic quilters, and not the creative processes that everyday quilters face. My research has certainly been influenced and guided by previous research, which is why I in particular pay attention to the average quilter, the leisure quilter, the most prevalent type of quilter as identified by two recent national surveys of U.S. quilters (Leman Publications 2003, 2006). My study involves mostly white, middle class, midlife U.S. women who quilt for leisure – fun. They do not profit from quilting as professionals do, and they do not have to make quilts to keep the family warm, as might have been the case in earlier times. In many ways, quilting is one of many leisure pursuits to choose from when women enter midlife (e.g., scrapbooking, knitting, golfing, and gardening). But, interestingly, quilting today for middle class, midlife women can transform family life in some quite surprising ways. The time I have spent with these midlife quilters has revealed a hidden social world that is not necessarily visible to outsiders. This is a world with tension and conflict, where women feel they have to negotiate their time and space with family concerns. This image of quilting is not what the general public would associate with their granny's non-threatening sewing circle, for example.

In Chapter 2, I consider myself as the researcher, noting how my dual positions as researcher and quilter merged as the study progressed, and I highlight this with images of some of my personal quilting experiences. Overall, quilters were more likely to talk with me once they found out that I was a quilter – the fact that I was a researcher was rather secondary. The potential bias of being a quilter, then, became an advantage and a point of entrée into the social world of quilting. After I discuss my insider status as a quilter, I then introduce the research setting and study participants, highlighting how quilting has changed for women over the past generation. I also discuss the methodological considerations for the study, including the research methods used, the difficulties I encountered while pursuing a study of quilting, and the gendered assumptions about quilting and qualitative fieldwork.

In Chapter 3, I focus on the sometimes painful process that midlife women endure when taking time from their work and their families to learn a new hobby. The women in this study have decided not only to try quilting, but also to continue quilting, to the point where they identify themselves as "quilters." Being a quilter can be a marginalized identity – one that is shared with a select few – thus many women hide their identities as quilters, unless they are around other quilters or non-quilters they know to be sympathetic. When women publicly self-identify as quilters, they also begin to define subjective careers around quilting – that is, women define personal successes in quilting that are not related to economic success. Making connections with others who quilt and maintaining kin ties through gifting quilts to others are not activities that are likely to win awards or make money.

In Chapter 4, I examine the guilty pleasures of quilting, including the deviant acts of hiding not only fabric, but also one's identity as a quilter from family members and others. For example, while fabric is the medium of quilting, quilters usually purchase more of it than is necessary for projects, slowly building up and hoarding a fabric stash. Because they cannot fully share their quilting with their families, they then strategize hiding places for their fabric. Women's anxieties surrounding acquiring, hoarding, and hiding their fabric stashes highlight their diminished ability, relative to their spouses and their children, to pursue leisure activities without a stigma. Collecting and hiding the stash become symbolic of women's attempts to carve out time and space for themselves amidst the multiple demands placed on them by families and by paid work.

In Chapter 5, I discuss both the leisure constraints women experience and the acts of resistance they engage in while practicing quilting. Even though quilting is a feminized and gendered activity, there are still time and space constraints in the traditional family that affect women's ability to quilt. Women resist such constraints and stereotypical notions of gender relations as they pursue quilting. They quilt first for themselves, and second to fulfill family and kin needs in gendered ways (e.g., to give homemade gifts that cement ties to family and friends, and to provide a material representation of important family events). Quilting highlights how women accept, reproduce, and negotiate traditional notions of gender in families.

In Chapter 6, I examine how women engage in carework both for themselves and others through quilting. They quilt for themselves as they quilt for their own enjoyment. Yet, women also use quilting as a means to care for others by gifting finished quilts. Although the women in this study pursue quilting as leisure (i.e., just for fun), giving finished quilts to others (e.g., family members and close friends) is a way to mark a significant family event in a highly personalized way, wherein the gift becomes a representation of the entire family's care for and commitment to the recipient. In this way, quilting, women are still caring for others as they care for themselves.

In the final chapter, I discuss how women quilters are cultural producers engaging in carework for self and others, and why quilting is an attractive activity for midlife women. Women regularly engage in carework for others throughout the life course, and quilting allows them to continue to do this, but it also becomes a form of carework for quilters and their families. When quilting is understood as a gendered form of leisure as I posit it to be, quilting reveals a great deal about the modern U.S. family and the modern woman's everyday struggles in finding time and space for herself within that family and within the broader society.

# 2 TRIPPING THROUGH THE TULIPS: DOING RESEARCH CLOSE TO HOME

## USING FEMINIST METHODS TO STUDY CONTEMPORARY U.S. QUILTERS

Given existing research on quilts and quilting, I purposefully centered my study on the perspectives of quilters and their creative processes, rather than quilts. To best understand their emic perspective (the insider perspective), I immersed myself in the quilting world (Blumer 1969; Geertz 1973, 1983; Harre 1979; Mead 1934). Emphasizing the emic perspective does two things to promote quilters, and the quilting process. First, by focusing on quilters, I wanted to know what they thought about the activity and their finished products, and not how outsiders did or did not value quilts (assumedly, many outsiders are oblivious to the quilting process as the quilters in the study indicate). Second, I was also able to see how quilters made meaning out of quilting processes, and how quilting revealed tension within the home and the institution of the family.

Getting to know women, and learn about how they engaged in quilting, required me to get my feet wet in the quilting world. This process of getting one's feet wet in the field is an important step in developing as a qualitative researcher (Geertz 1973, 1983). Gaining access to and developing rapport with research participants can be difficult, and, in reflection on my experiences, I have been able to see why some of my efforts were more fruitful than others. In this chapter, I discuss gaining access to and developing rapport with women quilters, and the gendered assumptions other researchers and I make about the populations we study. The local knowledge we seek to gain in conducting field research is influenced in part by the identities of the researcher, including his or her gender.

Guided by the tenets of grounded theory and a feminist perspective (Reinharz 1992), my purpose was to investigate the quilting process from the point of view of women who choose to quilt for pleasure, rather than as an income-generating activity. I chose grounded theory because quilting as a process was an exploratory concept, particularly in the social sciences. Scholars have examined quilts as cultural and artistic objects, but the process of making quilts and the gendered cultural production that occurs during this process have had very little academic attention. My background as a long-time sewer helped me make connections and conduct interviews with quilters. I used my insider status as a quilter to better establish rapport with women, and to reduce barriers between researcher and participant (Baca Zinn 1979; Hertz 1997).

## LOCAL KNOWLEDGE AND GROUNDED THEORY

In discussing the role of the qualitative field researcher, Geertz (1973, 1983) emphasizes the importance of understanding the native's point of view, known as *local knowledge*. Local knowledge contributes to the researcher's comprehension of basic rules and norms within social interaction settings, which is enhanced by immersing oneself in a group. Geertz (1973: 28) elaborates this point: "The aim is to draw large conclusions from small, but very densely textured facts; to support broad assertions about the role of culture in the construction of collective life by engaging them exactly with complex specifics." Understanding the native wisdom present within local communities of quilters can be time consuming, labor intensive, and theoretically challenging.

For multiple reasons, grounded theory serves this study on midlife women quilters particularly well. Quilting takes place in mostly unnoticeable places like the home, and quilters' efforts are generally hidden from mainstream society, making research access difficult. To gain the local knowledge of quilters, I needed to become part of the culture of quilting, and make public my personal quilting knowledge. Immersing myself in local quilting activities and developing my insider status as a quilter allowed me to understand better quilters' points of view. As Geertz (1983: 69) has contended: "In order to follow a baseball game one must understand what a bat, a hit, an inning, a left fielder, a squeeze play, a hanging curve, and a tightened infield are, and what the game in which these 'things' are elements is all about." To understand quilting today in the U.S., I needed to know the terminology, the equipment, and the techniques in order to immerse myself in the quilting world. Thus, I learned what a fat quarter was and how this cut of fabric was perceived by quilters. (A fat quarter is a piece of 100-percent cotton quilting fabric measuring eighteen inches by twenty-two inches, typically cut from a piece of fabric that is forty-five inches wide. It is a quarter yard of fabric, but is fat rather than skinny. A skinny quarter yard of fabric would measure nine inches by forty-five inches. Quilters often prefer this cut of fabric as it is more useful in quilting than a long skinny piece of fabric.) I also learned about new techniques, the preferences quilters have in hand versus machine techniques, color, and design, and even the width of the binding as having historical trends and preferences.

I also began to appreciate quilting as an art form. The immediate, local knowledge of "primitive" artistic communities has been overlooked and under-interpreted in sociological research (Zolberg and Cherbo 1997). This is the case especially for artistic communities consisting mostly of women and other marginalized groups. As my purpose in this research was to investigate the quilting process from the perspective of the women who do it, I centered on women's quilting experiences within a broader social context, to develop integrative theory drawing from gender, culture, leisure, and identity research.

Important and complex meaning-making activities occur in artistic communities. In art communities generally, and primitive art societies specifically, Western aesthetic formalism influences outsiders and researchers and their classifications of what constitutes "art." These assumptions can lead researchers to impose theoretical frames, interpretations, and analyses on research settings in biased and incorrect ways, thus impeding the discovery of local knowledge: "the giving to art objects a cultural significance, is always a local matter ... no matter how universal the intrinsic qualities that actualize its emotional power ... may be" (Geertz 1983: 96). Witnessing, understanding, and integrating local knowledge within sites of culture are crucial to valid social research. Quilting is a particularly interesting case to research, then, for it does not easily fit into established art categories, and it is a somewhat hidden cultural activity, often occurring in the home.

The importance of keeping an insider perspective on quilting became clearer to me when I began talking with non-quilters (and academic non-quilters) about my research. When I brought up *quilting* as a researchable topic to colleagues, these non-quilters generally responded with statements about how much they loved quilts, or told a story about a quilt they received from a grandmother, and asked me if I knew anything about a quilt that they owned – restoring or cleaning it. These reactions to my *quilting* research are quilt-focused, not focused on the women making quilts, and not about the creative process of quilting that happens before the quilt is a finished product. These continual quilt-focused responses to my quilting research interested me. I elaborated to outsiders the importance of the *process* of quilting, and continued to make more central the process of quilting and the social world of quilting in my research endeavors. In discussing my quilting research with outsiders, I had to find a way to convey the importance of this process and to deepen their focus of attention from the artistry or value of finished quilts to embody the critical, but often invisible, process that binds women I met to quilting as a form of gendered cultural production. For, in contrast to the non-quilting outsiders, quilters focus far more on the *process* of quilting, as artists would. The finished quilt is often gifted to family and friends, and sometimes only a photograph is kept of the finished quilt, with the quilter moving onto the next quilting project and process. My focus in this research on cultural production in women's lives requires an emphasis on *process*.

I interviewed self-identified quilters (those who would say, "I am a quilter"), allowing quilters at different levels of technique to define themselves as such. I avoided using an externally developed schema of what constitutes a quilter to recruit participants (e.g., a minimum number of finished quilts, or years spent quilting), for I soon discovered that the process of taking on the identity of a quilter is an important step for midlife women learning a new hobby and integrating it into already established home activities. I made note of the different aspects of the process and the product of quilting and the hierarchical framework of art/craft in which quilting can often reside. The outsider perspective of classifying quilts as art or craft is far less meaningful to quilters generally, as they often create both types of quilts, finding the outsider-placed art/craft binary less than useful.

I continue to struggle with the hierarchical nature of the naming and placement of art over craft in the mainstream art world. Although useful in analysis of the production of culture, specifically with high art examples such as oil painting, the art/craft binary does not fit well into current quilters' lives. For example, quilters typically create both art and craft quilts simultaneously and are not limited to one form within the medium of quilting – they often reject the binary both in their finished quilts and in their conversations concerning quilting. The integrative "both/and" strategy proposed by black feminist Patricia Hill Collins (1991) is important when applied to quilters' everyday lives. Thus, quilters create both craft and art quilts, and can be considered to reside in both camps, simultaneously, bridging the hierarchical (and often economical) divide. My research on quilting expands the limited way of thinking about quilts solely as art or craft to include a both/and theoretical framework, and considers quilts as both art *and* craft. Additionally, both/and thinking is necessary to envision both the process and the product aspects of current quilting activities.

Interestingly, when one looks only at the art/craft distinction within quilting, the women making the quilts begin to disappear, and the finished product emerges as the central focus. Without a person to make the cultural object of a quilt, there can be no quilts to admire, use, collect, or study. Although this may seem repetitive, it is imperative for readers to understand the importance of placing women quilters at the center of the research, privileging their decisions in terms of quilting, and understanding their lives inside and outside the quilting process. This conscious focus on quilting from quilters' perspectives highlighted the women in the study and pointed out to me, the researcher, what is important about the quilter's world. It illustrated the women as cultural creators in their own right, and focused the analytical lens on the process of quilting, and not the product. Finally, in examining the process of quilting from the perspective of quilters, I was "pivoting the center" of the quilting world to pay attention to any quilt producer who thinks of herself in that way (Aptheker 1989).

Since much of women's everyday lives and culture are oral (Fonow and Cook 1991; Gluck and Patai 1991), I used a feminist perspective to give voice to women quilters (Harding 1987; Hurston 1995[1942]). Writing about feminist methodology, Reinharz (1992: 248) notes some of the more remarkable goals achieved through feminist research: "Making the invisible visible, bringing the margin to the center, rendering the trivial important, putting the spotlight on women as competent actors, understanding women as subjects in their own right ..." Quilters, as the central focus of this study, inform the reader about the struggles they face in finding time for themselves as cultural producers of quilts.

Like countless others, I too began my research with incorrect assumptions about quilting. I assumed that quilt patterns had inherent and finite meaning in them, and that I could determine where quilt patterns came from, what they meant, and what they communicated to the mainstream public. However, I soon learned that quilt patterns' names changed as they were carried across the United States by white pioneers (Brackman 1993). So, talking with women about a specific pattern was not particularly useful, for each one had numerous titles, and depending upon which region of the country I was in, we may or may not have been able to discuss a quilt using one of the many names for that pattern. More interesting was the naming process of individual quilts by each woman, and not how the quilts looked.

I began my initial collection attempts with diverse contacts, having more success with white contacts in organized groups (e.g., quilt guilds). This happened perhaps because I am also white. I cannot explain why I had more success with white women in large groups and less success with women in small groups, or with women of color in small groups, but I speculate that quilting can be a very personal experience for women. I attempted to minimize differences as much as I could, but, certainly, there are specific characteristics to my identity that cannot be changed (e.g., race, age, gender). Regardless of my successes and failures in securing interviews with quilters, my collection strategies are similar to other feminist qualitative researchers, who note the importance of sharing similar backgrounds with research participants (Baca Zinn 1979; Beoku-Betts 1994; Reinharz 1992). The demographic composition of the sample has much to do with my purposive snowball sampling methods. As I proceeded to collect data in a grounded theory perspective, quilters recommended that I speak next with their friend or relative who also was a quilter. In this way, I encouraged quilters to reveal their friendship and quilting networks, rather than attempt to achieve an age-, race-, or region-based balance of participants. Therefore, I make no claims about quilting based on racial or regional comparisons because of said limitations in this study. This study is a base from which to continue research on women's creative lives, as well as the beginnings of a fruitful theoretical framework that incorporates gender and culture.

## METHODS AND DATA

I collected data using an ethnographic approach in which multiple sources and types of data were collected and included in the data set (Emerson, Fretz, and Shaw 1995). I conducted four years of participant observation and completed intensive unstructured interviews with seventy "self-identified" quilters – that is, women who have developed or were in the process of developing a quilting identity, and would identify themselves to others as quilters – those who admired quilting but did not practice it regularly would not necessarily have the same constraints to leisure as those who practiced quilting in serious leisure ways. I employed purposive snowball sampling to contact these seventy participants from seven states in four regions of the U.S. (Midwest, Northeast, South, West), as well as to complete informal interviews with hundreds of women quilters in the U.S. I targeted publicly visible quilt organizations such as quilt guilds and small religiously affiliated quilt groups to recruit participants.

I began the interview process at the quilt guild level, as this was the largest organization in the area. I contacted the local quilt guild, which numbered 150 members, and was granted permission to join the group as a researcher and as a quilter. The quilt guild met monthly and not all members knew each other well, or at all, though all shared the interest of quilting, self-identified as quilters, and practiced quilting regularly. Monthly guild meetings were business meetings that lasted two hours, and met in privately and publicly owned buildings that donated rooms for use by non-profit organizations. Similar to other non-profit organizations, the quilt guild meeting adhered to Robert's Rules of Order, and had elected officers with one-year terms, who served as members of the Guild Board of Directors. Comparable to other large quilt guilds, which can number 500 to 1,000 members, this guild collected annual membership fees, which funded national-level instructors and a quilt show every two years. I approached a few individuals involved at different levels in the guild and interviewed them. I intentionally selected members at different levels of involvement to avoid gaining a biased understanding of the organization, from solely the leadership or the membership perspective. And, I was not conducting analysis on the organizational structure of the guild, but instead I focused on the meaning of quilting in these women's lives – I hoped that by contacting women at different levels in the guild that I would also connect with different quilting networks, which proved to be the case. The first round of participants then recommended me to additional guild members to interview, which led me to meet more quilters from the local guild. The guild had both organizational and interest divisions within it, and from the diverse interests and roles of my initial contacts, I was able to understand this particular guild from many perspectives, which also informed me about differing perspectives concerning contemporary quilting practices.

Participants gave me the names of friends and family who quilted locally but did not belong to the guild, as well as quilting contacts in other parts of the U.S. Through this process I was able to interview women who quilt on their own, in small, unorganized groups, in religiously affiliated groups, as well as members of additional quilt guilds in different parts of the country. Participants put me in contact with three quilt groups who differed in geography and size from the original quilt guild. The three groups I successfully met with were affiliated with different faiths, and had varying purposes and procedures for their quilting, though all groups partook in some form of fundraising via their quilting efforts. These three groups were far less formal than the quilt guild, as they did not collect fees or have a quilt show, and they worked on quilts together in church facilities. A similar purposive snowball sampling process occurred within the three groups – I came into contact with a member of each group, who then referred me to others with whom I could talk. As I anticipated, not all group members wanted to talk with me, and most of those who were willing to participate wanted to be interviewed together while they quilted during their regularly scheduled weekday afternoon devoted to quilting.

The unstructured interviews for this research resembled guided conversations between two quilters rather than a structured interview between a researcher and a participant (Rubin and Rubin 1995). In these conversations I encouraged women to highlight aspects of quilting important in their lives. Feminist methodological strategies helped me to privilege participants' experiences as the center point of interviews, and to recognize women quilters as competent actors, and as subjects in their own right (Oakley 1987). Additionally, this research exhibits a feminist perspective as it topically makes invisible women quilters visible within a sociological perspective (Smith 1987; Wolf 1996).

Guided by feminist methodology (Reinharz 1992), I used intensive unstructured interview techniques to share voice, ownership, and order of conversation with participants. I also tried to minimize differences between researcher and participant by making my sewing and quilting background obvious (Hertz 1997; Baca Zinn 1979). I took extensive fieldnotes within twenty-four hours of each interview and fieldwork experience (Laureau 1989), and transcribed verbatim the majority of interviews myself. For those interviews hired out for transcription, I listened to the interview tapes while reading carefully through each transcript to ensure accurate transcription and comparable familiarity with each interview and transcript. After preparing transcripts, which ranged from twenty to fifty single-spaced pages, I completed member checks with participants and assigned pseudonyms to each participant to ensure confidentiality (Janesick 1994; Lincoln and Guba 1985).

The interview process most often occurred in women's homes, but sometimes we met in an office space where they engaged in paid work. My time spent at quilters' homes felt much like a social visit – we sat down in comfortable chairs to talk and occasionally had snacks. The unstructured format allowed quilters to emphasize what they personally felt was important about quilting in their lives. Most interviews were lengthy, and the time I spent with each quilter was even longer, as we took time before and after the interview to visit, have refreshments, tour the house, and look at the finished and unfinished quilting projects.

I compiled a list of open-ended questions that I used to guide me through the interview if necessary. I was able to use the list of questions as a checklist rather than a formal interview guide, for participants would end up covering the issues I wanted to discuss in an order that made sense to them, episodically rather than historically, for example. I began each interview with the question, "How did you get involved with quilting?" and asked follow-up questions based on women's answers, keeping track of which issues were being covered on the interview guide. When the women had thoroughly covered the list of questions in discussing their quilting activities, I asked (while keeping the tape recorder running): "Is there anything I haven't asked you yet that you feel is important about your quilting?" It was at this point in the interview process that many of the women began talking more comfortably as they felt explicitly in control of the interview. In general, participants appeared comfortable talking with me, were flattered that I wanted to interview them, and discussed in considerable depth their personal experiences and how they felt about quilting activities in their lives.

For the religiously affiliated group interviews, I spent one "quilting day" with each quilt group. Before I attended any group, I planned on a relatively unstructured focus group similar to the interviews I conducted with individual quilters. My original plan did not work with two groups as they were in the process of hand quilting a quilt top on a frame and strongly encouraged me to participate: "I arrived in the afternoon as the ladies recommended. They were in the first day of quilting on the quilt. It had already been set up and marked for quilting on the frame. They told me to pull up a chair and grab a thimble, needle, and thread and begin quilting. I did" (fieldnotes 1999). The women talked about quilting a bit, but spent more time on their other usual topics: their lives, families, friends, church goings-on, and local gossip. At times the conversation would pause and a woman would say, "Do you have another question for us?" I then asked another question about quilting, and the same pattern would happen, they would begin to discuss answers to my question, and then move into their regular conversation. Their non-quilt-related comments were revealing about their relationships with one another, the church, and the community. Their comments were also revealing about the role of research in everyday life – that many of the issues we as researchers worry about translate differently when we are in the field collecting data. My time with the groups ranged from two to four hours, average length three hours. These interviews occurred in church facilities, while the women were working collectively on the same quilt. I intended to interview each woman separately, but as interviews began to overlap, I moved around the quilt frame and talked to each woman as she sat quilting with the group. These interviews benefited from the memories of all the quilters present, and as many women were related or good friends, they assisted one another in telling their quilt stories.

I tape-recorded all but two of the interviews in person – the remaining two audio taped individual interviews occurred over the telephone. Individual interviews

FIG. 2.1. Church group, quilting in the rectory basement. Personal photograph.

ranged from one to eight hours, and church group interviews ranged from two to four hours, with the average length of all interviews three hours.

The collection and analysis of data were consistent with the constant comparative method, simultaneously collecting and coding data, with emerging understandings and theoretical questions guiding further data analysis (Glaser and Strauss 1967). I proceeded with analysis by going back and forth between data collection, analysis, and writing, and I found the process to be beneficial in my understanding of the meaning of quilting to women. This analysis approach is consistent with the non-linear nature of qualitative philosophy. As Janesick (2000: 389) states, "The qualita-tive researcher uses inductive analysis, which means that categories, themes, and patterns come from the data." Even in the earliest stages of data collection I began to see that although these women lived in different parts of the country and that no two quilters were alike, they discussed similarly how they came to choose quilting as an activity, the process of taking on the identity of a quilter, and the carework involved in making and gifting quilts.

I had continual contact with quilters during the research and writing process. My relationships with quilters who were and were not participants allowed me to get more involved in the field generally. It helped me to become aware of additional quilt-related resources such as quilt stores, websites, and other quilters to interview. I also had continual exposure to quilting, and quilting from the perspective of the people who do it. This exposure kept me abreast of quilting vocabulary and lingo, and also reminded me of the importance of getting at the emic perspective in quilting activities. After I had reached theoretical saturation with interviews, I began discussing with quilters some of my initial findings. This member-check process proved most useful as I was able to engage in a dialectical conversation between quil-ters, between me and the transcripts, and between me and the sociological and academic community.

## WHEN QUILTING IS ENOUGH: IMMEDIATE COMMONALITIES THROUGH QUILTING

Before entering the field, I assumed that I would easily fit into the "student" role to these midlife quilters. Because of my younger age relative to midlife women (I was then in my late twenties), I hoped that quilters would take me under their wings and instruct me about quilting. This was not always the case, as many women much older than me were just learning how to quilt, and relied upon me to guide them through the initial learning-to-quilt stages, which was sometimes awkward. Especially when we introduced ourselves to one another in group settings we often shared how long we had been sewing and quilting. In these situations I learned that my personal sewing and quilting experiences were often greater than the majority of women in the group. Because of my quilting experience, unexpectedly I often took on the teacher role instead of the student role (sometimes by coercion, sometimes by choice), instructing women of a variety of ages about sewing and quilting.

There were both advantages and disadvantages in sharing myself with these women. I enjoyed learning more about quilting and developing my skills and my artistic eye within the medium of quilting, and got my feet even wetter in the ways of quilting (Geertz 1973, 1983). I became close friends with many of the women I studied, blurring the line between researcher and quilter. To resolve some of the tension I was feeling regarding analyzing my acquaintances/friends, I began writing about my own quilting experiences as well. Putting myself and my quilting experiences under similar analytical scrutiny helped inform the sometimes fuzzy line between me and the quilters in my study.

My insider status and general knowledge of sewing and quilting helped me to participate in group events and serve as a knowledgeable volunteer at quilt shows. Publicizing my identity as a quilter was important in establishing my legitimacy as a quilter, and as a researcher. For example, before entering the quilt guild, the contact person (gatekeeper) strongly encouraged me to become a member. I agreed. I joined the guild the first night I attended and very soon discovered that my membership was an important indication of my commitment to the group. When the gatekeeper introduced me to members, a number of potential participants asked if I was a member, nodded their heads approvingly when I stated that I was. Then they agreed to an interview (fieldnotes 1997). Additionally, after I completed data collection, I continued my involvement with the group.

The quilters I interviewed were very interested in and aware of my extensive sewing and quilting background. In fact, we often spent a short time during interviews discussing current projects and asking one another for advice on quilting projects. During a majority of interviews, women also interviewed me to find out a few things: quilting skills and preferences, age, and marital status (with some women suggesting to fix me up with their friends' sons or even their own sons). With this information in hand, then, quilters willingly gave me advice on my quilts, how to proceed with my research, and, of course, guided me in my love life (regardless of if I wanted this advice or not). In some cases, if my quilting techniques were not up to par, or if I had a different perspective on what quilting was about, I found it difficult to gain entrée to a quilting group.

When meeting new quilters, I would first introduce myself as a sociologist and then as a quilter. They would focus on my being a quilter, sometimes even requesting to examine my quilting before they would agree to talk with me. My role as a quilter seeking more quilting knowledge was often essential to the success of the project more so than establishing myself as a researcher. However, at times my role and identity as a researcher prevented access to quilters, despite my quilting background. I did rely on my quilting background when interacting with quilters and this quilting identity seemed to counteract the negative assumptions that the women I encountered had about researchers. Specifically, there were times when quilters became quite aware and suspicious of my presence. I was denied access to some quilt groups because I was a researcher, with members of one group relaying the following response to me: "We don't want you here inspecting us and what we do. We don't know what you'll do with the research that you do, and we don't want any part of it" (fieldnotes 1998). Groups that did reject me were usually smaller than a typical group, met on weekends, and found this to be the only time they could "get away from it all." Understandably, these women's quilting time was precious to them and they felt having an outsider with them would disrupt their lives in an unacceptable way. These kinds of experiences were disheartening, but revealed the importance of quilting in women's lives.

In contrast to gaining access to quilting groups, talking in public with the hundreds of quilters I encountered during this research was relatively simple, even when introducing myself as a researcher and as a quilter. Often times, just being a quilter was more than enough to be accepted by other quilters, creating at least an artificial closeness or commonality. One example of acceptance occurred while checking into a hotel before a national quilt show: "During the hotel room cancellation fiasco, a woman [who was a quilter] turned to me and asked, 'Are you a quilter?' I replied, 'Yes.' She asked, 'Do you want to stay in my room with me since you don't have a room for the weekend?'" (fieldnotes 1999). Quilters generally enjoyed discussing their quilting experiences with an interested and informed listener, and especially another quilter. Yet, in some contexts when it seemed that quilting was the only thing women had in common, it alone was not enough to establish rapport (Baca Zinn 1979; Beoku-Betts 1994). Especially in attempting access to quilting groups that differed along race, age, education, and social class lines, neither my status as researcher nor my status as quilter could grant me access. Even preferences about color, style, and technique in quilting came to become divisive issues in these contexts. Again, such refusals contributed to my understanding that quilting spaces are close-knit and sometimes intimate settings.

## PIECING TOGETHER MY PERSONAL AND PROFESSIONAL SELVES

I have been sewing for thirty years and quilting for fifteen years. Growing up the second oldest in a family of six girls on a farm in rural northeastern Nebraska, I was encouraged along with my sisters to learn traditional masculinized skills, such as animal husbandry and light farming duties, as well as feminized skills like cooking, sewing, and quilting. My mother taught me to sew when I was about six years old, and my first quilting memory centers on my mom and her friends making a fundraising quilt for their alma mater.

I remember this day of quilting only vaguely, but I recall the women quilting in the basement having a good time, and being flattered that the local newspaper came to take their picture. Being quite young at the time, I remember wanting the women to leave so that I could have more of my mom's attention.

My mom and I struggled over my sewing lessons, as I tended to sew in my early years rather quickly, making lots of mistakes and risking my fingers in the path of the needle on a regular basis. To avoid injury, my mom would "strongly encourage" me to slow down on the machine, which, truthfully, I haven't really learned how to do to this day. Sewing became a source of tension in our relationship. And, in addition to teaching me how to sew, mom was also teaching my other five sisters to sew, which I can only imagine was a very taxing thing to do. Mom came up with a workable

**West Point**
# N E W S P A P E R S
Combining the Cuming County Democrat and the West Point Republican
### Page 1C   Thur, March 20, 1975

## Making Quilt for School

Some of the workers on the quilt for the College of Saint Mary in Omaha for its annual boutique are (left to right) Mrs. Hilbert Hunke, Mrs. Anthony Aschoff and Mrs. Paul Stalp. The children are Betty Aschoff, Mary Beth Stalp and Peggy Stalp.

FIG. 2.2. My first experience with quilting happened in my parents' basement in Nebraska, watching my mom's college friends making a fundraising quilt. I think I was more interested in the newspaper reporters who came that day than the actual quilting. Reprinted with permission of *West Point News*.

solution, though, for soon after learning to sew, my sisters and I joined a 4-H club, which further legitimated my mother's efforts at communicating the importance of sewing. My sisters and I eventually competed successfully in clothing construction through 4-H at the county, regional, and state levels. After we had mastered the basics of sewing from my mom, she enrolled us in sewing lessons with our neighbor, who is a professional seamstress, specializing in women's bridal wear, and has a sewing

FIG. 2.3. Kim's quilt frame in the kitchen. Personal photograph.

studio in her home. Despite the tense moments, I remember fondly the time I spent sewing with my family and my sewing teacher. While sewing, we did discuss sewing, but we also discussed many non-sewing topics, including our lives as women and girls, and, to date, we continue to share our sewing experiences.

Note that quilting had not yet entered my life path, but did so when I was a young adult. My dad's sister Genevieve, or "Aunt Jenny," taught me how to quilt when I was twenty years old, and a college junior. I thought my extensive sewing skills would transfer easily to quilting. I assumed incorrectly that quilting was a rather unsophisticated way of putting fabric together, especially in comparison to the complicated tailored clothing I could assemble by then. I learned that quilting requires precise sewing, design, and color theory skills. In addition, quilting encourages creativity and patience, and an appreciation of history. Through this creative learning process, I started and finished my first quilt, which I still use and of which I am proud.

Importantly, I learned much more than quilting techniques from my Aunt Jenny. We learned a lot about each other and formed a closer relationship by quilting together. I have been able to replicate this process, this woman-centered creative culture, with others in similar situations. When I travel to see my sisters, go to my parents' house, entertain family in my home, or visit friends who quilt, we typically carve out some time for what we term "crafting." Crafting as my sisters and I define it includes quilting, sewing, cooking, educating each other about new creative projects, shopping for creative materials, and most recently learning knitting and weaving. I envision that my three nieces will be destined to learn to sew and craft just as we did – at the very least they were bombarded at birth with homemade gifts from their aunties! Through engaging in creative work in shared spaces, we recreate the supportive environment in which we first learned to sew. This time for us is relaxing, educational, emotionally satisfying, and regenerates our energy for our multiple life tasks. This creative work can become the social glue that helps regenerate family social ties.

Being a quilter in contemporary times can require complicated negotiations with non-quilting family and friends. Because I had learned to sew as a child and it held a regular and respected place in my everyday life, I was fascinated while researching quilting that midlife women struggled with their family and friends in order to make time and space for quilting in their lives. Many women in this study referred to quilting as a now necessary component of their lives and central to their well-being. Quilters shared with me how they bought fabric, how they stored it in their home, and how they hid it from their families. Accumulated fabric is usually called *stash* or *fabric stash* and carries with it an air of secrecy (see Stalp 2006a, 2006b). Quilters advised me that when I finally "settled down," I would need to learn how to hide my fabric stash from those with whom I shared space (this would be a good example of the "love life" advice passed on to me from quilters). Little did they know that their cautions came to me far too late, for I had been purchasing and collecting fabric since childhood. My current fabric stash cannot be hidden from anyone successfully at this point, for it occupies a large bookshelf and a few random boxes and drawers in the half story of my home which is my quilting and sewing studio.

## GENDERED ASSUMPTIONS ABOUT QUILTING AND FIELDWORK

Quilting is difficult, not just technically, but artistically. Yet, before I had learned to quilt, I, like many others, discounted quilting as a challenging and creative outlet. When my late Aunt Jenny agreed to teach me how to quilt, I was faced with a number of learning curves. I will never forget the important lessons about color and design that I learned from this first quilting experience. After struggling about which colors were appropriate for a quilt (she liked pastels, while I prefer bold colors), we argued about the design of the quilt. Once I began to identify myself as a quilter, I also began to notice outsiders' responses to quilting – quite similar to my previously uninformed opinions. Acknowledging my earlier misinformed attitudes about quilting was helpful to me in that I could understand on a personal level about how quilters tend to keep to themselves when talking in detail about quilting, as they feel others will be unappreciative or even mocking of quilting, which I have also experienced. Although difficult at times to manage, having an insider/outsider perspective while doing this research was beneficial overall for I could see both sides of the situation while collecting, analyzing, and writing.

Quilters' consciousness about the devaluation of quilting was also revealed in the logistics of the interview process itself – typically, when I showed up to their homes to interview quilters, their families had either already left or were in the process of leaving. When I did try to engage family in the interview process, I either received looks of astonishment or disgust. Some participants revealed that their spouses did not understand why they were even being interviewed about quilting. In situations such as this, participants arranged an interview when we would be alone in the house. Some women also attempted to involve their husbands and children in the interview process. They tried to get their family members to comment on quilting, I believe to include them in the process, to make them less suspicious of me, and to emphasize the importance of quilting to them in and outside the home. Despite the validation I provided in interviewing quilters, few spouses or family members wanted to be involved in the interview process at all. When husbands were present in the house, interviews were likely to be shorter and women seemed more reserved with me than during our initial contact to set up the interview. With husbands away from the home, the women seemed more open to discuss quilting and what it meant to them.

Being in the field with quilters over a four-year period, I learned how to talk about quilts, and I also learned about how *not* to talk about quilts. For example, women consistently talk about quilts in relation to their selves, as well as their personal and family connections, aspects heavily emphasized in women's traditional gender roles. Any overarching linear concepts, such as time (e.g., hours, days, weeks, months, years) and quantity (how many quilts a quilter has made), are secondary to the meaning-making processes women used to measure and discuss their quilting activities.

#### HOW LONG DID IT TAKE YOU TO MAKE THAT QUILT?

Quilters are most likely to talk about a quilt in non-traditional measures, while non-quilters generally talk about quilts in linear ways. Upon viewing a finished quilt, outsiders to quilting generally ask, "How long did this take you to make?" Since quilters in this study do not consider traditional time measures while discussing their quilts, they often find it difficult to answer time-related questions in meaningful ways. As the quilters in this study quilt for personal reasons, they are not as concerned about how much time they devote to any one quilt as an outsider or a professional quilter might be, for example. Quilters are concerned about how to charge for one's time when quilting for others, but the activity of quilting for others is a minor element for the women in this study.

More often, quilters discuss a quilt and the quilting process as it relates to the person for whom it was made, or what they were experiencing personally while constructing a particular quilt. If women do discuss a quilt in terms of marking time, they are usually struggling with a new technique (e.g., "it took me forever to learn how to do this"), having trouble with fabrics, or frustrated that they did not have enough time to devote to it. And, when they do discuss time in this way, they are most likely sharing detailed quilt information with another quilter, or with an understanding outsider or sympathizer to quilting. Additionally, and important to note, the actual discussion of time remains secondary to quilters. The new quilt production technique or problem is at the forefront of the conversation, not the clock or calendar.

So, to answer this complicated question, quilters have various responses. Some state a standard hourly rate (e.g., 100 hours) to answer the meaningless questions quickly (meaningless to them, but more important to outsiders) and move onto a more salient discussion of the quilt at hand. When giving out a standard hourly answer, some quilters are careful to portray a quilting time frame "that will sound good" to the outsider, and fall in between the precarious and mystical time line of too much time and not enough time spent on any one quilt (fieldnotes 1999).

Spending too much time on a quilt puts the quilter at risk of being considered a time waster. Not spending enough time can leave her open to criticism. If the viewer does not like the quilt, the quilter is apparently at fault for not devoting enough time to do a satisfactory job. And, some quilters posit that quoting too little time on a quilt can make quilting seem too easy. This can result in the outsider scoffing at quilting as something that anyone could do (e.g., only that long? I could do that!), or the outsider trying to negotiate a no-cost or below-cost quilting arrangement with the quilter if it is a for-pay situation. Most women in this study chose to quilt for fun, and turned down money-making opportunities related to quilting (e.g., making a quilt for hire), as they felt that they would tend to enjoy quilting less when the process becomes more related to making money and less about creativity: "when I have quilted for money, it felt less like fun and more like work, yuck" (fieldnotes 1999). When quilters are asked about quilting for money by outsiders, they sometimes quote a price far above what outsiders are willing to pay for the service to turn them off to the idea and to leave themselves more time to work on their own fun projects (fieldnotes 2000).

### HOW MANY QUILTS HAVE YOU MADE?

Another common question outsiders ask is, "How many quilts have you made so far?" Interestingly, quilters do not keep track of their quilting in this way; they typically do not have the number of quilts that they have finished in their heads. Instead of using a mainstream conception of quantity to measure their progress in quilting, women refer to their personal relationships with others as a way to tap indirectly into the number of quilts they have made. Many women can recall how many quilts they have made by reviewing past events to jar their memory into a quantity mode of reporting them: "in the last year, I made a quilt for my grandson's birthday, a t-shirt quilt for my niece's high school graduation, and then I finished a commemorative wall hanging for my parents' fiftieth wedding anniversary, so I guess that's three quilts" (fieldnotes 2000). Specific quilts, the intentions behind them, and the relationships with those who received them rather than sheer quantity are the prominent gendered measures in quilters' lives.

Quilters also use event deadlines and goals to organize their time and their lives, rather than traditional time allotments. I use myself as an example: a number of friends from high school and college are currently having children. I have chosen to make crib-sized quilts, or baby quilts, for their children. This is a highly personalized and special gift requiring specific skills that establish a tie with the child, and indicate the closeness of my relationship to the parents. For myself, I make bed-sized quilts, taking considerably more time and materials, and I do not complete them at the same rate as baby quilts. When a friend calls with the happy news of a new arrival, I prioritize the baby quilt over other projects in the queue. The events surrounding others in my life (e.g., a baby's due date) often take precedence over quilts that I make for myself, and are consistent with the explicit carework of gifting quilts to others that is prominent in this study.

In addition to the gift-giving purposes quilting provides me, I also have personal quilting goals. I have noticed from my quilt research that the majority of quilters possess few quilts that they have made themselves – most finished quilts leave the home as gifts. Giving quilts as gifts is a gendered tradition within quilting. Additionally, giving gifts allows women to establish or continue a cultural tradition in their families, and individual women create personal and historical legacies. I want to have immediate visual and tangible evidence of my quilting talent in addition to giving gifts to important people in my life. I also sew some of my own clothes, and part of the fun of sewing clothes, beyond the enjoyment of the process, is being able to wear them proudly. Similar to sewing clothes, I want to have near me quilts that I have made, and be able to look at them daily, to feel a sense of accomplishment that I have created these beautiful items myself. Therefore, I have decided to invest considerable time into making bed quilts for myself. I want my quilts to be in good condition so that I can eventually pass them on to others who will value them. These quilts preserve my artistic and technical quilting talent, as well as exhibit the effort I put into my quilting. Just as published articles and books help academics keep track of their work progress (e.g., tenure and promotion requirements), quilts leave records of the people who created them, and provide tangible proof of quilters' marked and skilled effort. In this way, then, quilts record the continued importance of the gendered cultural tradition of the quilting process.

REVEALING MY QUILTING AND MY SELF

During the fieldwork process with the quilt guild, I tried to investigate different dimensions of the organization to see how quilting was done, including smaller groups that specialized in various techniques. I attended two that met regularly during my data collection stage: one met in the mornings and one in the evenings. The morning group was known as "The Friendly Starters" and the evening group called themselves "Contemporary Art." Each group had different members with no overlap, and the focus for each differed as well – the friendly starters were concerned with "getting going" on their quilting projects, and wanted to use the time both to start a group project and to continue to work on individual projects that were already started. The second group resembled a book club and we met to discuss contemporary quilting design and techniques, and we did not work on projects while there. It was the second group that provided me the opportunity to reveal my own quilting self.

In 1999, the contemporary art group devoted the year to making "concept quilts" – individual ten-inch-square quilts portraying a specific concept. At our first meeting, we each brought an idea with us to be conceptualized into a quilt. We assigned these concepts randomly, and began making quilts. This year-long challenge was to help us spark our creativity and develop new skills, and by restricting the size of the quilt to ten inches, it would not take long to complete each quilt.

The challenge for the month of June for all group members was "The Last Straw." I interpreted the concept to be about romance gone awry, and constructed a toilet with an interactive seat, one which could be snapped up or down. Through assembling "The Last Straw" I was making a statement about the struggle within romantic relationships between heterosexual men and women. I had recently ended a long-term relationship and felt this would be a good healing project. Admittedly, all of the concepts were challenging to put into fabric, and I had struggled with each one, as well as presenting my quilts to the group. However, this one was different – after hearing the concept, the image of a toilet with an interactive seat popped into my mind and I knew this would be the quilt I would make. I was certain to follow the few rules we had set up for ourselves: I met requirements of size (ten inches square) and layer (three layers, two of fabric, one of batting). I incorporated at least one new technique in this quilt (stuffed appliqué, hand quilting). Finally, as I found out through making this quilt, I was sharing my self, identity, personality, and sense of humor with these women. And I was fearful that my quilting would not be up to par, that my sense of humor would offend them, and that they might want me to leave the group.

I brought my quilt to the next meeting and waited nervously for my turn to share it, meanwhile viewing others' interpretations of The Last Straw. One woman depicted it by constructing a broken camel with a pile of straws weighing the animal down enough to break it in half. Another chose a pictorial scene, describing a typical situation where she and her husband reached the point of frustration around his fishing attempts where she actually had said, "This is the last straw. Either you clean the fish you catch, or you stop bringing them home." A third woman explained to us how her abstract quilt design represented difficulties she faced during the last month. Finally, it was my turn. I showed them my interpretation of The Last Straw and after witnessing their response; no explanation from me was necessary. A great squeal of delight erupted from the group. A few women shared that they were thinking of similar interpretations about the difficulties of romantic relationships, like two tubes of toothpaste, one rolled and one squished in the middle, and the like.

Up until that point, I felt like an outsider about my presence at the meetings, and questioned my identity as a quilter. Many of the quilts I had made up to that point were for my friends who were either getting married or having babies. These quilts were not about me, necessarily, and some came with their own restrictions (e.g., fabric to match the nursery, or s/he only likes this color). In my mind, that night was the first time I really felt accepted by the group. When I look at that quilt hanging in my house, it reminds me of being accepted as a quilter, by other quilters whom I respected.

This small group of women (twelve members when all were present) consistently kept each other informed about their lives. As a newcomer to the group, it took me a bit of time to be able to participate fully, meaning that I did not reveal much about myself to the group until I knew more about the group, its members, and how to go about sharing information about myself. Somehow I decided to share my self through my quilting, as this medium was something that we all had in common.

Sharing my self with them was both a personal and a professional risk. Ultimately, becoming more involved with the group helped me gain entrée into the group, and to establish meaningful relationships with individual women from the group. Soon after I had unleashed my quilt and my self to the group, I started feeling more support from the group. For example, at a guild meeting soon after, one woman from the group approached me: "She gave me a hug and asked me how I was doing. I said, 'Fine,' and she looked at me and said, 'No, really'" (fieldnotes 1999). This exchange led us to a brief but more meaningful and more detailed conversation about what was really going on in both of our lives, not just a surface level greeting like we had participated in before.

While I was in the writing stages of my dissertation, which was on quilting, I also relied on quilting to get me through the difficult times. My friends and I had started meeting weekly for quilting and sewing together, where we would gather with wine and chocolate to work on our current sewing projects (e.g., quilting, knitting, crocheting, and mending). I had run into some difficulty explaining my topic to my committee and convincing them that it was a worthwhile study, which continued even in my dissertation defense. To deal with this effectively, I had decided to make a small, personalized quilt for each committee member from my dissertation and master's thesis. I selected the pattern "Sunbonnet Sue," which pictures a girl with a bonnet in profile. I depicted her doing something that they each enjoyed doing (e.g., playing basketball, gardening). After sharing these quilt blocks with other quilters,

Detty, who is in her fifties, came up with "Oh Shit!" which indicates her aversion to the sweetness implied in the Sunbonnet Sue pattern (see Plate 6 and Pershing 1993 for a series of quilts that challenge the "sweetness" of Sunbonnet Sue).

Working on these quilts kept me busy and kept me thinking about the committee members' responses to my work and the dissertation writing process in positive ways, which I definitely needed at the time. *After* the defense was complete and I had passed and been awarded my Ph.D. in sociology, I pulled these quilts from a bag and gifted them to my committee members. They were pleasantly surprised, although I did not know until recently how much so. Throughout the years we see each other at national conferences, and they have each individually told me how much they value their quilt, how they are taking care of it, and where they have decided to display it. With the constant struggles I had faced with arguing the academic and sociological relevance of quilting, their positive responses were certainly a relief! As quilts occupy such a domestic and intimate space in our everyday lives, conceptualizing quilting as a worthy research topic is a bit risky. Williams (2000) notes how the second wave of feminism succeeded in gaining white women entrance into the paid workforce, but resulted unfortunately in the devaluation of women's unpaid family work – this devaluation can be thought to include women's quilting efforts, and especially those that are unpaid, like the leisure quilters in this study.

## WHEN QUILTING IS NOT ENOUGH: TRIPPING THROUGH THE TULIPS OF AN ACADEMIC CAREER

Through my experiences in sewing and quilting, I realized the wealth of knowledge and support present within women's spaces, specifically women's creative spaces. Sewing and quilting have been important anchor points in my life, and they are activities that I turn to repeatedly as a relaxing escape, to spend time with others interested in sewing and quilting, and more simply for leisure purposes. Nevertheless, it has been only relatively recently that I have realized the importance of quilting as a topic for sociological analysis.

Quilting as a topic provides a cultural and gendered setting in which I demonstrate the hidden but salient meaning present in women's lives, and within their sites of cultural production. Sociology of culture rarely addresses issues of gender, and it assumes that cultural practices are gender-neutral. Sociology of gender has given little attention to activities that are creative, unpaid, and part of the fabric of everyday life. Instead, both areas of sociology have emphasized meaning-making phenomena and activities tied to economic production. Neither pays much attention to activities pursued without the intent of economic gain, or activities that are pursued because they are enjoyable in their own right, those activities that provide an outlet for creative expression. My study focuses on women who pursue quilting, on their own or as members of groups, for reasons other than economic gain.

Initially, I had difficulty finding research in sociology that combined my interest in gender and culture. Early during my graduate studies, I began to retreat regularly into sewing sessions alone, with other quilters, and, when I had the opportunity, with my sisters. I soon realized that women's everyday and creative activities in the home are a neglected area of study within sociology, even within feminist sociology. I then began to see how my involvement in quilting could be brought under the lens of sociological analysis. Why did this activity – which was so central in the lives of my mother, her daughters, and my female friends and relatives – have no sociological visibility?

As a scholar interested in both gender and culture, I believe that encouraging a dialog between the sociology of gender and sociology of culture is critical to my work as an academic sociologist, and specifically introducing gender issues within a cultural framework. As a feminist scholar, I question how culture theorists conceptualize structure and culture, and their failure to incorporate gender fully in their analyses. Likewise, as a culture theorist I have questioned the sometimes narrow conceptualizations of feminist sociology that have tended to concentrate on male-dominated structures and economic spaces such as workplaces. Everyday privatized activities of women in non-public spaces are an important part of social and cultural life, yet they are too little studied.

Hearing, for example, Marty the tattoo artist, when he administered my first tattoo, talk about how "his old lady" was a quilter, and after checking myself in an eye roll, I patiently listened to him elaborate about the similarities between his wife's quilting and his tattooing practice. Marty had quite a firm grasp on his wife's quilting and his own tattoo process, and how they were similar and different than one another. Sitting there I realized that there were a lot of similarities between the tattoo artist and the quilter. Both had an artistic process, both were somewhat disregarded in contemporary society, but both had very rich stories to tell.

I am a sociologist, not a historian, and certainly not a quilt historian. Thus, I leave the particular discussions related to quilt history to my highly skilled colleagues in other disciplines. My discipline, sociology, is famed for viewing society without blinders on, and according to my Introduction to Sociology students, often much of what I have to say about society and its institutions is considered to be somewhat "harsh." That writ, my experience in doing this research has been that there are a variety of populations who do not care at all for what I have to say about quilting, and have been very explicit in letting me know this. I do not claim to know all the history surrounding quilting (revisionist, elitist, or otherwise), but I do lay claim to the findings regarding the midlife women in my study – viewed as a group, they do collect more fabric than they need, they do enjoy quilting to an extent that some might not understand, and yet they are not individuals with compulsive personalities who should be locked up for their "addictive" behaviors. These women are no different than anyone who has found a leisure activity that they enjoy to the point of avocation, and to the disgruntlement of seemingly neglected family members (e.g., football wives?). And yet, these women *are* different than other family members, for they have systematically put themselves and been put last in terms of enjoying personal leisure activities, and even when they are quilting, they are quilting in gendered ways – they are making gifts for others to cement important relationships.

At various professional venues over the years, I have been made quite aware that this research makes people uncomfortable. Quilting reveals numerous social facts about current U.S. society: midlife women who have chosen to devote their time and attention to their families sometimes want some of it back for themselves, which can upset the status quo of family dynamics (Lynch et al. 2007; Stalp et al. 2008). Leisure activities provide midlife women with such opportunities. Quilting is one of many options for midlife women to choose and become involved in at a serious leisure level. Thus, one can claim glibly that quilting practiced in its current form is a challenge to the family. To understand this claim, one must know a bit about current quilting practices, the family, and the life course of traditional women in the U.S.

# 3 IT'S NOT JUST FOR GRANNIES ANYMORE: LEARNING TO QUILT AT MIDLIFE

> I knew that I would always quilt, I just didn't know when, I put it off. When I was about forty-two, I guess, my kids were grown and so I thought, alright, now's the time I want to do it. And, so, I decided to make a quilt.
>
> Alice, middle sixties

Quilting is a time-intensive activity. Quilters put a great deal of time into it, especially while learning. Today, most quilters learn to quilt at midlife, through taking classes, or from a friend or family member, and not as children as our memories might guide us to think. Thus, for women who begin quilting at midlife, the quilting process can sometimes be painful as it disrupts family dynamics. The time and attention now devoted to quilting may have once been focused on family needs, unpaid and paid work. Contemporary quilting practices can challenge the status quo of the family as women have to deal with the new challenges that quilting brings to them and their already established lives.

Being a quilter can be thought about as a marginalized identity – an identity that is shared with a select few – many women hide their identities as quilters, often sharing their passion for quilting only with other quilters or sympathetic non-quilters (Goffman 1963). Women keep their quilting secret from others, as many misunderstand what quilting is, and have stereotypical thoughts about people who quilt. They juggle quilting with other responsibilities, and find that family, friends, and co-workers do not always understand the interest and passion women have for quilting. Like other identities, being a quilter involves a process of "becoming." When "becoming" a quilter, many women tried quilting and liked it, continued with it to the point that they considered themselves to be "quilters," and then began to self-identify as quilters. Noticeably, when women began to publicly self-identify as quilters (e.g., "I am a quilter") they also defined quilting on their own terms, and created personally defined measures of accomplishment, (i.e., subjective careers) around quilting.

Kelly is a quilter and an academic in her early forties. She struggles with being understood by outsiders in both categories. She is aware of the negative connotations attached to both aspects of her identity as a quilter and as a Ph.D. candidate. Her family has traditional notions of what women should be: "Nobody knows what academia is, nobody knows what a Ph.D. is. I don't have kids. If I had kids that would be part of the traditional American life that people understand. I really do think that this is a way that people understand me in a way that they don't understand other parts of my life." Kelly is quite aware of the gendered family expectations present, as well as the quilting and feminine stereotypes that outsiders to quilting present to her: "I think it is really odd in a way but it kind of makes me think maybe I shouldn't quilt because I don't want to be pigeon-holed in that way." Despite the paradoxes present in her work and her quilting life, Kelly continues quilting.

## LEARNING TO QUILT AS AN ADULT, AND NOT AT YOUR MOTHER'S KNEE

When midlife women discussed how they began quilting, they typically began with someone who got them interested in quilting, or someone who taught them how to quilt, such as a family member or a close friend (Lenz 1998). For example, I learned how to quilt from my Aunt Jenny. The mere act of learning to quilt, then, is directly connected to larger social memories of quilts, their role in women's lives, and especially the relationships formed through quilting experiences. Through various ways of learning to quilt, women draw upon familial memories in recalling their quilting ancestors and reasons for learning to or continuing to quilt. Women reach backward through their family trees to re-establish connections with once-forgotten quilters, or establish new quilting traditions that they hope will develop into family memories.

Women in this study learned to quilt in one of three ways: relying upon their quilting heritage, in response to the skipped generation of quilters, and as new quilters. Quilting heritage refers to the unbroken line of familial quilting ancestors, continuing to pass down the techniques and traditions of quilting among women. Women influenced by their quilting ancestors or quilt heritage choose to continue the already established and culturally strong family tradition of quilting. The skipped generation of quilters consists of the women who were not included in the passing down of cultural quilting knowledge, either by choice or by socio-historical circumstances. Women with skipped generations of quilters in their families note with regret the women relatives who never learned how to quilt. Missing out on the cultural knowledge of quilting from ancestors, these women typically learn from others outside the family. New quilters are those women without any quilting background in their immediate families. Aware of the personal and familial legacy benefits of quilting, new quilters begin quilting traditions in their families. As they learn to quilt, they seek to establish new traditions that will endure in their families.

### QUILTING HERITAGE

Women with quilting heritage are conscious of their cultural legacy activity as a form of cultural production. Throughout interviews women reveal that they have relied upon their quilting heritage to validate their quilting activities. Many of these women own and treasure quilts made by now deceased family members and are consciously preserving what they perceive to be a valued family tradition. Women with quilting heritage recall their quilting ancestors, point with pride to generations of women who quilted before them, and express gratification at knowing that they are perpetuating familial cultural traditions. Kim, who is in her seventies, noted that there was "always a quilt up on a frame" at home, and as she does the same, her frame only fits in her kitchen, making it difficult to cook. Theresa, who is in her sixties, recalled: "My mother was a quilter and we've always had quilts in the house. My mother had a quilt frame that hung from the ceiling and when she didn't want to quilt then she would just pull it back up and put it on the ceiling. I would thread needles and stuff like that." Similarly, Karen, who is in her fifties, learned to quilt while she was expecting her first child, from her grandmother: "My grandmother was a quilter, and her daughters quilted. My granny gave me my first fabric for my quilt. She said that every quilt needed to have yellow in it, a little bit of sunshine, and she gave me some yellow cotton fabric and some calico fabric to make a quilt with."

Karen recalls her first quilting lessons affectionately, as she also remembers spending quality time with her grandmother. Likewise, Kim, who is in her seventies, remembers:

> I started [quilting] during the 1930s during the Great Depression. My mother quilted for the public. She had a quilt up nearly all the time. I was just tall enough to reach the frame standing up and I begged her to let me have a quilt. She would say, "No, but when I put up one of my own you can quilt." So when she put up one of her own, well I started quilting and I've been quilting ever since. I was quite young.

Denise is in her forties, and has a long-standing quilting tradition in her family: "I come from a long line of quilters." Her grandma was an avid quilter, and pledged to give special gifts to her grandchildren: "My grandma had said that for all the cousins, when they married, they could have a set of silverware or they could have a quilt." Denise never received a quilt specially made by her grandma: "Grandma died when I was in high school and needless to say I did not get a quilt or a set of silverware." Fortunately, for future quilters in the family, the tradition of quilting did not end with her grandma's death: "My mom felt so bad. There were probably fifteen of us that never got a quilt. She felt that she could do that, so she started making quilts for my cousins and I." Denise's mother picked up the tradition of quilting more actively, to finish the promise of tradition that her own mother had begun. Yet, with all this quilt activity in the family Denise still had not learned to sew or quilt. Until she was newly married, she had little interest for fabric outside of collecting it. Denise taught herself how to sew and quilt as an adult, first for necessity and then for pleasure. She is currently quite active in quilting, and is carrying on the traditional aspects of quilting as she is teaching her children to quilt.

These women are able to recall their familial and gendered cultural past in discussing their sewing and quilting heritage. Learning to quilt from family members cements the ties among women in families, especially cross-generational ties. However, there are women who have renegotiated the traditional notions of quilting, changing within quilt families how women learn how to quilt, and also the kinds of quilts that they make.

Ginny is in her forties, and her mother and grandmother both quilt using hand techniques. She had little interest in learning how to quilt by hand, yet Ginny admired her family members and the work that they did. A friend, a quilter who used the sewing machine, taught her how to quilt by machine as an adult:

> A friend asked me if I would teach her daughters how to play piano, and in return she would teach me how to quilt. She taught me two things that were really important. One is that I could use my sewing machine to make it and secondly it didn't have to be a full sized bed quilt in order to be a quilt, it could be something smaller. I realized, hey, I don't need to made bed quilts. I am an only child and my mother has forty million of them already so I don't need to make bed quilts.

In this exchange of skills Ginny learned how to quilt and is carrying on the quilting tradition in her family. Ginny uses a sewing machine, while both her mother and grandmother continue to quilt by hand, an important difference in the quilting world. Similar to Ginny, Chelsea is also in her forties, and she learned to quilt in a non-traditional way, too. After learning to quilt, Chelsea started teaching others how to quilt as an instructor. Here, Chelsea shares how she first almost did not learn how to quilt:

> I didn't know anybody [here] at all and I didn't have a job. I was standing outside the grade school with one child in a stroller waiting for another child to come out and there was another mom, same situation. She said, "Would you be interested in joining a small group of women. We are going to invite somebody to teach us how to make quilts and we are going to get together." I thought neat. We had one lesson. She gave us the lesson and said, "I'm really sorry, but I've got to go into the hospital, I won't be able to finish teaching you." So I went to visit her in the hospital, and I said, "Well, how about I be your gopher? I'll be your strength and you be the knowledge." And I picked things up pretty quick. We taught classes for a while team teaching and I learned all the stuff. I just really took to the medium because it's got so many aspects to it.

Chelsea has since taken to quilting, has become a successful instructor, and takes great delight in passing on quilting to others. Together, these women's quilting heritage experiences (which are both traditional and non-traditional) symbolize a way of carrying on treasured family traditions. Within their accounts of learning to quilt, women reveal the personal, familial, and historical importance of continuing quilting traditions.

### THE SKIPPED GENERATION OF QUILTERS

Quilters are often aware of the missing women in their quilting heritage, referring to these women as the skipped generation of quilters. Quilting traditions may skip over entire generations of women for personal, historical, or cultural reasons. Personal reasons include personality differences, lack of interest, upward mobility, and paid-work demands. Personality issues might also come into play through the detailed and stereotypical perfectionist techniques that quilting requires.

Kathy is in her forties, and she indicates that her mother did not teach her how to sew, as she did not have the patience to do so:

> My mother knits, my mother does not quilt. She sews. She sewed all of my clothes as a kid. My grandmother made like one quilt. My grandmother was sort of like that do one each kind of thing. There is like one quilt [in our family that she made]. She did a lot of embroidery and that kind of stuff. My mother did not have the patience to teach me [how to sew]. I taught myself.

Similarly, Judy's entrance to quilting did not come through her family line, but through taking a quilting class. Judy is one of five women in the study who are under forty years of age, but her and others' experiences mirror midlife women's quilting in many ways:

> I never really knew a lot about quilting, but I always thought it was cool. My friend saw an ad for a quilt class in continuing education, and she suggested that we take it together, so that was about three years ago. I had done some needle-work and cross stitch, but the only time I'd ever used a sewing machine was in my home economics class. I know in a lot of other families, their parents, their mothers quilted. My mother hated sewing, she had a sewing machine and, the first time we ever heard her swear was when she was sewing! (laughter) She made some curtains and put the sewing machine away, and that's the last we saw of the sewing machine. My great grandmother and my mother's aunt quilted because we have one of her quilts, but other than that I never knew anybody who quilted growing up.

Additionally, Diana is in her fifties, and attaches her quilting to a great grandmother who quilted, but she did not learn from a family member:

> I really never had anybody in my family who was a quilter but I relate to other grandmothers and great grandmothers who did. I did have one quilt that was passed down to me from my great grandmother, it was my grandfather's mother who made it sometime around the turn of the century, and it's very worn. They were just going to throw it out and the family knew I liked quilts, maybe I would want it? Are you kidding! Don't throw that thing out, that's worth a lot to me!

Hannah is in her fifties, and learned to quilt by taking classes as an adult, despite the fact that both her grandmothers quilted. Her mother disliked quilting as a child and is part of the skipped generation of quilters in her family: "My mother told me, 'When I was a little girl, I would attend quilting bees with your grandma. When she quilted at home she'd have me start quilting with her but she'd take out all of my stitches if they were too big. And since she took out all my stitches all the time, I wasn't inter-ested.'" Hannah notes that both her grandmothers quilted, but that she did not grow up with quilting surrounding her as Theresa mentioned earlier. Hannah considers the historical reasons why her grandmothers quilted, and why her mother did not quilt:

> My mother was really what I call the "skipped generation" of quilters, in terms of sewing. She came of age after the Second World War and even though she grew up with a mother who quilted, she herself never took up quilting as a practice. She went to work full time when I was four years old. Even though she sewed it wasn't really that much of something that held her, and quilting just didn't interest her.

Similarly, Karla is in her sixties, and her family history includes quilting, but skips over her mother and her grandmother:

> I am the only one in my family that does it. My mother doesn't sew or quilt, neither one of my sisters sews or quilts. My grandmother didn't either, now she may have sewn clothes or things like that but she didn't do quilts. So there was nobody in the family that I could learn from. I have since learned from my mother that her grandmother quilted and she remembers that her grandmother had made a crazy quilt but she has no idea where it is.

Women like Hannah's and Karla's mothers and grandmothers lived through the Great Depression and the Second World War, and are predecessors to today's generation of quilters. Although women have always worked in both paid and non-paid positions (Amott and Matthaei 1996), women engaged in paid work in the first half of the twentieth century did not have the public support that some working women enjoy today. These women faced a set of socio-historical demands different from contemporary women. Additionally, when women experienced upward mobility, handmade items were replaced with newly made products from the extensive production of new goods during the post-war economic upswing.

Sarah is in her thirties and is, like Judy, among the small number of younger quilters (younger than midlife), who began quilting earlier in their lives. She took up quilting in her thirties as a way to avoid going to the local bar every night. Sarah began quilting because she had an interest in it, and she wanted to establish some adult behavior in her life, claiming that "quilting saved me from a life of drinking." Despite hearing vague family stories about quilts being thrown out after the Great Depression, she had seen no actual evidence of quilters or quilts in her family history. Intrigued by quilting, Sarah decided to (re)start the quilting tradition in her family she had heard so much about. Having a family quilting heritage is somewhat expected among quilters, as Sarah experienced when she joined her first guild:

> Some of the ladies were a little bit surprised that someone in my age group would have picked up quilting without there being a quilting tradition. Others thought that I was kind of creative, through that my quilting interest was good, a good avenue for me to explore. I know my mom wanted to have quilts so she encouraged me.

Sarah's mom does not quilt, but she appreciates them enough to encourage her daughter to learn how to quilt. After quilting for a number of years, Sarah noted the number of quilts she had made, and considered the advantages of learning to quilt when she was younger (rather than at midlife):

> One of the ladies said, "I wish I had started quilting when I was thirty." And I said, "Really?" She said, "Oh yeah, just think of all the quilts you'll be able to make by the time you're my age." I think that was the first time that it really dawned on me that I have a whole lifetime ahead of me to make quilts. Women who get started in their fifties don't have a whole lifetime. I wish I had started quilting when I was four.

Sarah is passing on the tradition of quilting she has begun in her family by giving her nieces and nephews quilts as gifts, involving them in her quilting process when they visit her, and teaching them how to sew and quilt.

### NEW QUILTERS

In explaining why and how they learned to quilt, women reveal what quilts mean to them, and the important role quilts and quilting play in their lives. Women without a quilting heritage or even a skipped generation of quilters still manage to find out about quilting in a variety of ways. Certainly, women cannot control their ancestors' participation in and passing down of quilting traditions. But, many women have chosen to begin to establish the tradition of quilting in their families. This impetus for being a new quilter can come from educational experiences with sewing (e.g., home economics courses in school), marrying into a family with quilting heritage, and having or meeting friends who are quilters.

Michelle, now in her fifties, remembers being interested in history when she was young. She took a home economics class in the eighth grade, when she was fourteen, and really enjoyed it. At sixteen years of age, she taught herself to quilt: "I just had this old book that somebody had given me, it was a paperback book about quilting and it just fascinated me." Neither her mother nor her grandmother sewed or quilted, but Michelle's interest in history and sewing encouraged her to learn quilting. Although she has been quilting now for over thirty years, Michelle still notes with sadness the absence of sewing and quilting heritage in her family's past:

> One thing that makes me really jealous is if I go over to somebody's house and see this really old quilt and they say, "Oh my grandmother made that" or "my great grandmother made that." I wish I had something like that, but sewing is just not in my past. It's just me and I'm hoping that my daughter has an appreciation for it. I wish that I had come from that kind of family that had a history, but nobody sewed in my family, and I don't know why.

Through her quilting, Michelle hopes to secure family heirlooms and to reinforce the values of homemade items to her children. Interestingly, Michelle and her sisters all sew, although their mother does not. And following Michelle's example, her sisters are also picking up quilting: "All of my sisters sew and they have all started to quilt after visiting me as an adult and seeing some of the things that I've made and given them." Encouraged by this, Michelle has taught fifteen women to quilt since she taught herself, ensuring the beginning of a quilting tradition in her family and friendship networks. She hopes to someday be the answer to the question, "Who taught you how to quilt?"

Leaving a legacy behind for their children was a reason women gave frequently for becoming involved in quilting with no preexisting background. Emma is in her early forties, and found herself attracted to quilts, and even more so when she realized she could make quilts as lasting gifts for her children: "I always liked quilts, and I had a neighbor who was quilting and I thought it was really neat. But with two little kids I thought it was not possible. At that point I decided that I was going to make them a quilt by the time they graduated from high school." The combined network connections and the desire to make memorable gifts for her children were why and how she got involved in quilting.

Yet, there are also women in the study who just wanted to learn how to quilt, like Lisa, who in her fifties found more success with quilting the second time she learned how:

> The first time was about twenty years ago. I took a class in adult education, and I think it was during a time when I was working part time and I got my little project and did it and then I started working full time and it just kind of laid there. And I've always admired patchwork in quilting but I didn't really ever get back to it again until 1997 or so.

Work demands put constraints on Lisa's success at quilting. This was not the case for Linda, who was in her early sixties when she learned about quilting through her workplace:

> Some co-workers mentioned to me that they were going to be taking a quilt class and asked if I might at all be interested. The thing that intrigued me most about it was that at the end of this class, which was four Tuesdays, that we would have a double-sized quilt pinned and ready for us to finish when we got home. And it was for thirty-five dollars. I thought this is really great because I have sewn for quite a while. I started making my own clothes when I was about nineteen and then made maternity clothes and baby clothes and Halloween costumes. Since my daughter is grown up I really hadn't done a lot of sewing and this was one way that I could use my machine and get back into that and I found that I really enjoyed it. So what started then has just really brought me a great deal of joy.

Work ties also linked Carrie up with quilting, and in her opinion, she benefited from working at a fabric store when first learning how to quilt in her forties:

> I basically started quilting when I started working at a fabric store and I remember folks coming into the store and picking out the fabric and really

taking the time, and I really didn't appreciate fabric like I do now. Well, you know, once you get hooked, you're hooked. And I really like it and just learned from the store and feeding off the interest and the enthusiasm of the other people, customers and employees that was really nice and sharing and learning was really nice, too.

Currently, the majority of women come to quilting as adults, and mostly at midlife. Women at this age are better able to invest time and money in quilting after retiring from paid work, when their children attend school or leave home, as was the case with Karla, who was inspired to learn how to quilt from a friend:

> I never sewed a stitch until I started quilting. I had a friend who started and she was taking quilting classes. And I just envied her and I wanted to quilt and I could not afford to go to the store and buy one. And I wanted one that I could be proud of so that is why I wanted to start and it is fun.

Learning to quilt is closely linked to women's identities. The cultural transmission within quilting occurs between women through the institutions of family and the quilting community, both local and global. Through the family, quilting techniques are passed down through generations of women. In learning to quilt, women develop aspects of their selves and begin to engage in meaning-making activities that elaborate identities. They make connections with other women who quilt, and can make historically meaningful connections to legacies of women (both familial and non-familial) who have engaged in quilting generations before them.

Life course, human development, and generativity scholars note that at midlife, many women take the time to assess their current state in life and re-create themselves (Kotre 1984; Miller and Stiver 1997). If women choose to make a more serious commitment to work, or to a leisure activity like quilting, there can be tension in women's lives: "It is the nature of the conflict between caring and autonomy which imparts a distinctive character to women's life cycle and determines the particular constraints women face at mid-life" (Notman 1980: 106). As women reach midlife, they begin to focus on their own needs instead of only focusing on the family's needs. With such changes, the existing family structure, spouses, and children can feel confusion, anger, and resentment toward the primary caretaker.

In terms of quilting, there are both objective measures of success and subjective measures of success. Objective measures are those that outsiders to the activity can understand easily, such as selling a quilt, teaching a class, building an artistic reputation, and winning quilt show awards (and accompanying prize monies) – coincidentally, these objective measures typically also involve economic measures of success. A subjective measure of success is based in the personal and not necessarily the economic. For example, quilters value learning new techniques, building skill sets, making connections with others who quilt, and maintaining kin ties through gifting quilts to others.

## MIDLIFE WOMEN AND QUILTING

Society generally expects contemporary women in traditional family settings to engage in both paid work and unpaid carework for others (Hochschild 1989), which leaves little time for leisure such as quilting (Mattingly and Bianchi 2003; Wearing 1998). While most women manage to combine paid work and unpaid carework successfully, many accept the inability to pursue independent leisure or pleasurable activities (Crosby 1991; Green et al. 1990; Herridge et al. 2003). Yet, when women in traditional settings reach midlife, life circumstances change – children leave home, spouses retire, and women themselves near retirement (Shapiro 1996). At midlife, women may finally be able to pursue interests that exist outside the family.

A study of quilting includes both traditional femininity and carework. As quilting is historically considered "women's art" it has also been relegated to the feminine, the private sphere, and the home, rather than the art museum, as compared to other forms of art when examined historically. As such, quilting practices today merge femininity and carework, for although women do choose quilting for relaxation and creativity purposes as other artists might approach artwork, quilters approach quilting in very gendered ways as they often go through the quilting process to make gifts for others, to create family heirlooms, and to maintain family ties (Cheek and Piercy 2004; King 2001). Through quilting, then, women do carework for themselves and carework for others (Johnson and Wilson 2005), which is discussed more thoroughly in Chapter 6.

Quilting maintains and challenges traditional notions of contemporary femininity. When quilting becomes a regular leisure activity in their lives, women often develop quilting as a *subjective career*. Subjective careers in quilting focus on personal goals that are separate from external measures of success such as salary or artistic recognition that professional quilters might possess.

## SUBJECTIVE CAREERS

A subjective career can be understood as a coherent line of activity that is important to identity but is self-defined and is not always visible to outsiders. Subjective careers can be developed in many places, and in any kind of work that is important to an individual's identity, is self-defined, and is not always visible to or understood by outsiders. People can develop subjective careers in places such as paid work, carework, voluntary organization participation (Kendall 2002; Ostrander 1986), and creative endeavors such as quilting (Cheek and Piercy 2004; Stalp 2006a, 2006b, 2006c).

Evetts (1996: 3) considers subjective careers to be especially valuable in understanding the experiences of women and men scientists, as they individually interpreted their objective careers: "The subjective career focused on individuals' experiences, how they saw the constraints and opportunities, how constraints and opportunities were negotiated and managed, how individuals perceived the problem and the possibilities, the influences, the turning points, the key events and decisions."

Scientists in Evetts' study were being evaluated objectively by supervisors as part of their paid work, their "objective career." What Evetts points out, though, is that scientists interpreted their own paid-work careers with subjective measures – they decided what was important to them on a personal level. At times the subjective goals contradicted the objective goals. However, these scientists believed it was important to place personal-level measures upon themselves. An example of this is in negotiating promotion while avoiding management duties:

> In general, then, avoiding management or being persuaded into other kinds of posts and developing a professional specialist career was one way of achieving promotion as well as accommodating private and personal responsibilities, and, in addition, pursuing a particular kind of occupational identity. Promotion and career in organizations was dependent on merit; building a reputation was a viable objective for both women and men. (Evetts 1996: 114)

Individuals pursue subjective careers for personal reasons (Evetts 1996; Stebbins 1979, 1996), and are defined and understood subjectively (e.g., by the individual). Although subjective careers can be related to the prestigious paid work of research scientists, they can also be understood in relation to less prestigious or lesser paid work, much like that of jazz musicians (Becker 1963), river guides (Holyfield and Jonas 2003), and even unpaid work, or serious leisure activities, such as in the case of amateurs generally (Stebbins 1979) and barbershop singers specifically (Stebbins 1996). Subjective careers represent a subjectively defined social world closely linked to identity and self-worth, which can anchor one's life (Stebbins 1970, 1971).

Midlife women develop subjective careers as quilters, which centers quilting in their lives, and replaces the time and attention formerly spent on family concerns. External and mainstream measures of success and failure (such as salary or artistic recognition) are not as important as those established by individual quilters. For example, midlife women choose quilting because they enjoy it – their efforts are not focused on gaining income, and they are not working toward the status of professional quilter.[1] Subjective-career quilters often define themselves as artists and develop a creatively centered identity as a quilter, that is independent of family and work obligations. Quilters establish personal goals and measures of success that are important only to themselves (and may be misunderstood by non-quilting family and friends).

## LEARNING TO QUILT AT MIDLIFE

Women can often make time for themselves at midlife. At this time, women and their spouses are nearing retirement from paid work, and grown children are leaving the home for educational or work purposes. Quilting trends illustrate that the majority of women take up quilting at this point in their lives (Leman Publications 2003, 2006). Midlife women who choose quilting are setting aside time for themselves in the form of leisure and self-fulfillment. Additionally, midlife women have been engaged in paid work most of their adult lives, and have access to more discretionary income than women had in previous generations.

Angela is in her fifties, and she makes the following observations from attending regional and national quilt shows, reflecting the high numbers of midlife and older quilters present: "At these quilt shows you realize the heavy population of older women. I suppose a lot of it has to do with the fact that they are not raising children and a lot of them, even though a lot of them work, a lot of them are retired by the time they can pursue going to these shows." Angela's observations are in line with research on quilting trends that show an increase in women's leisure activities once other competing gendered responsibilities are minimized. Nora is in her sixties and began quilting after her children were grown and she had gone back to school: "I had finished a graduate degree and had decided to do something for myself." When Nora began quilting, she and her husband had recently both retired from paid work and bought their retirement home in a new region of the country. Nora used learning to quilt as a way to establish roots in her new community: "I joined a [quilt] guild here to meet women. When a woman moves to a new place there are certain ways you meet other women. Having small children is one of the big entrées, other than that you try to find an organization where you will meet women with your like interests." Realizing how women can meet one another and become friends, Nora carefully found women with like interests such as quilting to meet and befriend.

Meg is currently in her seventies, and she had sewn and quilted throughout her life, but she found more time for quilting when she and her husband retired from paid work. When they travel by recreational vehicle (RV) in the U.S. during the summer, Meg brings along her sewing machine. Meg quilts for artistic purposes as well as personal goals that she believes are related to her increasing age: "I've gotten to the age where I don't want to waste anything I do. And I don't want to take the time just to do something that isn't going to be of use or within the line that I'm focusing on. I quilt to create beauty, to create something of myself." Meg's reasons for quilting definitely fall within the tenets of a subjective career. Her quilting goals are self-defined, and she creates something not to satisfy an external audience, but to satisfy herself. Earlier in life, Meg was recognized for her oil painting and found herself wanting to be just as successful in her quilting (e.g., recognized artistically, externally, and economically). To be successful objectively as a quilter, Meg would have to create quilts by a set of standards based on artistic/economic success. Instead, she decided to focus on her personal quilting goals: "to create beauty, to create some-thing of myself." In defining quilting on a personal level, Meg admittedly has little time for outside measures that an objective career might highlight such as creating a quilt that will show well or bring a high price. Instead, Meg makes quilts as gifts for her family and friends.

Karla has also reached a stage in her quilting where she selectively makes quilts for others, with no external pressures or time lines: "Quilting is something for me to enjoy. I just want to do what I want to do. But I have no great pressures on me to do anything."

## BECOMING A SELF-IDENTIFIED QUILTER

The collective aspects of quilting (e.g., Amish quilting bee, sewing circle) are commonly and mythically known as are the finished products of quilts. However, many aspects of quilting, such as the actual piecing together of a "quilt top" or the quilting together of the "fabric sandwich," take place for women when they are alone, in the home, in the car traveling with family or driving carpool, and while on family vacation. In teaching each other how to manage time and family quarrels over time, space, and money that arise around quilting (see Stalp 2006b), quilters also provide support for one another, affirm their new identities as quilters, and encourage the creative process.

During the research process I was exposed to a variety of women's quilting experiences, including quilt shows and exhibits, guilds, small group gatherings, fabric stores, and women's personal quilting spaces. In these spaces, women revealed their passion for quilting, something often concealed in other contexts. In these "safe" spaces occupied mostly by quilters or quilt supporters, quilters were able to nurture interested women into becoming self-identified quilters. Out of the quilt guild, a small group formed with six women (including myself) that focused on starting new projects. We met weekly at one woman's home for coffee, and then we would work on our individual projects while hanging out together until early afternoon. Of the six women, four were beginning quilters, struggling with finding enough time in their everyday lives to devote to learning quilting.

Once women identify themselves as quilters, they take on additional behaviors related to quilter identity. Quilters mentioned repeatedly that they began to think mostly in terms of quilting (e.g., their heads would swim with ideas for new quilts, they envisioned quilt patterns everywhere including in nature and architecture, and they would solve problems with their quilts while engaging in other activities) (Csikszentmihalyi 1990). Women learn the process of quilting, which includes designing, fabric shopping, and spending time with others in guilds and working groups.

At one of the weekly meetings I attended, one woman in her fifties, Veronica, expressed her understanding of becoming a quilter:

> One morning, Veronica arrived at the quilt bee, grinning from ear to ear. She told us breathlessly, "I finally get it. *I am a quilter!*" She told us that she had spent yesterday in her quilt space, simply getting to know her fabric. She had spent an entire day playing with her fabric, experimenting with ideas, colors, and projects. She was entirely focused on the process, not the product. "When I came down from my quilt room to make dinner, my husband asked, '*Did you get anything done up there?*' I was so mad at him!" The women looked knowingly at one another. One woman commented, "She's got quilt fever." Then another woman said, "Join the club." Then they all laughed as they congratulated Veronica. (fieldnotes 1999)

Veronica was frustrated at her husband's question because it focused on a final product, when she was just learning how to enjoy the process of quilting. If she had something tangible to show for her time spent with fabric, he would understand and approve of the time she spent, much like an objective measure – time spent at an activity could produce a finished product. But, as Veronica focused on the process of quilting and not the product, she had no visible evidence of how she had just spent her time, except for her conscious choices to use a subjective measure. Additionally, Veronica had only spent a few hours in her quilt room, and planning a quilt can take weeks rather than hours, especially for a beginning quilter. Her husband's comments revealed that he was uninformed about how much time actually goes into making a quilt. His expectations were that she had visible proof of how she spent her leisure time, away from the family. When she returned to the family space, she would immediately begin to transition into meal-preparation duties for the family.

Before her transformation, Veronica had been feeling guilty because she had not finished any of her quilting projects. She considered herself a beginning quilter, and felt that she lacked the advanced skills and confidence necessary to accomplish a quilt project on her own. Veronica joined the small quilting group to meet other women, to learn from them the basics of quilting, and indirectly to have a supportive ear when she came into conflict with her family over her quilting activities. While the more experienced quilters supported Veronica and the slight difficulty she was having with her husband, they also encouraged Veronica as she developed her identity as a quilter. They understood the significance of Veronica's interaction with her husband and could relate to the moment when Veronica's husband challenged her. Veronica realized how meaningful quilting was to her. As Veronica's husband seemingly placed more importance on the quilt product than the quilting process, she understood the value of simply having time to devote to her self and to her creative needs. Defining the meaning of quilting for herself marks the beginnings of Veronica's subjective career in quilting.

Melinda is in her forties, and faces similar resistance from her family to her quilting, and notes that her husband's stained glass hobby is a complicated comparison:

> It's not until something gets done that they're like, "Oh I actually understand what you see about [quilting]" because my husband is doing stained glass. He's got an eye for piecing something which in his case is glass and I piece fabric so I know he knows how much work is really involved, but it's not until the actual product is done that they appreciate it. And for him to do stained glass, he can get his done in a month, I don't know, he's more focused or something, but I've got so much other stuff going around that everybody's in wonderment, "Oh, when is she ever going to get that done?" So it kind of puts a negative thing to it.

The more women increase their involvement in quilting, the more quilting activities shape their lives and the more they reaffirm their newly found identities as they receive validation from other like-minded quilters (Stone 1981). Once women discover that they enjoy quilting, they spend a great deal of time not just quilting on their own projects by themselves, but also sharing the activity with friends. Also, self-identified quilters develop additional behaviors akin to more experienced quilters and become exposed to and involved in more quilting activities.

Quilting as a form of women's art- and craftwork provides physical and mental benefits (Anderson and Gold 1998). Delaney-Mech (2000: 6), a physician and a quilter, notes:

> A simple sewing task, such as sewing together two patches, lowers your heart rate and blood pressure. It sends a wave of relaxation throughout your whole body. This calming is important because of all the pressures we encounter in our daily lives. We are wives, mothers, care givers to our aging parents, wage-earners, and volunteers. In the course of our days, we face snarled traffic, new technology, financial pressures, and the challenges of raising children. We need the health and life-giving benefits of quiltmaking.

Quilting provides inner peace, creative outlets, and time for reflexive thinking. For some women, quilting is the relaxing equivalent of taking a bubble bath, having some alone time spent at their own choosing.

Quilting benefits women emotionally, leaving them with a calmness and focus not achieved through other requisite, everyday activities such as childcare, laundry, meal preparation, or housework. For example, Angela explains the role that quilting plays in her life, emphasizing the social support among friends and artistic inspiration she receives from quilting:

> Quilting is my life, that's my friends. Almost all of my friends are quilters. I have developed a large part of my life around quilting. I find it stimulating to be around creative people and there are a lot of creative people in my group. There is always something to learn. There are always a lot of laughs with these people. They are very supportive of troubles in your life. If you need a shoulder to cry on they are always there to listen and help.

Similar to Angela, Sarah quilts because it brings her a sense of personal accomplishment and support from other quilters. Specifically, Sarah, in her early thirties, noticed she was spending an inordinate amount of time hanging out in bars with her friends. She decided to make some changes in her life and she decided to learn how to quilt. She enjoyed quilting a great deal, especially in comparison to her everyday work life. Here Sarah notes the differences between her work life and her quilting life:

> You start working, it's the same stuff day after day, your boss might say that you did something good, but you know tomorrow he's just as likely to yell at you and you don't get that sense that you've actually ever completed anything and then I'm spending all my time in bars doing absolutely nothing, so now I look back and say that my quilting saved me from a life of hard drinking (laughter).

Sarah juxtaposes her quilting experiences (where she sees valuable accomplishments occurring) to her paid-work life (where she finds little success in externally defined pursuits). In comparison to her work life, Sarah details her first quilt guild experience:

> I still was a beginner in my own mind and I thought that everybody would be like real tight lipped and wouldn't want to talk to anybody who hasn't been quilting for twenty years. These were all middle aged and older women and they kind of adopted me. They really welcomed me into the group. That's one thing I really like about being in a guild is the praise that you get from other people who actually quilt themselves and understand how difficult something is.

Heather is in her forties, and notes how quilting improves her as a person, that it provides a level of calmness and peace for her:

> My mother made a comment that she likes me better when I'm quilting, so, I think it's really good for me. It still seems like when I spend three or four hours and don't notice where the time has gone, that's kind of like what I am always looking for, that's the goal, that's where I'm trying to end up, is to have spent time and have that sort of calm, contented, satisfied feeling when I'm finished.

Heather's comments echo many quilters' testimony that quilting provides inner peace, creative outlets, and time for reflexive thinking, much like the *flow* state discussed by Csikszentmihalyi (1990, 1996). The repetitive motion, or flow, of quilting exhibits religious or trance-like properties. For some women quilting even has a spiritual nature.

In addition to providing midlife women a successful conduit to aging (Schofield-Tomschin and Littrell 2001), quilting provides a creative outlet, control over one's time, and a way in which women can give of themselves in relationships with others. Individually, midlife women provide specific answers as to why they quilt, and what benefits it provides them. Collectively, these reasons coalesce around the personal, familial, and artistic themes in women's lives. Quilting, for example, is necessary to Chelsea's sense of well-being, and she notes that her mood is negatively altered when quilting does not fit into her daily schedule: "I have to quilt. It's funny, though, if I don't do it, I get really irritable." Likewise, Cassie is in her early thirties, and strives to quilt everyday, for it provides her with positive emotional and physical experiences: "My true love is quilting. I know when I'm really stressed out that more times than not, one of the reasons is because I haven't been quilting. Ideally I would like to quilt for one to two hours every night. But normally it's two to three times a week." Quilting everyday is a goal for a number of women, and nearly all in this study try to quilt several times a week.

Heather's comments reveal her commitment to quilting and to herself as a quilter: "I'm just going to keep making quilts and keeping myself happy because that's all that there is." Likewise, Eileen is in her sixties, and states, "It's just a challenge and it's just exciting. I mean it's truly exciting to make quilts for somebody." Quilting also has spiritual meaning for women. Diana reveals the spiritual connections involved in her quilting activities:

> To me there is a spiritual significance to quilting, too. I guess I see that God created me and he gave me certain abilities and so I feel like I am blessing that to God and to others to create. I feel like whatever I have done or accomplished God has given me that ability. I quilt everyday and I ask God to give me time to work, to give me ideas. Then I thank him for that.

Diana takes pride in practicing her quilting everyday, and thereby acknowledging that her work is significant beyond just herself. Her daily activities contribute to her personal spirituality, and to her commitment to her home and family. Denise describes her discovery of quilting as a life-changing experience: "Quilting is one of the few experiences in my life I've ever had where it was as if somebody hit me upside the head and I said to myself, 'I was born to do this.'"

Emma, a mother with three young children, values her time spent quilting because quilts have more permanence than many other parts of her life:

> When I started quilting I was at home with the kids and lots of the stuff that you do is repetitive. Before you have the dishwasher empty, there are more dirty dishes, same thing with the clothes. The house is always a mess; the grass always needs cutting. You never see that you're getting anywhere, or you correct the kids and they do the same thing five minutes later; it's like you're not getting anywhere, whereas if you make a quilt at the end you have something tangible. That's what really attracted me and the fact that you can make it exactly the way you want it, and there's really no right or wrong way to do it, and it's something that you can give to somebody else, which is really neat too. I get the pleasure while I make it and then at least hope the other people will enjoy it too.

Emma feels that her efforts at quilting are more obvious and last longer than other duties she tends to daily for her family in the home, furthering the integration of quilting into women's lives. Loretta, in her fifties, explains how central quilting is to her everyday life: "It's so much a part of me now, it would be unthinkable not to have it a part of me."

Beyond learning new skills and becoming involved in new activities, quilting is a meaningful activity that encourages women to become creative individuals. Women use quilting to place their personal-level interests more centrally in their everyday lives, and develop quilting into a subjective career. However positive this process is for the individual quilter, being a self-identified quilter is not something that everyone will easily understand. There are women who protect their being quilters very carefully, only sharing it with those they feel will appreciate this part of them. They fear being misunderstood or judged negatively for participating in such a traditional and highly feminized activity. To participants, quilting is important – they decide individually how it is important to them, thus affirming a subjective career in quilting.

## AFFIRMING A SUBJECTIVE CAREER IN QUILTING

Learning a new activity often involves adhering to externally produced measures of success and failure, and others' expectations. Certainly many quilters follow these measures, but once women have learned to quilt and are comfortable with it, they begin to make their own rules for quilting. They define success and failure in quilting subjectively and independently from one another.

As women become more involved with quilting, they also discover that they must cloak their quilting identity from non-quilting outsiders as well as family members. In addition to the personal satisfaction that women gain from quilting, they also guard their quilting identities from others whom they feel do not understand what quilting is about.

Karla describes the tension with her mother regarding the efforts she puts into her quilting: "My mother doesn't understand how long it takes. Even though she has been here a few times and has seen me working on quilts and everything else she just doesn't have a clue as to how much time it takes. And people that don't do it don't know unless they have sat and watched." Cassie is particularly careful with whom she shares her quilting interests in the workplace. Cassie's colleagues certainly appreciate the quality present in the finished quilts they have hired her to make for them, yet they are openly suspicious and even hostile about the time she spends quilting. They accept the finished quilts as valuable cultural objects, but according to Cassie the time and effort she has spent on them is what they question and judge negatively. Cassie is particularly cautious about sharing her quilting interests with outsiders: "I need to be careful of the people that I show my things to." She explains how people at work react to her as a quilter when she reveals her finished quilt products:

> I don't want them to say, "Oh god, I don't do anything, you must do every-thing." That's not the image. So I try to make sure it's someone who's not going to say, "Well, when do you have the time? You work just as hard as we do!" I brought in a quilt that I had made and showed a couple of people and they did say, "Well, how can you do that?" It's a patronizing kind of remark, "Well, how do you do that *and* everything else?" So then I'm justifying it, because here I am not trying to self-promote and then it seems like I'm self-promoting, so I say, "Well, I don't have kids and I really don't have any hobbies besides running and so, this is what I do to relax," which is all true. But I'm justifying why I'm doing something like this. I try to minimize it, but it does kind of get that response. I think more from the men it's, "Oh, you quilt" meaning kind of old-fashioned, or fuddy-duddy.

Interestingly, the excerpt from Cassie's interview demonstrates the multiple standards for contemporary women. Her co-workers' knowledge of her quilting interests brings to light that Cassie feels she cannot be too successful in her quilting endeavors, or have too many time-consuming activities beyond paid work (not including children). The final insinuation by male co-workers that Cassie might be a fuddy-duddy because of her quilting even causes her to be conscious of the potentially negative nature of her outside-work interests. Cassie's co-workers, both male and female, are similar to her family and friends as they appreciate the quilt as a finished product, but not the quilter as she engages in the actual process. Logically, without the quilting process, one would not have a quilt as a finished piece. To have a finished quilt, someone has to make it.

Hunting and fishing provide an additional and important parallel experience to developing the identity of a quilter. People experience freedom when participating in activities which they enjoy, hunters and quilters included. Madson (1996: 133) discusses hunting from the perspective of a hunter, and provides an inner under-standing of enjoying a non-mainstream activity:

> The genuine hunter is probably as free as it's possible to be in this technocracy of ours. Free not because he sheds civilized codes and restraints when he goes into the woods, but because he can project himself out of and beyond himself, out of and beyond the ordinary, to be wholly absorbed in a quieter, deeper, and older world.

Although people engaged in marginal activities perceive the mainstream as wary of their interests, participants in these closely identity-linked activities remain passion-ately committed to them: "But as much as anything else, one of the greatest urges impelling such a hunter is his search for freedom, and for the genuine personal adventure inherent in such freedom. Just as game species may be the truest indica-tors of quality natural environments, so hunting can be an indicator of quality natural freedom" (Madson 1996: 132). A similar theme of commitment is articulated in this discussion of a man's fishing life with a questioning outsider:

> A friend, a naturalist, who has not fished since he was a teenager and won't, on "moral grounds," asked me recently if I *had* to fish to be closer to nature ... Though I have fished since before memory and have never needed a "reason" ... I realized I don't really go to rivers to "connect" with the natural world; I go to catch fish ... I go to the river to catch trout. Everything I do depends upon that one fact. I am happy to think I am better skilled now than when I began, so many years ago. There may be sunsets, wild-flowers galore, rainbows in the sky, good fellowship, good fishing, or lousy fishing; but what has drawn me here, the fulcrum of the entire equation, what will always draw me to water, is the simple prospect of catching a fish. (Lyons 1999: 72–73)

Viewing quilting from women's perspectives and understanding the subjective careers of quilters underscores the relevance of quilting in lives of individual women. It also demonstrates how quilting connects women quilters to one another, as well as to non-quilting outsiders. Quilting, along with other unpaid subjective careers in which women and men traditionally engage (e.g., scrapbooking, doll collecting, hunting, and fishing), are often easily misunderstood by outsiders. Quilters perceive outsiders to be dismissive, even explicitly negative, toward their passion for quilting.

Angela describes the encompassing position that quilting currently has in her life, and recalls how others often respond to her passion:

> People ask me, "What do you do now that you are retired?" I tell them, "I quilt." And they look at me like, "Well you can't possibly spend all your time quilting." They have no conception that you really could. No, you are not sitting in a chair putting a needle in and out of fabric all the time, but there are so many aspects involved in quilting that you literally can spend your entire life totally engrossed in quilting and I am awfully close to doing that.

In developing a subjective career as a quilter, Angela has had to renegotiate the stereotypes attached to quilting and other leisure activities. Quilting has complex and layered meaning-making activities within it, not always obvious to the outside perspective. Alice, now in her sixties, also notes how quilting is integrated into her life activities, and the important place quilting has in her life:

> No matter where you go, if you pull the quilting out, people will stop and talk to you. And they'll ask questions, and they'll tell you about their grandmother, and they'll tell you about Aunt Jane and they'll say I have a quilt top, do you want it? And no matter where you go, there's going to be a quilt store, and you go in one you've instantly got friends, and it gives you, you feel accomplished and you feel energized and you have goals all the time.

Karla states her reasons for quilting, noting the creative freedom she garners from the activity, highlighting her own self-satisfaction and a pressure-free environment as successful components to her subjective career as a quilter: "It's fun, I thoroughly enjoy it and it is like my therapy. [In quilting] I don't feel pressured to do anything that I don't want to do. I see me doing this forever, if the arthritis stays away and the hands are still able to work. I just do it strictly as pleasure and for my own self-satisfaction." Additionally Karla enjoys quilting as a subjective career in that she does not put externally generated constraints on herself, like producing so many quilts per year or quilting through the pain. She simply implies that if her arthritis becomes unmanageable, she will find something else that she wants to do just as much.

Although often stereotyped to be rigid and rule-based, quilting actually has great freedom within it as a creative activity. Eileen reflects upon the freedoms present in her quilting process: "One of the things I learned throughout the years that I was sewing and quilting, it's wonderful to not to have to be perfect. So what if the little corner isn't exactly right? So what? It's okay. And life has been a lot easier since I discovered that." Eileen's critique of perfectionism affirms how she has developed her own goals and measures of success through quilting. When she states, "It's wonderful to not have to be perfect" she is stating her subjective measure of success: "It's okay. And life has been a lot easier since I discovered that." Eileen's personal measure of success manifests itself positively in other parts of her life, and is evidence of a subjective measure – she is not, for instance, concerned if "the little corner isn't exactly right."

When talking with others about her quilting, Heather used to express the worth of her quilts through the traditional measures of time and money, measures used in objective careers like a professional quilter. She has since become more critical of such objective measures which focus mostly on external product-related standards. Heather now talks about her quilts in subjective-career ways. She values her quilts and the quilting process in ways that are important to her – ways that emphasize her personal, artistic, and self-expression standards:

> I stopped talking about my quilts in terms of their value simply because of how long it took me to do it. It's like quantifying something of value based on math rather than based on the thing. I used to feel like I had to justify why I considered them worthwhile. I hope that I talk about them more based on how I felt doing them, if I like them, if I think they're successful, what I like about them. Just be more willing to interact with them and speak about them from that intuitive side rather than that efficiency side.

Heather traces the growth of her commitment to quilting, realizing how her relationships with her quilts and her quilting process have become more complicated over time. By focusing on the connections she has to her quilts and the quilting process, Heather highlights the deep meaning embedded within them, and articulates the subjective-career goals and measures of success she has developed around quilting.

Meg offers a thoughtful reflection on her development as an artist and as a quilter. Implicit in this reflection is a critique of outside standards imposed on her and her work as a quilter:

> At one time I really wanted to be accepted as an artist because I had been accepted as an artist for my oil paintings and I wanted my quilts to be accepted as art also. And then I got to thinking, that's putting the values in the wrong places. If I don't do this to please myself, who in the world am I doing it for? And you're not in competition with anybody but yourself, and a lot of people lose track of that.

Meg's realization that she is only in competition with herself rather than seeking recognition from others helps her manage criticism coming from others and from her self. Admitting the pleasure she derives from quilting, knowing the limits she places on her own quilting and continuing in it for personal reasons keeps Meg going in her quilting efforts.

Women value quilting on many important levels, yet they do not expect nonquilters to be interested in, or value, quilting in the same ways that they do – they measure their quilting activities outside of economic and family-centered standards – this is evidence of how women develop subjective careers around quilting. Quilters state that it is difficult to articulate why they quilt in a way that makes sense to nonquilters. Some women in this study have been quilting for so long that it has become a fundamental part of their lives, confirmed in the intensity with which they talk about quilting as an avocation. While non-quilters who admire quilts often focus solely or primarily on the product – the finished quilt – quilters give far more emphasis to the *process* of quilting, for it is the process as well as the product that women enjoy (for example, recall Veronica's realization about process and product and how Melinda's family value her finished quilts but don't quite understand or appreciate the process of quilting). How a quilt is produced is often as important, or even more important, than the finished quilt itself, especially in considering quilting as a subjective career.

## QUILTING AS IDENTITY WORK

The development of quilting as a subjective career for these midlife women coincides with changes in the life course. As women progress through the life course, their focused energies adjust from being family-centered to include themselves and their personal interests. Earlier in their lives and especially in traditional settings, women choose to devote time and energy to their families, often at cost to their personal creative selves. Despite marked advances in paid work and career development, we still expect primarily women, not men, to tend to the family. These expectations take a daily emotional and physical toll on women and can limit their life course opportunities, as well as their leisure time. Research indicates that women experience less leisure time and on a less regular basis than do spouses and children, and some women actually regret the personal sacrifices they have made throughout their lives to tend mostly to family needs. Interestingly, quilters combine carework for selves and others through quilting.

When beginning to quilt, women in this study slowly "became" quilters, and began to self-identify as quilters, owning the activity at least to other quilters and sympathetic non-quilters. As these women became quilters, they negotiated their identities and developed the creative identities of quilters. Quilting was a leisure activity, one that provided respite and relaxation to them, and they left the activity of quilting feeling calmer and rejuvenated. This feeling of calm was important enough to the women in this study that quilting became an everyday part of their lives, and was something that they would turn to for relaxation on a regular basis. Quilting also provided women a place to "do gender" effectively, for as they were relaxing and doing something for themselves, they were also making gifts for others, further cementing important relationships and engaging in carework for others while caring for themselves.

Leisure activities are gendered, and quilting is certainly no exception. Inequitable divisions of domestic labor assign women a "second shift" of labor at home in comparison to men (Hochschild 1989). Mattingly and Bianchi (2003) demonstrate that this trend has not changed, for through time-diary data collected in the U.S., married men have, on the average, one month more of leisure per year in comparison to their wives. As a process, quilting provides a respite from the demands of the everyday lives of contemporary women, and it provides a mechanism for women to see themselves as part of a larger culture, a community of culture creators with a past and a future, and not simply as consumers of culture.

Quilters in this study match up with the research on how men and women are able to access and engage in leisure differently. Even though the participants in this study choose to quilt for fun (e.g., non-economic cultural production), they still practice it in gendered ways. Women talk about quilting as a good way to connect with family and friends through gifting finished quilts, rather than to contribute to the family economy, or to make a name for oneself as a professional quilter. Although many participants suggest that quilting is a personal activity done for their own benefit, they also reveal that quilting has a double (and somewhat contradictory) purpose: As women care for themselves, they also care for others. Quilters care for others as they care for themselves, through the "just for fun" reasons they cite for getting into quilting. Basically, women in this study quilt because it is simply fun for them; they are not concerned about making money for themselves or their families through this activity (and they certainly are in financially stable enough positions to be able to engage in leisure like this regularly).

These midlife women have learned to quilt for personal enjoyment, and they have also gained great satisfaction from giving handmade gifts to family and friends. Recall Eileen's resistance to perfect corners, and Meg's reluctance to pursue quilting in professional ways as she once did with painting – both of these women have defined quilting on their own terms. As they practice it more intensely and more consistently, they self-identify as quilters, and consequently develop subjective careers in quilting. They base their enjoyment in quilting upon personally constructed goals and measures of success, which are independent of external measures produced by family, friends, and the economy.

## EXTENDING THE SELF: QUILTS AS FINISHED PRODUCTS

What a quilt means and how it is to be used are different for every woman who makes them. Generally, though, quilters want their quilts to be used and enjoyed for their appropriate purposes, including comfort, display, and commemoration. Women speak positively about people to whom they have given quilts as gifts. They are hopeful that the recipients use the quilts appropriately, or in accordance with the makers' expectations. The quilts can serve as an extension of the quilter, representing her artistic creativity and her connection to the person who receives the quilt. When gifted quilts are used differently from the makers' intentions, they have to deal with the additional meaning attached to the quilt and the relationship, but the symbolism surrounding the quilt is still present. The finished quilt is so much a part of the quilter, when a quilter gives a quilt as a gift, she is giving something of her self, thus, when people mistreat a quilt in quilters' eyes, they feel as though they themselves are being mistreated, as is their relationship with that person.

Quilters are attached to both the process and products of quilting. What happens after the quilt is finished is also part of the quilting process, with quilters continuing to be involved in the meaning-making process of defining its function. The purposes can include use, display, or putting the quilt away for safekeeping. Women intend certain things to happen to quilts when they are finished, and can become disappointed when quilts are used in ways other than their original intentions. In many ways, how people respond to gifts represents how people respond to the gift giver, and can often cause anxiety in the giver (Schwartz 1967; Wooten 2000). If quilters perceive that their hand-made gifts are misused, they can take it personally as disrespect for their creative efforts, and a mishandling of the existing relationship between them. Recipients mostly see the finished product, and can usually only imagine the process. Recipients tend to focus on the finished product of the quilt and are not typically privy to the richly detailed and meaningful process embedded in every stitch.

Quilts are meaning-laden objects. As a quilt is passed from its creator to its receiver, ownership changes, and new meanings are attached to the object. As far as the quilter is concerned, even though it is a gift, a quilt carries with it the meaning the maker attached to it, as Meg states,

> My daughter has a lap quilt that I made for her and whenever I am there I always get under it, and it just feels like you're at home and I think, the love that goes into them, carries on. Just because you've finished it, doesn't mean that it is the end of it, I mean you really do feel that aura of the maker.

When women give quilts as gifts, the recipients have ownership of the quilt, and they also have the opportunity to interpret the quilt and attach their own cultural meanings to it. Sometimes the multiple meanings attached by maker and recipient concur, while other times they clash. Quilters perceive and share these additional meanings attached to quilts.

Karen gave one of her early attempts at quilting to her mother: "I decided for Christmas that year, I'd give that quilt to my mother. She thought it was so pretty, but that was the ugliest quilt (laughing)." Learning to quilt was challenging for Karen and she was not entirely happy with her finished products, but she enjoyed the process, and felt good that her family members valued them.

Carrie also gave the first bed-sized quilt she made to her mother. Her mother died soon after, and Carrie placed the quilt in the coffin with her mother's body. She shared the reasons why she decided to give her mother the quilt, and how people reacted to this:

> I gave it to my mom and everybody really made a comment, "Your first quilt and you're giving it away?" Well yeah, I didn't think there was anything wrong with that. My mom had always done so much and it was the least I could do. The poor thing, I'd never made her anything. She was always so cold and I didn't want anyone else to have it, it was hers. My husband thought it was really nice, but that's about it. I don't really tell anybody, I don't know why, I don't really talk about it, but it meant a lot to me because it was just for her, nobody else. I didn't want my sister to get it, I didn't want my brother to go and ruin it and put it underneath a car.

Carrie is particular about who receives her quilts. She bases her decisions somewhat on how she thinks they might care for them. Carrie also preserves family quilts and plans to give them to her children when they are older and probably more appreciative of them:

> Even the little quilts that my grandma made my kids who are now seventeen and eighteen years old, I still have them and I won't let my kids have them because I'm afraid that they won't respect them. I just keep them in the closet because it's just respect. Someone took the time, they thought about somebody and they made it for that person.

Similarly, Melinda shares concerns in giving quilts away as gifts to people who might not appreciate them:

> I don't know if the people I'm making it for will really appreciate it. One thing I'm a little concerned about is giving my seven year old this quilt. He's still pretty young. Jumping on the bed will probably rip out all those stitches that I did, but he's so proud of it, he knows it's his. And eventually maybe he'll take it to college and he'll remember me and all this kind of stuff and maybe it'll even be loved even if it gets ruined or something, he'll remember how long it took mom to make this.

Melinda's fears are not outlandish, especially when considering how other quilters react when their quilts are actually used in ways that conflict with the quilters' intent. For example, Emma recalls discovering that a child was not allowed to use a quilt that she had made for him:

> I was kind of disappointed when I went to see my friends. My daughter asked, "Where's the quilt?" And the lady said, "Oh, I put it away so nothing happens to it." I asked, "Why did you put it away like that?" She said, "Well, it's so pretty I don't want anything to happen to it." But, then nobody got to enjoy it because it was just stashed away. So, I decided to make less elaborate things so that people would feel more comfortable using them.
>
> *Now when you give quilts away, do you talk to people about how you put it together and what you intended it for?*
>
> Yeah, actually now when I send a quilt, I send a little sheet and I explain why I picked that pattern and how much fun it was to make it, and I hope the kids will like crawl on it and stuff. I also explain how you wash it.

Note that Emma has not stopped making quilts for others. Instead, she makes quilts for others more appropriate for the use she has in mind, and provides necessary cleaning information.

Other women are also aware that their quilts are not used in the ways they intended. Theresa speculates about her daughter-in-law, for whom she has made a bed-sized quilt: "My daughter-in-law doesn't use it very often and I keep telling her to use it. She says, 'Mom, it's too good to use.' And I say, 'No, it really isn't.'" I asked Theresa why it mattered to her what people do with gifts she has made them. She responded as follows:

I don't know, I just really want them to use the quilts. My grandchildren all have my quilts hanging on the wall, and they're to be touched and loved and hugged and if they want to drag them around I don't care, that's what they're for. And it really pleases me when I go to their house that they're hanging on the wall instead of the cupboard.

Cassie shares her response to discovering that her handmade gifts were being stored and were not being used regularly. Importantly, Cassie realizes that she relinquishes control over how the quilt is used once it is finished and given as a gift:

I was babysitting and looking for pajamas to change the little boy into. I pulled open a drawer, and there was the quilt that I had made with a couple of afghans I had made. It first kind of gets you in the stomach before you think, "Oh, maybe they just really didn't like it," and then you think, "Well it probably serves its purpose at some point." Of course, I would want every little child to take my quilt and have it be the one that they are attached to but I know that doesn't happen. I'm fine with that. I'd love to say that I'm more reluctant to give it to people that don't quilt, but that's not true. I don't really make that judgment.

Cassie is aware of the effort and intent behind the gifts that she gives to others. In giving the quilt away, she hopes that those receiving the quilt will appreciate it and find use with it. The disappointment Cassie expresses initially, "It first kind of gets you in the stomach," becomes less important than the actual gesture of making and giving the gift.

Quilters also share the joy they feel when their quilting process and products are appreciated and validated by others. For example, Loretta made a commemorative quilt for her son as he completed his military duty. Making this quilt was a deeply emotional process for her, and as she gave it to him, she was pleased with his response:

I think he was awestruck. He just kind of looked at it, he didn't really believe it. He's so proud of it. He would show it to everybody and it's got the place of honor. That's his quilt. When he first got home he took it out and would lie down on the couch and curl up in it. After a while he would fold it back up and put it in the safe we've got so it's in its honored position. He's real excited because we're going to have it in the [quilt] show this year. If it does win something, I think it will thrill him to death. I think it will thrill him more than it will me.

Once quilts are finished, many quilters give their labors of love away to friends and family members. The relationship between the creator and the receiver of the quilt is important (Griswold 2004). Women sometimes take personally what happens (or does not happen) to the quilt once they give it away. Quilters indicate that they are still somewhat attached to the quilt as a cultural object, they have their own meaning attached to it, while the receivers are also creating meaning and attaching it to the quilt. Women's comments reveal that in some instances, quilts are extensions of themselves and represent the carework that they are doing for others through their quilting efforts. As women give quilts away as gifts, they are also giving part of themselves away to the receiver, and want to be treated with respect, in accordance with the production and gifting of said quilt.

## NOTE

1. Professional status within U.S. quilting can be understood in at least two ways. First, the typical notion of supporting oneself through an activity is present with professional quilters. A second, and lesser-known aspect of professional quilting is that of a "Master Quilter," one who does not necessarily make a living from quilting, but one who is regarded as having highly advanced skills, and who wins awards at shows and contests. The participants in this study are primarily amateur quilters – they neither make a living from quilting, nor do they seek awards at shows and contests. Their focus is based on internal, personal goals, rather than economic goals as salary or public, artistic recognition.

# 4 THE GUILTY PLEASURES OF THE FABRIC STASH

Three of anything makes a collection.

Anonymous

Women I interviewed value quilting on many important levels, yet they do not expect non-quilters to be interested in it, or value quilting in the same ways that they do. Because of this, some quilters thought it unusual that I as a researcher would want to interview them about quilting. Many quilters said they found it difficult to express to non-quilters why they quilted. Some women have been quilting for so long that it has become a fundamental part of their lives, demonstrated in the intensity with which they talked about quilting as a passion. Others had never been asked, respectfully, about what quilting meant to them. While non-quilters who admire quilts often focus solely or primarily on the product – the finished quilt – quilters give far more emphasis to the process of quilting. To a quilter, *how* a quilt is produced is often as important, or even more important, than the finished quilt itself. In the process of quilting, fabric plays an important role.

Viewing quilting from quilters' perspectives highlights both the relevance of this leisure activity in lives of individual women, and how women feel constrained when pursuing it. Although the quilters in this study live traditional lives and use finished quilts mostly in family-linked ways (e.g., bedcoverings, small wall hangings, and gifts for family and friends), the process of quilting takes up women's attention and time, as well as space in the home for the fabric stash.

## QUILTING AND FABRIC COLLECTING

People engage in the hobby of collecting for numerous reasons (Belk 2001). Some collectors display prized collections in living spaces (Csikszentmihalyi and Rochberg-Halton 1995), while others commemorate life events (Mavor 1997), or bond as a community of collectors, such as at Pez Dispenser collector conventions (Fogle 2002). Collecting and leisure activities share common ground, specifically in defending the time and space used to store materials to others not involved in the activity, including family members (Bartram 2001; Siegenthaler and O'Dell 2001). For example, dog sports competitors experience difficulty in negotiating boundaries between dog sports activities and paid-work demands (Gillespie et al. 2002), and marathon runners and their spouses have sometimes conflicting perceptions regarding leisure time and family activities (Goff et al. 1997; Major 2001). Even romance readers (Brackett 2000; Radway 1991) and quilters (Abrahams and

Pannabecker 2000; Doyle 1998; Gabbert 2000; Stalp 2006a, 2006b, 2006c) must engage in subterfuge to successfully enjoy their hobbies under the radar of other family members.

Today a typical American quilter is a middle aged, middle to upper class woman who learns how to quilt as a leisure activity. She takes quilting classes, collects fabric, and makes use of her fabric collection for quilting (Stalp 2006b). Quilting is both a leisure activity and a form of collecting. Like "found art" collectors, who collect and make use of their collections by transforming them into new and/or different forms, such as a collage (Rothbart 2004; Zolberg and Cherbo 1997), quilters make use of their collections of fabric to produce quilts. Quilters collectively refer to their collections as "fabric stash." They hoard fabric over time, and together strategize about hiding places for the fabric stash in their homes. Collecting, hoarding, and hiding fabric stash is a normal activity for quilters, and yet these acts seem deviant to non-quilters, particularly those who share living space with them. Having a stash legitimates many women's claims in identifying themselves as quilters and pursuing a leisure activity independent from their family members. The presence of the fabric stash in the home also establishes the need for women's leisure space in the home. Why do midlife women quilters collect, hoard, and hide fabric?

I explore how and why women collect, hoard, and hide fabric in the home, exploring the "guilty pleasures" of quilting, including the deviant acts of hiding fabric and quilting identity from family members. While fabric is the medium of quilting, quilters purchase more fabric than is necessary for specific projects, slowly building up and hoarding a fabric stash. Then they strategize hiding places for their fabric. Collecting and hiding the stash become symbolic of women's attempts to carve out time and space for themselves amidst the multiple demands placed on them by families and by paid work. Women's anxieties surrounding acquiring, hoarding, and hiding their fabric stashes highlight their diminished ability, relative to their spouses and their children, to pursue leisure activities without a stigma.

## STARTING A FABRIC COLLECTION

> I don't know why I love fabric, I just do.
>
> Emily, forties

A quality collection of new 100-percent cotton fabric is an essential component of many quilters' lives. Certainly, some quilters make use of vintage fabrics, but the majority of new quilters use almost entirely new, 100-percent cotton fabric for quilting. A painter puts paint to canvas, a potter throws clay on a wheel, and a quilter creates quilts with fabric. Many quilters describe quilting as "a way of painting with fabric." In order to paint with fabric, quilters told me they need access to and possession of a large variety of fabrics. Many of the fabrics are new, rather than scraps of family clothing, for example. In this way, then, quilters are both creators of collectible objects (quilts), and collectors of found art (fabric). As we have seen above, quilters refer to their fabric collections as *fabric stash*, or *stash*.

FIG. 4.1. Eileen's fabric stash hidden away. Personal photograph.

The concept of stash is not restricted to quilters, for other crafters such as weavers, knitters, and crocheters also refer to their collection of raw materials necessary to their type of cultural production as stash (for examples of quilting and knitting books, see Gervais 1995; Lydon 1997; Macdonald 1988; Mainardi 1975; Myers 2001; Parker and Pollock 1981; Radner 1993; Ryer 1997; Stoller 2004a, 2004b, 2006; Torsney and Elsley 1994). The fabric stash represents important and revealing elements in quilters' lives. Fabric collections and the space they take up reveal the primacy of women's identities as quilters within the home.

Depending on quilters and their spaces, they arrange fabric in a way that best suits them: project, color, or fabric type (e.g., solids, patterns, reproductions, hand dyed, marbled, batiks). Regardless of how much money most quilters have, when able, they are willing to devote substantial resources to equipment. Many women with permanent quilting space in the home store their fabric in a cleaned-out clothes closet or utility closet somewhere in the home, and arrange fabric by color.

By arranging fabric by color, quilters can easily see what their fabric palettes will provide them. They then can quickly assess which fabrics will work with any given project, or if they need to shop for new fabrics. Importantly, by having their fabric stash available in this way, quilters simply have to open the closet door to have immediate access to their fabric. Those without permanent space rely upon plastic storage bins, cardboard boxes, or plastic garbage bags to store their fabric. These women are not able to see their palette at a glance, and, in comparison to those with permanent quilting space, spend extra time sorting through fabric before beginning a project.

Women are quite attached to their fabric collections and spend a good deal of time organizing and browsing. Women shared with me the importance of a good fabric stash, joked about how large their stashes are, and gave tips on how best to hide fabric purchases from others. Once discovering that I was also a quilter, women even gave me suggestions about how to hide fabric. They said that when I finally settled down with a spouse, that I would need to learn, as they did, how to hide a stash and new fabric purchases. In such jovial discussions, women often justified their fabric collections, or rationalized a fabric purchase. For example, in an interview setting with her husband sitting in the next room Meg justified her large fabric stash because she lives in the country, away from town and fabric stores:

> The fabric stash is your palette. See, I justify it [fabric stash] because I live so far
> out. I can't just run down the street and get thread or get another piece of fabric.
> If I don't have it, it's an effort to get in the car and go for half an hour to get
> fabric. So I have a *real* justification for all my stash (laughter).

Other women justified their stash by saying, "I know I will use this soon, which is why I bought so much of it."

Quilters often engage in this somewhat joking, somewhat serious line of fabric stash justification, and compare quilting to other activities, or habits: "Hey, I could be drinking, gambling, or smoking – quilting is much healthier." When criticized by others for their quilting and fabric stash purchases, women are quick to make comparisons with other potentially addictive pursuits, demonstrating the harmlessness of quilting compared to the potential danger of activities in which they could otherwise be involved.

Quilting is such a pleasurable activity for women though, that some describe it as an addiction that takes over much of their lives. Patricia is in her fifties, and shares her addictive quilting experiences:

> Three years ago I had a quilt on the frame and I got so addicted to it that I was
> quilting late at night, and I actually got tendonitis in my wrist. I had to quilt, I
> would just think, "one more block, one more line." I overdid it. I did it until my
> wrist was very, very sore. I could hardly move it.

FIG. 4.2. The Sow's Ear is a lovely yarn and coffee shop in Verona, WI, that combines the two potentially addictive elements of knitting and coffee. When I shop here I get doubly fixed! Feed Your Addictions, The Sow's Ear. Artist: Carey Armstrong-Ellis. Permission granted.

Patricia is not alone in her addictive experience with quilting. Sarah also devotes serious time to quilting and claims, "I would say quilting is bordering on an obsession (laughter)." And, Judy has this to say about quilting, fabric, and addiction:

> My friend says, "When they have little fat quarters all cut up, it's like crack for quilters." I think it gets to be like an addiction, because I say, "I have to have that fabric" and I've gotten better about just buying the fat quarter. If it's

something I really like, I'll buy a couple of yards, because then at least you can use it for a bigger thing. A lot of times I really don't have any reason for buying stuff, but I do anyway. My brother makes fun of me for that, I told him that I was going to get fabric this weekend, and he said, "Well it's not like you don't have enough fabric!"

When women participate in quilting activities, they are able to take time for themselves. Karla likens quilting to therapy: "I enjoy it and it is therapeutic. I mean, if I am not reading, I am quilting, and if I'm not quilting, I am reading. I have to have something and I prefer doing things with my hands." Other quilters echo her sentiments, like Judy:

> It's always more fun to go to a quilt shop with others. When I travel by myself for work, I'll look up on the internet beforehand the quilt shops, and then I'll go by myself. When I'm traveling with others I don't try to do that, unless I know that they quilt. I remember fabric – that I got it at this store in San Francisco, or I went to a store in Wisconsin and it was so cool.

Although not often compared to drug users, the behaviors of quilters do parallel those of drug users in some ways – secrecy about their identities, the activities they pursue to obtain and use drugs, where they store their drugs, and how they talk about their habit in public. Referring to fabric as "stash" as well as women's guarded behavior around family does link quilting to other deviant acts, like illicit drug use. In fact, I have found that in discussing my quilting research regularly in the college courses that I teach, that some students begin calling their illicit activities and hidden paraphernalia "fabric" rather than "weed" or "stash." While quilters legally collect fabric, they keep it hidden from others. If their passion for fabric were to be revealed, quilters expect to be criticized by others who neither quilt, nor understand their passion for quilting.

This was certainly the case for Cindy, who is in her eighties, and whose husband and grandchildren were at home one afternoon while I was there for an interview. She had already prepared a meal for them before I arrived, and they were busily eating in the kitchen when we started the interview, sitting together in the living room. Interestingly, in the middle of the interview, Cindy told me she had something to show me. She took me from the living room to the back bedroom, locked the door, and opened the closet to reveal the secret stash of quilts she had made throughout her life. While locking the bedroom door she said she didn't want us to be interrupted, but I think she did not want her family to see how much quilting actually meant to her. For, despite the stash of beautiful quilts she had made over her lifetime, the family still opted to use comforters and bedspreads rather than the quilts she had made for them. Because of these and other reactions by family members, women continue to hide and to some extent criminalize their quilting. They disguise their quilting identities, downplay how active their quilting lives are, hide fabric, and disguise their conversations about their fabric stash.

## STASHING FABRIC

Hardware commercials and print advertisements in particular provide us a mental template to understand how quilters set up their quilting spaces. A hardware commercial advertises gifts for "the special man in your life." It pictures a workshop space with a waist-high table and a pegboard panel covering the wall. As the commercial proceeds, the pegboard wall slowly fills up with workshop tools: a hammer, pliers, drill, saw, etc. These tools are generally part of our common culture. Even if we do not personally handle hardware tools, we most probably know what they are. We are surrounded by "men's" things, like easily recognizable hardware tools, and it is legitimate that such items take up storage space in the home.

The public is less familiar with the tools of quilting. If women's quilting spaces were advertised in similar ways, it is not clear that the general public would be able to recognize and name the difference between a quilter's basic tools (e.g., sewing machine, quilt frame, needles, thread, rotary cutter, cutting mat). Women are aware that while most outsiders recognize what a finished quilt is, many non-quilters are quite unfamiliar with both the processes and tools involved in quilting. For example, an advertising campaign for "quilted" toilet paper originally depicted quilters sitting around a piece of toilet paper, quilting it with knitting needles instead of quilting needles. Knitting needles range from eight inches to fifteen inches long and are used with yarn, while quilting needles range from one to one-and-a-half inches long and are used with thread. Only after an immediate negative response from quilters nationwide did the company remove the television commercial and alter it. The cartoon quilters were then using quilting needles, but ones that were the same size as knitting needles. Currently, the commercial depicts needles more in proportion to the cartoon quilters' bodies (Stalp 1999).

Quilting fabric is controlled by supply in terms of what kinds of fabric are produced each cycle. If a quilter were to need a specific print from last season, chances can be slim that she would be able to find it. Thus, quilters admittedly overdo it when buying fabric: "When I see something I like, I buy a lot of it because I know if I don't, it will be gone when I come back to buy more" (fieldnotes 2000). Quilters buy fabric for multiple reasons: for a specific project, it was on sale, or they need a particular color or type of fabric to add to their collections for future projects. Sometimes, quilters are coaxed by an encouraging quilt shop sign to buy fabric, and, sometimes, fabric just catches their eye and whispers to them in the store to bring it home. Acquiring fabric can be a gleeful experience, comparable to that of collectors of rare cultural objects. For example, Beth is in her sixties, and describes her friend who became ecstatic about her fabric purchase: "My friend had ordered fabric from a national company through the mail and when her fabric came it was like GASP! I said she was having an *orgasm* just looking at the fabric! She said, 'There are *solids* I have *never seen!*'" Kelly is in her forties, and she has a routine that she follows when in quilt shops. Before looking at the bolts of quilt fabric, she will stop by the fabric already cut, also known as "fat quarters." Admittedly addicted to fabric collecting,

Kelly uses addiction terminology when talking about her fabric shopping. She refers to fat quarters as crack cocaine, calling the fat quarter tables set up in the front of the shops as the "crack tables." Once when shopping with her, she said, "Let's check out the crack table first, and then move on to the bolts." Any outsider privy to this conversation might have been tempted to report "two nice-looking girls" to the police as potential crack users.

Family members question why quilters need to have so much fabric collected that is not being used to make quilts. One woman's husband regularly questioned her about why she kept accumulating fabric and did not ever seem to use any of the fabric stash: "I said to him, 'This is my hobby. I collect fabric. Would you ask a stamp collector to mail a valuable stamp?'" (fieldnotes 2000). Quilters are stuck between a rock and a hard place as both collectors of fabric and participants in a serious leisure activity.

Admittedly, women who quilt collect more fabric than they will probably ever use. This is partly due to how fabric is manufactured, and how it is available seasonally to quilters. Women buying new fabric for quilting on a regular basis must rely on the fabric market for what colors, patterns, styles, and designs are attainable and affordable. The majority of quilters purchase new 100-percent cotton fabric designed and printed specifically for quilting from readily available outlets: general fabric stores that also sell quilting fabric, quilt shops which specialize in quilting fabric, and websites. Fabric companies produce particular designs by season, and most stores have a limited supply of any given fabric. Dye lots and designs of quilt fabric change over time and in examining a quilter's fabric stash over a number of years, women are able to approximate in which decade a certain piece of fabric was produced – as with clothing, shoe, or automobile production, planned obsolescence also exists in the quilting world – fabrics from the 1970s may noticeably clash with fabrics from the late 1990s. Similar to how an artist might discuss raw materials in terms of need for future projects Denise describes how fabric fashion trends influence fabric selection in her quilting fabric purchases:

> Lately I've been buying tans and browns and greens that I know I can't get in two or three years and I buy them ... I'll use some of them for projects now, but in two or three years I'll have them in my stash. You buy what you know you will need in the future even if you know you don't need it right that second.

Theresa realizes that she has a lot of quilting materials, evidenced by the amount of money she's invested in quilting: "I have far too much money wrapped up into my quilting. But it's really been cheap entertainment." Although she feels she has gone a bit overboard on collecting quilting materials, Theresa implies that her positive quilting experience is harmless entertainment. Kelly discusses the role quilting plays in her life in similar ways: "Quilting has become quite an obsession that I wouldn't have expected it to be." As quilters strategize with one another about how to assemble and defend their fabric collections among the constraints of family life, as women at midlife, they are also concerned with what will happen to their carefully collected stashes if no family member takes a similar interest. Supportive of this notion is

PLATE 1. My first quilt. I made this "trip around the world" quilt with help from my Aunt Jenny, 1991. Personal photograph.

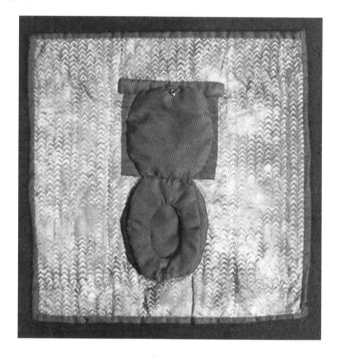

PLATE 2. "The Last Straw," down position, 1999. Personal photograph. I made this 12 × 12-inch quilt as a testament to how romantic relationships can end. This small interactive quilt was part of a year-long concept challenge for an art quilt group to which I belonged.

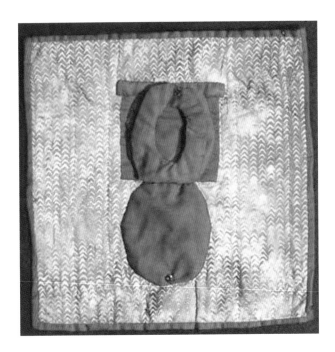

PLATE 3. "The Last Straw," up position, 1999. Personal photograph. This small 12 × 12-inch quilt demonstrates how romantic relationships can end. After presenting this interactive quilt to the art quilt group I belonged to, other members quickly and humorously suggested other ways in which relationships can end.

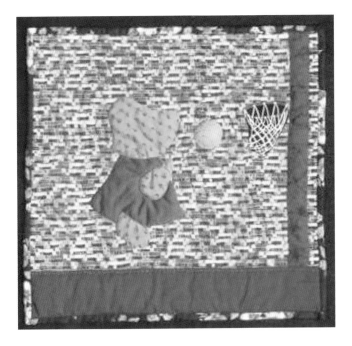

PLATE 4. "Sue Does Hoops," 2001. Personal photograph. This small 12 × 12-inch quilt was part of my dissertation series, where I constructed Sunbonnet Sue doing a favorite activity of one of my committee members, in this case, playing basketball.

PLATE 5. "Sue Does Music," 2001. Personal photograph. This small 12 × 12-inch quilt was part of my dissertation series, where I constructed Sunbonnet Sue doing a favorite activity of one of my committee members, in this case, playing the guitar.

PLATE 6. "Oh Shit!" Betty's humorous take on the seemingly innocent quilt pattern, Sunbonnet Sue.

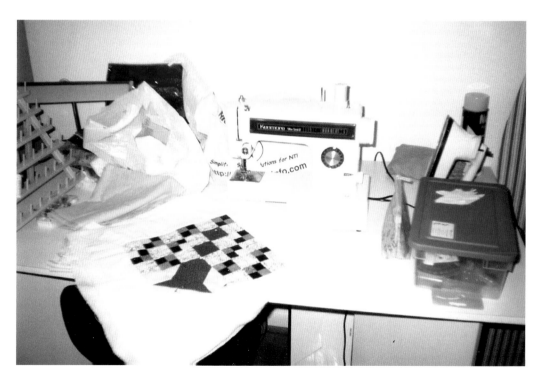

PLATE 7. Kelly's sewing space is quite small, and is often invaded by her cats. Personal photograph.

PLATE 8. Loretta's design wall. Quilters who have design walls like Loretta can get needed perspective on their quilts, and have a permanent space to store quilts-in-process. Loretta secured her quilt room after her children moved out of the home for educational pursuits. Personal photograph.

PLATE 9. Judy made this quilt for her brother, which he hangs on the wall in the dining room of his home. Quilting can play a visually central role in the home, as this quilt indicates. Personal photograph.

PLATE 10. Judy made this quilt out of bug fabric, and cleverly titled it, "You've got a bug on you." Personal photograph.

PLATE 11. This picture portrays a rather traditional understanding of inter-generational craft learning through a weaving demonstration, 1999. Personal photograph.

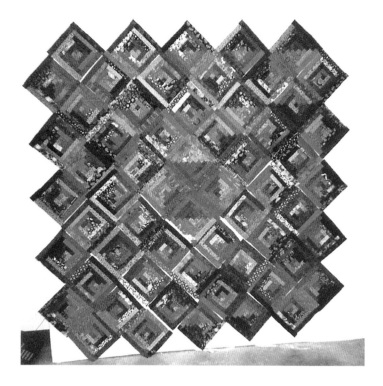

PLATE 12. I made this quilt while I was working on completing my Ph.D. I called it "Dissertation Quilt. Vampire Quilt," 2001. Personal photograph.

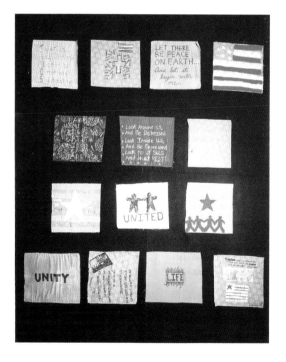

PLATE 13. "Black 9/11 quilt," University of Georgia students, 2001. Personal photograph.

PLATE 14. "Red 9/11 quilt," University of Georgia students, 2001. Personal photograph.

PLATE 15. Theresa enjoys a great amount of space in her quilt room to display her fabric by color. This acts as her fabric palate, and she can pull fabric when she needs it. Such permanent spaces allow for this freedom in the quilting process. "Theresa's fabric stash by color," personal photograph.

PLATE 16. This quilt shop sign is one of many located within quilt shops that encourage the overbuying of fabric. Personal photograph.

PLATE 17. This bumper sticker appeals to more than just quilters, and is supportive of building up of one's stash. Photo taken at Waechter's Silk Shop, a decades-old business for fine, natural fiber fabrics (www.waechters.com). A sure place to collect beautiful and special fabrics to help keep you alive and sewing longer. Photograph by Pattiy Torno. Permission Granted.

PLATE 18. This storefront in Rochester, MN, near the Mayo Clinic brings together those with fabric interests, and provides a supportive and therapeutic creative environment. Ginny's Fine Fabrics and Support Group, 2006, permission granted.

PLATE 19. Karen's quilt room is envied by many of her friends. She was able to build this quilt room from two standard-sized bedrooms, which provides enough space for her to keep her sewing machines, ironing boards, design wall, fabric, and books out and available permanently. Personal photograph.

PLATE 20. Angela's quilt room is similar to Karen's in that it is permanent. A bit smaller, this quilt room is one bedroom's worth of space that she secured in her home. Personal photograph.

PLATE 21. Sewing room, 2006, personal photograph.

PLATE 22. At first glance, one might think this quilter has an interest in frogs, biology, the environment, or entertaining children. However, Sarah's Frog quilt documents her unsuccessful dating life by including lots of frogs that she dated while she was single. Personal photograph.

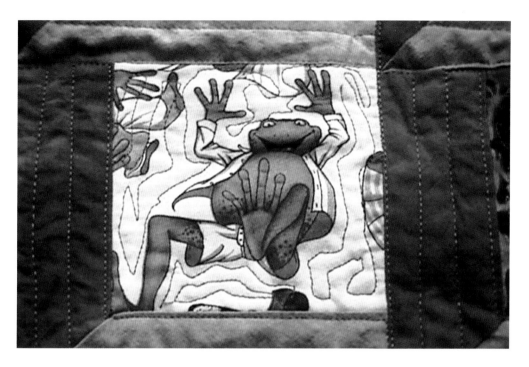

PLATE 23. Closer examination of the quilt, Sarah's frog quilt, close-up 1, shows cavalier and sad frogs, perhaps direct identifiers of some of the frogs she dated? Personal photograph.

PLATE 24. Sarah's frog quilt, close-up 2, again shows the types of frogs that Sarah dated while single. Now that Sarah is married, she no longer collects frog fabric. Personal photograph.

PLATE 25. There is more to a quilt than what is on the surface, as indicated in Emma's anger quilt. Recall that she only works on this quilt when she is frustrated with one particular person. Personal photograph.

PLATE 26. Leslie's divorce quilt uses soft and calming colors, and Leslie uses it for comfort to curl up in while she heals. Personal photograph.

PLATE 27. Oftentimes, friends send pictures of their children with the quilts that women make, as is the case with Henry on his baby quilt. Personal photograph.

PLATE 28. Being present when gifting quilts is a real treat, especially when a quilter witnesses such joy, as expressed by Deven and Derek enjoying their new quilts. Personal photograph.

PLATE 29. I once attended a weekend quilting retreat, where a group of quilters, myself included, pretty much worked only on quilting projects for two and half days continuously, breaking just for food, drink, and a trip to a quilt shop to stock up on supplies. Personal photograph.

PLATE 30. After gifting quilts, quilters are happy to see how the recipients use them as Caleb does. He sleeps with his quilt and likes to jump on it, too. Personal photograph.

Figure 4.3, "The Quiltmaker's Will" that was hung in many women's quilting spaces, and was also referenced in multiple conversations with quilters.

Note that in "The Quiltmaker's Will" there is explicit acknowledgment of non-quilters lacking the proper understanding of a fabric collection: "_____hasn't the least appreciation for or for that matter knowledge of my extensive fabric collection – which collection is suitably deposited in sundry places for safe keeping." This lack of appreciation is also illustrated in the directives of the will, pointing the fabric inheritors to the most likely resting grounds of a misunderstood quilter's fabric stash: "…before the dumpster, search out my collection which is similarly stored. That said collection should be rescued and stacked in my quilting studio," and providing

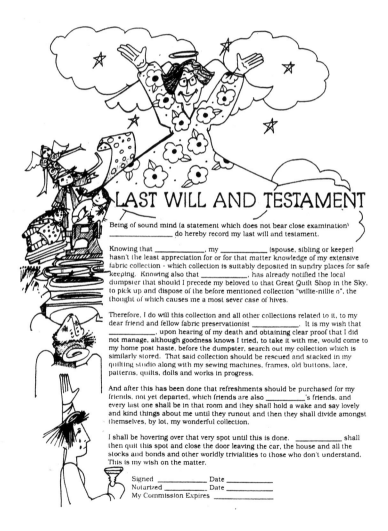

## LAST WILL AND TESTAMENT

Being of sound mind (a statement which does not bear close examination) _____ do hereby record my last will and testament.

Knowing that _____, my _____ (spouse, sibling or keeper) hasn't the least appreciation for or for that matter knowledge of my extensive fabric collection - which collection is suitably deposited in sundry places for safe keeping. Knowing also that _____, has already notified the local dumpster that should I precede my beloved to that Great Quilt Shop in the Sky, to pick up and dispose of the before mentioned collection "willie-nillie o", the thought of which causes me a most sever case of hives.

Therefore, I do will this collection and all other collections related to it, to my dear friend and fellow fabric preservationist _____. It is my wish that _____, upon hearing of my death and obtaining clear proof that I did not manage, although goodness knows I tried, to take it with me, would come to my home post haste, before the dumpster, search out my collection which is similarly stored. That said collection should be rescued and stacked in my quilting studio along with my sewing machines, frames, old buttons, lace, patterns, quilts, dolls and works in progress.

And after this has been done that refreshments should be purchased for my friends, not yet departed, which friends are also _____'s friends, and every last one shall be in that room and they shall hold a wake and say lovely and kind things about me until they runout and then they shall divide amongst themselves, by lot, my wonderful collection.

I shall be hovering over that very spot until this is done. _____ shall then quit this spot and close the door leaving the car, the house and all the stocks and bonds and other worldly trivialities to those who don't understand. This is my wish on the matter.

Signed _____ Date _____
Notarized _____ Date _____
My Commission Expires _____

FIG. 4.3. "The Quiltmaker's Will." Reprinted with permission of Elinor Peace Bailey. All rights reserved.

instruction of what is to happen to the fabric stash: "they shall divide amongst themselves, by lot, my wonderful collection."

Throughout countless interviews, women joked about how when they died their
families would not know what to do with their fabric collections, and they were
afraid their collections would get thrown away. This concerned them beyond joking
about it, as many women had planned to open up their houses to quilting friends
who could collectively determine what to do with the fabric collection, or put
quilting friends in their wills so that they would have some control over what would
happen to their valuable fabric stash. For example, Karla states,

> I don't know when I will ever get to use it all but as they say, "the one who dies
> with the most fabric wins" and I have a will in there on the wall that when I pass
> away my husband is to call five or six different people and they are to come at
> once, not to buy but to take fabric. They can just have whatever is in there.

Fabric hoarding practices, such as Karla's, result in a long-term overabundance of
fabric. Judy witnesses this when a plethora of fabric was brought to a quilt guild
meeting, for the taking – this influenced her to think about what would happen to
her fabric stash when she died:

> This woman brought a bunch of fabric to the quilt guild that had belonged to
> her mother and said that her mother had died and that she had all this fabric
> that she didn't want to go to waste and brought it in for us to use. And my friend
> and I looked at each other and we're like, "Oh my god, if I die, you get my stash,
> okay?" And so we both decided that if we both die, then my niece gets our
> stashes. That's what happens to your stash when you die. And then I have
> another friend who doesn't quilt but she cross stitches and she's told her friends
> that after she dies, just start throwing her unfinished projects onto the coffin and
> then throw the dirt in.

What to do with one's fabric stash or one's unfinished projects is something many
aging quilters are contemplating. They want the fabric to go to someone who will
appreciate it, and will cherish it as they have over time. Similar to family heirlooms,
the fabric stash carries sentimentality with it. Yet, this heirloom is not going to the
family, but to quilters outside the family, for as quilters witness the disdain some
family members have for the quilting process, they certainly want their materials to
end up with an appreciative recipient.

## THE STIGMATIZED STASH AND HIDING ONE'S QUILTING IDENTITY

It's amazing what you do to hide fabric.

Melinda

Women often strategize with other quilters to deceive family members about the
costs of their quilting activities. They distort information about the amount of

money they spend on fabric and other quilting materials and the accumulated fabric stash they have already purchased. Interestingly, women also hide their fabric stash from family members, and assist each other in devising ways to keep fabric hidden from others.

One legendary tale was passed on in a group interview where the women were sharing their "stash stories." These women worked together at a fabric store in the western U.S., and were remembering their more colorful customers. Tracy, late twenties, shared that "one woman took all of the food out of her freezer and lined the freezer bottom with fabric and put the food on top so her husband never knew." While discussing this fabric-stash-hiding genius, the women seemed somewhat conflicted. They admired her for finding such a good hiding place, but were also saddened by the deceit they practice in order to continue to quilt.

As the conversation progressed, Carrie recounted her own dilemma about having to hide new fabric purchases from her family. Since Carrie works at a fabric store, she is perpetually tempted by fabric. She came home after working late one night and unexpectedly encountered her still-awake husband. Faced with exposing her most recent fabric stash purchase to him, Carrie thought quickly to hide it:

> I brought home a big bag of fabric and I'm thinking, he's usually asleep. I come in and he's awake, and I have this huge bag. And I remember opening the door and I said, "Oh, you're up." I dropped the bag, so it's sitting out on the front porch, under the mailbox. So I'm thinking I'll just get it when he goes to bed. We'll watch Friends and we'll go to sleep, or he'll go to sleep. Well, he ran outside to the van to go get whatever, his planner or something, and he comes back in and he says, "Did you forget something?" I went, "Oh." And he just put it on the couch and shook his head and said, "Good Night." That was the last time I hid fabric. I was so embarrassed because he caught me. He caught me.

This passage proves particularly interesting, as Carrie documents that it is through the family framework that she feels limits and she then passes judgment on her own serious leisure activities. Carrie's statement of, "I was so embarrassed that he caught me. He caught me," indicates her guilt and feeling that she should not perhaps be participating in an activity that she feels she must hide from her family. To some extent, quilters feel that their activities are deviant to normal family activities; they carry a stigma with them concerning their quilting, and choose to keep it a hidden activity from family and friends.

Since this event, Carrie no longer hides fabric from her family. Yet, despite her attempts to make more public her interest in quilting (and therefore trying to legitimate and normalize the activity for her family), her extended family continues to tease her about her fabric stash and quilting in ways that make her uncomfortable:

> I have a section of the basement now. I took up the dining room for about four years and I was really embarrassed the other day. My sister-in-law said, "When did you buy that?" referring to the dining room table, and I said, "Four years

ago." It was embarrassing. I said, "Didn't you know that's what my fabric sat on?" I mean, they knew my fabric was sitting on there, why couldn't they figure it was sitting on something? My father-in-law said, "Hey, you moved your stuff." I said, "Yes." I didn't know it was so big.

Carrie used to keep her quilting materials on the dining room table as a temporary quilting space. When she was finally able to move her materials to a permanent quilting space in the basement, her extended family noticed, leaving her with feelings of embarrassment. She was embarrassed for reasons other than quilting, though. Her passion for quilting had revealed the neglect of keeping the house up to her in-laws' standards. Therefore, Carrie felt that perhaps her in-laws were not simply commenting on her fabric stash, but that her fabric stash was getting in the way of her other wifely duties, like keeping a clean house and entertaining guests with regular use of the dining room table.

Similarly, Melinda, who also works at a fabric store, remembers the first time she hid fabric from her family:

I read a book about fabric-aholics and I thought, "Oh, I'm getting to that point." One day I worked an evening shift, I left some of my fabric in the car, in the back of the car, and I thought, "Oh, I'll just get it tomorrow, my husband will be gone." I think he had the day off and I'm thinking, "Oh, this plan is not working because now he's going to see me bringing it in during the day."

When Melinda and other quilters discussed their hiding strategies, they indicated the extent to which they were attached to their fabric purchases and quilting practices. Continuously hiding fabric also reveals the household tensions concerning women's abilities to engage in quilting in open, common family spaces.

Loretta, for example, hides her fabric in similar ways to Carrie and Melinda, although she states that her husband and family are fully supportive of her quilting:

I have fabric in the trunk of my car, and it's so dumb, my husband does not care. I'll go buy stuff and leave it in the trunk, and after everybody goes to sleep I'll go get it and take it in the house. Now why? They don't care. It's just like you know that you're obsessed, so I guess it's like a bulimic person, you don't want anybody to know that you're eating, although they know you are, so you sneak it and you hide it, and then when it gets melted in there with everything else nobody knows.

*Does it have anything to do with the fact that it's yours, it's just yours?*

Yeah. And it's just mine, because when you're raising a family, you are doing for everybody else and making quilts gives you an accomplishment.

Loretta likens her quilting activities to the eating disorder of bulimia in terms of hiding and hoarding her fabric, stating that she knows she is obsessed with fabric, and is choosing not to reveal her obsession to her family. Although Loretta indicates that she has support from her family for her quilting activities, she still feels the need to guard this part of her life from the non-quilters in her family, as if she were hiding a stigmatized addiction. The link Loretta makes between her enjoyment in quilting and family constraints that limit her time doing it also supports the notion of families as greedy institutions.

## QUILTERS' FAMILIES AS GREEDY INSTITUTIONS

Sociologist Lewis Coser (1974: 6, 11) argues that the modern middle class family best resembles a "greedy institution," one which makes unequal demands upon the wife-mother in comparison to the husband-father:

> Greedy institutions are characterized by the fact that they exercise pressures on component individuals to weaken their ties, or not to form any ties, with other institutions or persons that might make claims that conflict with their own demands ... This patterned greediness, however, conflicts with other institutionalized arrangements in modern society and introduces instabilities and incongruities. These arise from incompatibilities between modern and traditional definitions of social roles.

Women in traditional heterosexual relationships are encouraged to strengthen ties within the family unit, and to weaken or eliminate ties with organizations that exist outside the family and may pull women away from expected family duties and roles. The greediness of the family structure pressures women to keep interests tied closely to family interests.[1]

Although Coser first wrote about families as greedy institutions in the early 1970s, more recent social science research indicates that this phenomenon has, unfortunately, not dissipated for women in traditional heterosexual families. In contemporary society, traditional heterosexual married women have less free time than their husbands on a daily basis (Green, Hebron, and Woodward 1987; Mattingly and Bianchi 2003), and women are still overwhelmingly burdened with the second shift of unpaid housework in addition to paid-work responsibilities (Hochschild 1989). Therefore, as it consistently eats up women's leisure time, the institution of the traditional family can be successfully conceptualized as a greedy institution in relation to women's leisure opportunities.

When women attempt to carve out time for themselves for quilting, they feel guilt in doing so, and carry with them the stigma (Goffman 1963) of their serious leisure activity by hiding evidence of quilting (i.e., new fabric purchases) from family members (Stalp 2006a, 2006b). Quilters, though not often thought to be on parallel with pot smokers, do have something in common with them – secrecy about their activities. Howard Becker (1963: 66–67), a sociologist, documents such secrecy practices involved in regular marijuana use, detailing that:

> Although the user does not know what specifically to expect in the way of punishments, the outlines are clear: he [sic] fears repudiation by people whose

respect and acceptance he requires both practically and emotionally. That is, he expects that his relationships with nonusers will be disturbed and disrupted if they should find out, and limits and controls his behavior to the degree that relationships with outsiders are important to him.

Women who quilt expect similar consequences from family members while participating in quilting – they expect that relationships with non-quilters (e.g., family members, friends, and co-workers) will be affected negatively should their quilting processes be revealed publicly, including collecting, hoarding, and hiding fabric. Note also that quilters make marked effort to conceal their quilting identities from friends and co-workers who they believe will not be supportive. Additional gendered stigmas abound from friends and co-workers, including self-promotion, being old-fashioned, and fuddy-duddy.

The language quilters use to describe and defend their serious leisure activities indicates that the family is a greedy institution for the women in this study. For example, the definition of a fabric collection as a "stash" associates the fabric and the activity of quilting to other deviant or marginalized activities. The stigma women feel while participating in leisure is further evidence of their limited options to pursue leisure activities. As members of traditional families, women quilters, in trying to pursue quilting, reveal the greediness of families, for families not only limit women's leisure pursuits, but family members also question the value of the activity. The greedy institution of the family provides a framework through which to understand the development of deviant stigma surrounding women's leisure, and further promotes the deviance of the hidden activities involved in fabric collecting, hoarding, and hiding.

Carrie, who was caught hiding fabric from her husband and whose in-laws teased her about her fabric stash taking up the dining room table, has this to say about living with the stigma of quilting:

> Why is there such a stigma on women? I mean, it's because of women that people are here, period. I mean, we bear children, we mother children, and men couldn't do what they do without us. I'm just like, give us credit, we work our butts off, and I am probably the most lax, lazy mom that I can think of, but if it wasn't for me, my kids wouldn't be who they are, my husband wouldn't be the way he is. It's because of women. And, okay, so we happen to enjoy getting together to spend an afternoon talking about quilts, what's so wrong about that? My husband spent a whole day last weekend hunting a bird.

Carrie's frustration with the deviant label is clearly present in this excerpt. Carrie recognizes that her husband stigmatizes quilting, as in his eyes her time and effort spent on quilting take away from other expected household duties. Yet, she questions this stigmatizing of her chosen hobby, 'What's so wrong with that?' The language family members use also reinforces this stigma. Cassie has a fabric stash, but what fabric she has on hand does not always meet upcoming projects. This makes it necessary to go shopping for more quilt materials. She realizes that her husband views the stash differently than she, as he negatively refers to it as a "stock-pile" rather than a stash. To acknowledge her husband's insinuation that she has an abundance of fabric, before embarking on a new quilting project, she checks her stash to see if what she has will work: "I always out of guilt go to the stash first. I'll at least go through it before I look at a store to buy more fabric."

Contemporary quilting practices reveal much about women's leisure opportunities. There is overlap between fabric collecting and the leisure activity of quilting. Quilters collect fabric, but they also make quilts, using fabric from their collections. Women quilters collect to establish a fabric stash, a base from which to properly engage in their serious leisure activity. Similar to artists, quilters need a set of raw materials from which to draw. And yet, similar to other collectors, quilters are emotionally attached to their fabric stash, and are not willing to cut some of it up for quilting.

Hiding the fabric stash reveals how quilters perceive the lack of support from outsiders, family, and friends. Quilters feel that they must squeeze in their leisure practices among other everyday familial duties. Akin to illicit drug users, quilters engage in secret practices such as hoarding and hiding fabric to keep from their families the extent to which they are engaged in this activity. As they feel pressured to place quilting last in a day's scheduled events, quilters feel that their families do the same thing – place them and their leisure interests last in a list of valued daily items. Convinced of non-support while alive, they also predict that their families will disrespect their fabric once they pass on. Simply hiding the stash is no longer the answer. Instead, women make arrangements with other quilters who value the years devoted to the fabric collection stored in the house, as evidenced with "The Quiltermaker's Will" (Figure 4.3).

Quilters in this study collect fabric and under-report both the amount of fabric purchased and the related cost to family members, which is similar behavior to that of others engaged in serious leisure pursuits. They also hoard fabric because they see it as a limited commodity, produced in specific amounts and guided by fashion cycles. Finally, women quilters hide their fabric stash from family members, being unwilling to divulge the vastness of their collections to non-quilting outsiders.

Women's leisure pursuits are typically ranked last both by family members and quilters themselves. By examining women whose leisure pursuits have risen up the leisure ladder of importance, we can also see the struggles women confront as they continue to quilt and continue to participate as active members of the families. Women carry the deviant stigma of quilter as they engage in subterfuge to collect, hoard, and hide fabric. Because in contemporary life quilting is not a necessity (and indeed may be a luxury), it is not always legitimated as an activity worthy of time, space, and resources, as other well-documented non-utilitarian collectors and hobbyists experience. Thus, contemporary women performing a traditionally feminized needlework craft, such as quilting, sometimes have to struggle and engage in subterfuge to do so successfully. That women are less free to use family resources to pursue traditionally feminized activities such as quilting reveals the still-gendered configuration of home and family life, and contributes to the understanding of collectors and collecting in contemporary society.

## CAN THE FABRIC STASH EVER COME OUT OF THE CLOSET?

One of my mentors has a vinyl album collection that he treasures. He is upset that no one in his family seems to appreciate his carefully collected music as he does, and he wonders what will become of it when he dies. He claims that "no one understands how important it is" to him, and he bemoans the neglect he feels from family members. Yet, he criticizes his wife for her collecting passions. She collects many different things, mostly knick-knacks of various sorts, and displays her collections throughout the house, which apparently annoys him a great deal. She most often shops at secondhand stores and garage sales to add to her collection. But, after numerous conversations about quilters and their stashes, the light dawned for my mentor when he finally realized that his wife's collections mean as much to her as his record collection means to him. He soon understood that referring to her collections as "junk" probably wasn't the most sensitive or appropriate thing to do. I am not certain of the status of respect for either of their collections, but I do know that he became more enlightened about other people's collections than he was before we met.

I have a collection of 1950s aprons and kitchen linens. I also collect old purses and hats, and I collect fabric, rocks, and books. Most academics like me probably also collect books but we may not think of ourselves as book collectors because we make use of our collections regularly. When students first come into my office, they stare at the overflowing bookshelves that line the walls. "Gee, you have a lot of books," they say. I first respond, "Of course I have a lot of books – this is my profession." But, then I also say, "I've been *collecting* them ever since college, and I *use* them." In thinking about others people's collections, I personally know people who collect t-shirts, mugs, refrigerator magnets, shoes, animal skulls, lovers, Beanie Babies, Longaberger baskets, Disney paraphernalia, bumper stickers, cars, pets, dolls, coins, spoons, thimbles, baseball cards, and figurines of various sorts. Collecting fabric, then, is not that unusual, and, I suspect, not that deviant.

Understood within the family setting, quilting reveals the greediness of the institution and the limitations of current gender roles. As long as the wife/mother is relegated to caretaking duties, the family will background her interests. When midlife provides women opportunities to stretch and grow into new activities and interests, this upsets the existing order to which the family is accustomed. Developing a serious leisure activity before midlife is especially difficult for women in traditional settings. Quilting should be an activity that easily fits into the family structure as it provides direct and indirect benefits to the family. Women even justify quilting to their families, arguing that they make quilts for family members, give quilts as gifts for the family, and they even model traditional feminine behavior and gender roles through their quilting. Yet, at midlife, women appear to be foregrounding personal-level benefits of quilting over family needs. It is the foregrounding of quilting that becomes problematic, not quilting itself.

Can the fabric stash ever come out of the closet? Or will women forever hide their quilting identities and fabric collections from family members? Carrie, who was caught hiding fabric and teased by family members about her fabric stash, decided to stop hiding fabric, and she now makes her quilting interests more public to the family. Public recognition of quilting does not ensure respect for it, but Carrie feels it is a good place to start. Sarah advises women to learn how to quilt before getting into a serious relationship, because quilting takes up time and space not just in the lives of women who pursue it as serious leisure, but also in the lives of family members and friends. Those quilters who share space with others in a family setting are more likely to face resistance to their quilting – not because they are fabric collectors who quilt, but because that serious leisure quilting takes up time and space formerly focused solely on the family and its needs. Until the family can come to recognize the direct and indirect benefits of having a quilter in the family, quilters will continue to bear the brunt of the stigmatized identity of quilter, collecting, hoarding, and hiding fabric secretly.

At a writing retreat a few years ago, I made my first attempt to write about how and why quilters hide their fabric. During the evenings we met as a group and read aloud something that we had written that day. One night I shared some writing about the stash with the group. In response, one woman said, "We all have a stash. I collect pens, I buy them, my husband buys them for me, and I have them all over the house. My husband built me a special shelf for my favorite pens. The fabric for these women is like me and my pens." I think she is right. Most of us probably have some sort of stash that makes us happy. Whether or not others value it the same say we do is another story entirely.

## NOTE

1. In extreme situations, such as domestic abuse, the family can be understood not simply as a greedy institution, but as a total institution (Avni 1991; Goffman 1961). The women in this study, certainly, are not in this situation. This study is not an attempt to diminish cases of domestic violence or other instances of oppressive family environments.

# 5 QUILT RHYMES WITH GUILT: FINDING THE TIME AND SPACE TO QUILT

> This is mine. Quilting is my reward. Once the toilets are clean and the dishes are done it is quilting time. And like tonight, I'll sit and watch the baseball game all night and quilt.
>
> Sandy, fifties

Personal creative space can provide important insights into women's lives. Quilting activities and the spaces in which they occur in the home denote such creative spaces, signaling women's freedom to engage in personal leisure. Creative spaces devoted to women's leisure challenge the historical patterns of distribution of space by gender in the contemporary household and can be viewed as a form of resistance. Typically it is men's leisure activities – more so than women's – that receive more leisure space in the home (Spain 1992).

Quilting space fulfills a number of needs for quilters. It makes room for fabric and quilting equipment (e.g., sewing machines, ironing boards), and provides a private haven in which women can spend needed leisure time. Women's quilting spaces range from a designated chair or corner of the living room, the kitchen table during allotted times of the day, a quilt room that doubles as a guest room, and, for some women, an entire room in the house is reserved solely for quilting. The space itself and the time that women spend in it (as well as the time that women spend outside the home in quilting-related activities) are indicators of how involved women are in quilting and/or the space they have been allotted in the traditional family setting to pursue their own goals. The physical space, as well as the spending of time quilting inside or outside the home, can become a point of contention for quilters and their families as women carve out such resources for personal leisure activities. Through their interviews, quilters reiterated the importance of having personal creative space that they can escape to during their hectic, everyday lives.

Developing and maintaining a quilting life comes with challenges as the quilters I interviewed revealed to me. Challenges stem not only from the enjoyable creative struggle to quilt, but also from friends and family. To alleviate family difficulties, many women try to merge their quilting into already established family activities. They break down quilt projects into smaller units that they can take with them when they leave the house to tend to family duties (e.g., carpools, family vacations, and taking children to extracurricular activities). Just as a quilter pieces together fabric to make a quilt top, she also pieces together different components of her life. These components are sometimes pieced together peacefully, and sometimes not. How the creative spaces in the home are used (if they exist at all) provides important insight into families, gender relations, and women's freedom to participate comfortably in quilting activities.

## QUILTING SERIOUSLY

Quilting can be understood as a serious leisure activity that women turn to primarily for escape, relaxation, and creativity. As noted by Stebbins (1979: 3), serious leisure is: "a systematic pursuit of an amateur, hobbyist, or volunteer activity that partici- pants find so substantial and interesting that they launch themselves on a career, centred on acquiring and expressing its special skills, knowledge, and experience." Women who engage in serious leisure quilting as participants in this study do typ- ically learn to quilt as adults, pay others for quilting instruction, and make quilts as individuals rather than in groups (e.g., quilting bees). Quilting, like other serious leisure activities, is aptly considered superfluous to the household economy.[1] Most contemporary American quilters learn and practice quilting in serious leisure ways – they pursue it voluntarily and intensely for individual pleasure. Women also quilt because it helps them relax from paid work, unpaid household work, and other familial carework duties. For further clarification, Stebbins (1996: 46) outlines six characteristics of a serious leisure participant:

> 1) Serious leisure is leisure in which its practitioners encounter the occasional need to persevere, although this need is significantly less acute than in some occupations and significantly more acute than its opposite, casual leisure; 2) Moreover, a career awaits the serious leisure enthusiast. It consists of a history of turning points, levels of achievement and involvement, and a set of background contingencies; 3) Third, personal effort is common in such leisure, as based on extensive skill, knowledge or experience and oftentimes a combination of these; 4) Those who engage in serious leisure derive various durable benefits from it, including self-actualization, self-enrichment, feelings of group accomplishment, and enhancement of self-image; 5) Further, they find in connection with each serious leisure activity a unique social world composed of special norms, beliefs, values, morals, events, principles, and traditions; 6) These five distinguishing qualities are the soil in which the sixth takes root: practitioners come to identify strongly with their avocation.

Women's quilting experiences in this study comply with each of the six character- istics that Stebbins (1996) proposes. First, quilters express the need to find time and space for quilting and they take steps to negotiate with their families to quilt. Quilters, then, persevere for their activity as is suggested in the first characteristic (Doyle 1998; Stalp 2001). Second, quilters establish non-economic personal-level goals within quilting. They first identify themselves as quilters and develop personal creative goals, and they also use quilting as a way to cement ties with family and friends by gifting finished quilts (Stalp 2006c). Third, quilters develop advanced skills in quilting, including experience with sewing, fabric, and color. Many consider quilting as a way to paint with fabric and quilters spend time to learn new quilting skills (Stalp 2001). Fourth, women derive personal, social, and familial benefits from quilting (Stalp 2001), including all that Stebbins (1996: 46) mentions: "self-actualization, self-enrichment, feelings of group accomplishment, and enhancement of self-image." Fifth, when women self-identify as quilters, they also take on the externally generated meanings of being a quilter within the quilting social world (Stalp 2006c). In other words, quilters take on the "norms, beliefs, values, morals, events, principles, and traditions" of the quilting social world (Stebbins 1996: 46). Finally, the women in this study frame quilting as a passion or avocation (Stalp 2006c), which is in line with Stebbins' (1996: 46) sixth and final characteristic of a serious leisure participant: "practitioners come to identify strongly with their avocation."

American women's serious leisure quilting experiences demonstrate women's resistance to preexisting familial constraints, such as adequate time and space in the home for leisure. Women choose to quilt, and although quilting is thought to be more of a traditional activity than not, at present quilting does not appear to "fit" into the family structure, as quilts are no longer necessary household goods. Despite its traditional feminine history, quilting is more like any other modern leisure activity that takes time, attention, money, and space away from the family routine and toward one's individual routine. In this way, although once a traditional activity that supported the family economy, quilting as it is practiced in serious leisure ways can be considered a non-traditional activity as another hobby would, for serious leisure quilting does not contribute to the family economy. This particular leisure activity occurs within the home and affects family members in ways different than when an individual pursues leisure outside the home (e.g., golf and football widows). For example, Collis (1999) notes in her study of a small Australian mining community that married men working four twelve-hour shifts like to hang out in pubs and drink alcohol during their off nights. This, too, is a traditional and gendered activity, and it removes the individual from the family and familial activities. Disrupting the family status quo is a considerable factor as leisure is studied both within and outside of the family structure, whether traditional or non-traditional families are being studied (Shaw 1997).

Women quilt first for themselves, and second to administer to family and kin needs in gendered ways (e.g., providing gifts that cement emotional ties to family and friends). To acknowledge the constraints and the resistance present in women's leisure, I draw on Shaw's (1994: 9) integrative approach to studying women's leisure, one that: "sees women's leisure as offering possibilities for resistance. The argument for resistance arises out of the definition of leisure as a situation of choice, control, and self determination. When leisure is seen in this way, women's participation in activities, especially non-traditional activities, can be seen to challenge restrictive social roles." Shaw (1994) focuses on non-traditional activities, which quilting in its present form can certainly be considered. As a non-traditional activity, quilting takes away from traditional needs of the home. When chosen and pursued in a serious leisure fashion, quilting affords women benefits that other leisure pursuits offer.

Midlife women quilters both experience leisure constraints and resist those constraints as they find the time and space to quilt within and outside other gendered familial duties. When women secure space for quilting in the home, it typically happens after other family members' space needs are met, regardless of social class background. As women in this study *both* quilt *and* spend time with their families, they reveal the important gendered sites of negotiation for women and leisure in contemporary families; that is, the constraints and resistance present in American quilters' lives. In this chapter, in line with Shaw's (1994, 1997) integrative framework, I examine the constraints of time and space for quilting, as well as the resistance strategies that women use to integrate leisure with family activities within American serious leisure quilting, practiced in a traditional family setting.

As a leisure activity, quilting takes up a lot of time and space. And, because quilting mostly happens in the home, the time and space issues become apparent and can cause tension in the home. To deal with this tension, many women juggle quilting with other family duties, and quilt at the kitchen table, in front of the television, and while waiting for children when driving carpool. Women make quilting fit into the rest of their lives, which is both positive and negative. Fitting quilting into everyday life is positive because women get to spend time doing something they enjoy, amidst family activities that they also enjoy. However, this can also be negative because as women have made quilting appear to be such an everyday activity, it can then be considered mundane and not special enough to warrant its own space and time. Quilting might be viewed by family members to be replaceable by another everyday activity such as cleaning, cooking, or tending to the family. Women try to manage the guilt they sometimes feel while quilting because they believe (as some of their family members do) that their quilting interests "take away" from family responsibilities.

Denise is married and the mother of two children, and she has a separate space for quilting in her home. Yet, when cutting fabric for a quilt, rather than spending time alone in her quilt room, she moves to be near the family so that she can both cut fabric and be with her family: "I have a little tiny space that has a cutting board and I will work in there, but I get lonesome for my family. So I will basically go where my family is." Denise chooses to spend time quilting and to spend time with her family. She chooses *both*. However, Denise fills the role of caretaker before the role of quilter, as she places being with the family over quilting – she does not move her family to her quilting area. Additionally, Denise's storage system for when she is working on a specific project is shaped by her husband's organizational style: "My husband is a very precise person, he likes things tidy and I do not, so I keep all the fabric from one project in a box and then I'll carry the box with me and then put everything back in. That's helping, but not really." Note how Denise first describes her husband's organizational preferences, then her own, and next she includes how she has changed her ways to fit her husband's ways. In both of these passages, it is clear that Denise is modifying her quilting based upon her family and her family's needs and preferences, and integrating both leisure and family. Denise's actions are typical of women in traditional families pursuing leisure.

## NOT ENOUGH TIME

Quilting is a labor-intensive process, and it is sometimes difficult for others to see or measure progress from a single session of quilting. Michelle, who is in her fifties, married with children, notes the time she spends with each quilt: "I feel like every quilt that I have made, part of my heart and soul went into it. I guess you work on them for so long. It will probably be two years from start to finish that this one is done. It is a part of me." Other gendered home tasks, such as cooking a meal, doing dishes, or washing clothes can be done rather quickly in comparison to the highly skilled and labor-intensive process of constructing a quilt from start to finish. General housework efforts are more easily detected and recognized by family members who benefit from eating a home-cooked meal off of clean dishes, or wearing clean clothes. In contrast, family members do not necessarily benefit immediately, directly, or even personally from women's quilting efforts.

According to quilters, family members sometimes see time spent on quilting as "wasted" time. Quilters reported that their families misunderstood their quilting time, and that they wanted the quilter to be doing something more directly related to the family. For example, Tina is in her early forties and she enjoys quilting above watching television, which sometimes upsets her family and friends:

> They don't like to see me spend so much time on it. It seems that they'd like to do more things with me, but then in reality the things that they really want you to do sometimes are just sitting in front of the TV and stuff like that. My boyfriend right now, he's really jealous of me doing quilting.

In Tina's case, time for quilting has become an issue. Misunderstandings and sometimes resentment about time spent on quilting can extend to other activities that involve one family member (Baldwin and Norris 1999; Baldwin et al. 1999; Gillespie et al. 2002; Goff et al. 1997; Major 2001). Women incorporate quilting into everyday activities, they steal time away to quilt, and feel guilty as they devote time to themselves when there are other family-centered activities in need of attention.

## NOT ENOUGH SPACE

Women's quilting spaces in this study existed on a continuum, and ranged from temporary public family space to a separate, private space such as a bedroom, or even a rented-out space away from the home. For those who have private spaces, there are both temporary and permanent categories. Having a private quilting room does not mean that women go to the room only to quilt. Rather, women want to have a space in their home that they can call their own, where they can leave a mess and close the door if company comes over. Additionally, a small number of women rented space outside the home to use only for quilting activities. Seen through the allocation of space in the home, women without permanent quilting space work to garner space around other home activities for quilting. Such setting up and taking down and setting back up again takes valuable time out of a quilter's already limited leisure time.

In this study, forty-eight women (just over 68 percent) had no space in the home where they could quilt regularly. Most women had small, hidden spaces such as closets and cupboards to store materials and equipment. These women had to find both time and space to quilt, taking out stored quilting equipment, set up in a common space such as the kitchen or the dining room. Once quilting time had passed, these women took down equipment and stored it. This process of taking out and returning equipment took time that could have been spent quilting, and was layered with the frustration of not having a space, even a small one, to call their own.

Thirteen women (just over 18 percent) from this study had semi-permanent quilting space in the home, and often were in rooms that had additional purposes, such as guest rooms, junk rooms, or vacant bedrooms. This type of space permits some equipment to be set up and left out in the open, but as it is temporary, when the space is needed for other purposes (e.g., guests), the quilting equipment gets taken down and stored away, similar to when women have no space.

Only seven women (10 percent) had permanent quilting within the home. Here they were able to have equipment set up and ready to use. These spaces were located away from common space, in a spare bedroom, basement, or attic. Carrie is in her middle forties, married with three children, and she talks about the process of obtaining a permanent quilting space: "I have a section of the basement now. We have the computer room, my sewing stuff, and my sewing stuff supplies. I took up the dining room for about four years." Recall that Carrie's family ridiculed her for how much space her quilting stash took up in the dining room.

An even-smaller number of women rent space for equipment storage and a place to quilt. Only two women (3 percent) in this study fit this definition of space, and both were unusual in that they had economic goals linked to their quilting – they planned to teach classes, which justified the rental space.

## THE SPACE "HAVE-NOTS"

Quilters without specific quilting space lamented first that they had no permanent quilting space in light of women who do. Secondly, though, they talk about the practical advantages of having a permanent space. Without it, women spend time unpacking their materials, setting up, working, and then taking the equipment down again, so that the family could again use the space. Patricia, who is in her sixties, married with four adult children who no longer live at home, longs for a more convenient space in which to quilt. She lives in a two-story farmhouse, and has her equipment spread throughout the house:

> Well, I have a sewing room; it is kind of a room upstairs at the top of our steps.
> It is kind of a half hallway where I have my sewing machine. I've had my sewing

machine downstairs, too, but I put it upstairs a couple of years ago. Most of it I do up there although upstairs is still not set up really well. That room isn't big enough for cutting out and then I have to bring everything down to the kitchen table to cut it out and then take it up to the sewing machine. Handwork and stuff I just sit by the chair and a lamp. I usually have a basket full of stuff sitting there. But I would say that all of my machine work is done upstairs.

The upstairs room, where Patricia set up her sewing machine, is not large enough for all her quilting tasks beyond sewing such as designing, cutting, and ironing fabric. Patricia uses other common family space to hand quilt and has even used the kitchen table to sew on. The kitchen is large enough, but because it is the kitchen and used frequently for other purposes, Patricia must take down her equipment for family needs:

My daughter and I set two machines up on the kitchen table. We both sewed at the same time and had the ironing board there and everything. But you know as far as having a really nice sewing space I don't have that. I see a lot of people that have a big room and they have their ironing board, they have everything right there.

Patricia realizes the potential of a quilt room and sees other quilters with specific and adequate space in which to quilt. She wants "a really nice sewing space."

Negotiating space generally, and quilting space specifically, is a challenge many families face, especially newly married couples. When Sarah married, she moved into her husband's house, which does not have a permanent quilting space. Before she married, Sarah was living alone and she had permanent quilting space in her apartment. Sarah comments on the amount of space it takes her to quilt effectively:

The more space you have though, I think it is easier to work on stuff. Now especially I have to almost work on what I'm working with and then put it away, and drag out something else. I mean it's alright, I'm getting it done.

*So if your husband ever goes away for the weekend, what would happen?*

(laughing) There would be fabric from one end of the house to the other. I think I would just use it as an opportunity to spread out more.

Having a specific space leaves quilters to experience their quilting process more freely. A temporary space such as Sarah's current space shapes how she now experiences leisure in comparison to how she used to be able to "spread out more" while quilting. When Sarah's husband is at home, then, she works with her materials in a more contained and presumably less than ideal space. Sarah feels more able to spread out her fabric and equipment, as she needs them, when her spouse is not at home. Sarah uses general family space to compensate for the lack of permanent space, and when family members re-enter the home, she spends time packing up and storing equipment away.

Cassie is newly married and her quilting space is considerably smaller than most spaces in this study, comprising just a corner in the living room around a reclining easy chair, and yet this small space is powerfully meaningful to her:

> This is my little quilting area, which I love. I feel like this little corner of the world is mine and I try to keep it organized. If I'm sitting here and can just pull it up and that's it, then I can start going and do it for a half an hour, that's a half hour more that I would get done.

Cassie's quilting corner takes up little space in the living room, especially since she does all her sewing and quilting by hand, and does not need additional space to set up a sewing machine either temporarily or permanently. As she stores her materials in a cabinet in a different room than her quilting corner, only the project she is currently hand piecing or hand quilting is out in the open. Occasionally Cassie works on projects that require more space than her corner allows. Cassie and her husband argue about how much space her quilting takes up in the house, although her husband currently occupies the extra bedroom as his home office and definitely takes up more square footage of the apartment than she does:

> He does complain when quilting takes over [the apartment], or especially when I have a quilt out for six weeks. I'll say, "Well, unfortunately, this is common space." I definitely don't try to be bitchy about it, but I told him that when we buy a house I'm having my own sewing room and it's going to be mine and he can come in sometimes.

In sharing her frustration about the space issues with her husband, Cassie discusses how she plans to resolve the space issues with a quilting room of her own:

> I have these visions of what I want and lots of light and baskets full of fabric and a chair that's so comfortable, with pretty walls with quilts on the walls and a tile floor. I have it all mapped out in my mind. Whenever we look at a house and we see a standard formal house and there's a side room that some people make into a breakfast room I say, "That's going to be my quilting room, that's going to be it. You've had your own room for a long time." I want a space that's mine.

In her mind, Cassie has moved beyond just talking about the room. She has planned out what it will look like, and she actively shares that vision with her husband (who has always had a home office since they married) as they make plans to buy a house.

## RHYMES WITH GUILT: FINDING THE TIME TO QUILT

Time is an important issue for quilters. The women in this study challenged time constraints and embraced contemporary family dynamics as they simultaneously quilted within family time. Rather than resenting their families for the energy and time put into managing family and work responsibilities, women instead use their quilting activities as a strategy to achieve both family and leisure. That is, they *both* embrace their families and friends *and* they continue to quilt, both complying with and resisting traditional gendered family roles.

While spending time quilting, some women feel that they are using time selfishly that could be devoted to the family. Realizing this, Meg (middle sixties), who is currently retired from paid work and spends time traveling to visit her children and grandchildren, taught quilting classes, and designed projects that had quilters' busy family-centered lifestyles in mind:

> I taught lap quilting where you quilted one block at a time and then put the quilt together with the blocks already quilted. This appeals so much, because women could take it with them, while they were waiting for kids, while they were carpooling. Those that work could do it at their lunch hour; they could do it watching television at night. It kept them within the family instead of taking them out of the family. Because I think women don't necessarily like to be pulled out of their families to do their hobby. But this you can take with you. The nice thing is that you can carry it with you and you don't feel quite as guilty about doing something for yourself. Because you know women are full of guilt. That's how we're raised.

Meg's comments indicate that she is conflicted in balancing her quilting activities within her family – she wants *both*. First, Meg is conscious of the struggles women face to get quilting done in everyday life, and she designs quilt projects that will work for women with families, challenging family roles but also supporting them. Next, she defends her decisions, affirming traditional family roles: "Because I think women don't necessarily like to be pulled out of their families to do their hobby" and normalizes women's guilt: "Because you know women are full of guilt. That's how we're raised." Meg acknowledges the difficulties women experience with personal leisure, she develops a solution to combine family and leisure, and then defends her guilt while she encourages women to continue to quilt among other family responsibilities.

Tina, who earlier claimed that her boyfriend is "really jealous" of her quilting, describes a typical situation in which she compromises what type of quilting project she will work on when her boyfriend wants to go on a driving trip over the weekend:

> I've never had a fight about it or anything and if he decides [that we're going] someplace, it takes away from the sewing machine time that I would like to have done that weekend, but then I'll go ahead and carry something else with me to just try to compromise that way. I don't always get exactly what I want, but I'll get something done.

Note that Tina continues to quilt and does not compromise entirely. Instead, Tina alters which project will get her attention that weekend, as does Beth who has three children that no longer live at home: "I like handwork because I can do it in the car." Other quilters have similar project choices to make when including family activities and limited amounts of time.

Emma finds that although she enjoys quilting greatly, it is difficult to squeeze it into other family activities. Struggling to find balance between her identities as both a good mother and a good quilter, she talks about how she spends a typical Sunday: "Between church and Sunday school I have a little time to kill, and when the kids go on the playground I would quilt then, and then after Sunday school we would meet their friends and we would play on the playground so I would sit and quilt, and that's kind of how it is." In addition to bringing her quilting along, Emma has also altered her quilting projects to be smaller and less complicated: "I know I don't have much time, and I can't stay with something too intricate because I get interrupted so often. I've got to do something that's simple but I don't want it to *look* too simple." In this way, Emma's quilting is more portable, and it is still satisfying to her. It is important to Emma that she spends time with her family, but also that she is seen by other women as a skilled quilter.

Meg shares her strategy for negotiating quilting into her family activities: "I try to save the handwork for evenings, so I can watch television and spend time with my family in a more general sense. My husband doesn't like it when I go into the other room to work when he's watching television at night." Making time for both family time and self time (quilting time) is important to these quilters. As some women have recognized their work as a perceived threat to a collective family time, they make marked efforts to arrange their quilting schedule so that they can spend time with family members when the family is home.

### FINALLY! NEGOTIATING A ROOM OF ONE'S OWN

Having a room of one's own in which to quilt is related to age, marital status, children, and affluence in this study. Young newly married women, women living with roommates or women with small children at home were more likely to have temporary quilting areas rather than quilt rooms in their living spaces. Young single women, married or unmarried women at midlife, retired married women, and widowed women were more likely to have permanent space for quilting. This breakdown of space allocation indicates that when women are living with others, their personal and/or creative needs often receive lower priority, and this is consistent with current family and leisure research (Chafetz and Kotarba 1995; Freysinger and Flannery 1992; Green, Hebron, and Woodward 1990; Herridge et al. 2003; Larson et al. 1997; Marks et al. 2001; Mattingly and Bianchi 2003; Thompson 1999; Walker 1996). Yet, the age and space breakdown do not ensure women quilting spaces, for the majority of women I interviewed have no space in the home where they can quilt regularly.

Those with guest rooms and home offices were sometimes able to use these spaces as semi-permanent quilt spaces. Others converted children's bedrooms into permanent quilting spaces once their children left home. Women in the situation of looking for a new house or building a house made certain to select or build one that included a sewing room, or at least a guest bedroom that could double as a quilt room when guests are not visiting: "they bought this house which is a split level, and the bottom floor is one large room and the garage. The large room is hers to work in, and she said that they bought this house with the intention that this room would be hers" (fieldnotes 1999).

However, not even differences in social class can resolve the issue of women's space in the home completely. Even the most affluent women in this study obtained their quilt rooms *after* their children had left home, or *after* they had moved into a larger house. For example, Karla is currently retired from paid work and shares how she secured her quilt room. After their children left home, Karla and her husband bought their retirement home and she planned on it having a quilt room:

> I have a [quilt] room. When we bought this house my husband had said, "We only need two bedrooms." I said, "No, we don't, we need three." He asked, "Why?" "Well, I need a room, and we need a guest room." He finally agreed, but he did not know my ulterior motive was to have a sewing room, a craft room.

Although Karla neglected to inform her husband what her room would be for, she did negotiate a space for her quilting. Linda (middle sixties) was entirely clear with her husband about her quilt room. Linda's quilt room was a space that she and her husband planned for when they built their new house, after their children had all left home: "We built the home that we are living in now and I decided that I wanted to have a room that I could have for my sewing. I could spread out my work materials and I could just shut the door. So I have a beautiful table, and a walk-in closet that has shelving for my material." The priority of space devoted to women in the home is revealed in how participants discuss having a space, or not having a space. Women with different quilting spaces, therefore, are not just discussing the quilting space or lack thereof, but also the priority these women's leisure experiences are given in the family household. A quilting room to some extent is an accomplishment of having one's personal creative needs recognized.

Women describe their quilting spaces in great detail, and demonstrate the important role that quilting plays in their lives. In describing her newly obtained quilting space, Loretta notes that it was once her daughter's bedroom:

> Well, when one of my kids moved out I took her bedroom over, and it's probably twelve feet by twelve feet, and it is so crammed full. I have a table with a sewing machine and the closet is now shelves with fabric stash, shelves all around the walls with batting. I just love the solitude. And it's kind of like an oasis away from everything. I can sit for four or five hours without moving and quilt and the time just flies by, it's a catharsis. Just soothing to your soul, it really is.

Loretta comments on how she felt when she was able to allocate space in the home for her quilting: "I can think of the accomplishment I felt within myself when I finally got a sewing room. And it's just mine, because when you're raising a family, you are doing [things] for everybody else and making quilts gives you an accomplishment."

After meeting the needs of other family members, Loretta is finally granted a quilting space of her own as she nears retirement from paid work.

Some quilters referred to their quilting areas as their quilt studio, their place to keep their quilting materials whether or not they actually did work in that space. Having the space was important to these women, because it was *their* space. For example, Beth appreciates having a quilting space that is all hers:

> It's kind of nice having this room. I don't have to quilt on my kitchen table, so I'm real lucky to have this space. My husband has his computer space, so why shouldn't I have my sewing room? There is nobody else at home and nobody else accountable so I can do stuff like that which is kind of good, I do what I want to do.

Beth's comments prove particularly interesting as she highlights both space issues with her husband and priority issues in terms of her entire family. In claiming that "nobody else is at home and nobody else accountable" Beth reveals that with her children gone, she can finally have some time to herself, to use it the way she chooses. Additionally, Beth compares her space to her husband's computer space, noting that her husband's space came before hers. She also expresses that "it's kind of nice having this room" for she no longer has to use family space such as the kitchen table for quilting – she now "gets" a room of her own so that she can do what she wants to do. Beth's statement of "I do what I want to do" only stands, though, after other family members are taken care of – after her husband got his office, and after her children have left home. Recall that quilting is both time and labor intensive, so if a quilter is tending to family needs, she is not tending to quilting. When some women begin quilting, they do so with such intensity that family members are noticeably upset – they were once the object of such intense attention and can sometimes feel displaced.

Leisure opportunities for women quilters are hampered by space in the home (or lack thereof) for quilting. An overwhelming 68 percent of women in this study have no permanent space for personal leisure pursuits, and only 10 percent have permanent spaces, or quilt rooms to call their own.[2] Importantly, regardless of social class background, quilters secured permanent leisure space *only* after all family members' needs were met – after their children left home, or when their spouses established a home office. Additionally, the presence of personal leisure space does not resolve leisure issues within the household, for women with permanent spaces continue to plan their quilting activities so that they can spend evenings and weekends with family. Some women indicated that time constraints to leisure would not disappear if space constraints were diminished. For example, Cassie suggests that once she secures her permanent quilt space, her husband will continue to call her fabric collection "a space-hogging stockpile" rather than necessary quilting materials, as she views them (fieldnotes 1999). The larger issues of legitimating time and space for women's quilting, as well as those surrounding women's leisure generally remain.

## FROM A ROOM OF ONE'S OWN TO A LIFE OF ONE'S OWN?

> Hobbies are a good thing it seems. Yet, one apparently contradictory side of
> serious leisure, given the culturally dominant belief that all leisure is casual
> activity, is the paradox that those who engage in it encounter costs and rewards,
> both of which can be sharply felt.

> Robert A. Stebbins, *The Barbershop Singer*

The costs and rewards of quilting as a leisure activity are complicated, but worthwhile, according to the study participants. Women find it difficult to locate time and
space for leisure activities, especially those that occur in the home, as quilting does.
To accommodate family interaction, women alter how they practice serious leisure
quilting – they break down larger projects into smaller, travel-friendly ones which
accompany women as they run daily errands. Women also save handwork for
evenings so they can watch television with the family as they also work on their
quilting projects. Faced with time and space challenges to their chosen leisure
activity, women do not abandon quilting. Instead, they alter it so that they can
interact with their families while they enjoy the personal stress-relieving benefits of
quilting. By carving out both time and space to quilt within existing familial structures, then, women resist familial constraints and yet simultaneously comply with the
gendered structure of the traditional family.

Serious leisure quilters put great amounts of time and effort into quilting, and
once they begin to self-identify as quilters, they integrate quilting into other components of their lives (Stalp 2006c). For example, Angela states, "Quilting is my life,
that's my friends. Almost all my friends are quilters. I have developed a large part of
my life around quilting." Here Angela not only describes the role that quilting plays
in her life, she also emphasizes how quilting benefits her through social support
among friends and artistic inspiration. Because quilting is a serious leisure activity,
women will go to great lengths to ensure they have adequate time and space in the
home to practice it. I speculate that women who may quilt but who do not self-
identify as quilters will not need to resist the constraints of time and space as regularly as serious leisure quilters will.

Although not immediately obvious to the outside eye, family negotiations over
women's serious leisure quilting carry hidden gendered components. American
women in traditional heterosexual families are often expected to support and care for
others at the expense of leisure pursuits. Within-home and non-economic aspects of
women's serious leisure reveal the importance of women-centered cultural activities,
those that women engage in for personal reasons. This analysis of serious leisure
quilting sheds light on the power dynamics in contemporary families, where women's
activities that cannot be defined as either market work or direct family carework are
not validated. Parker (1984: 215) elaborates upon the gendered components of
women's serious leisure constraints and resistance in her study of British embroidery:

> The role of embroidery in the construction of femininity has undoubtedly constricted the development of the art. What women depicted in thread became determined by notions of femininity, and the resulting femininity of embroidery defined and constructed its practitioners in its own image. However, the vicious circle has never been complete. Limited to practicing art with needle and thread, women have nevertheless sewn a subversive stitch – managed to make meanings of their own in their very medium intended to inculcate self-effacement.

Similar to British embroiderers, American quilters challenge the traditional feminine stereotypes affiliated with quilting, for when practiced in serious leisure ways, the individual quilter benefits directly from the experience, and family and friends may benefit indirectly. Men's leisure pursuits in families are more supported than women's leisure, as noted by Collis (1999) in her study of men frequenting taverns during off-work hours, and by Stebbins (1996) who demonstrates how barbershop singers' wives will accompany them to conventions and become involved in other supportive roles. Likewise, researchers note how women experience hostility in the home toward reading romance novels (Brackett 2000; Radway 1991), watching televised soap operas (Harrington and Bielby 1995) and telenovelas (Barreras and Bielby 2001), and, according to Stebbins (1996), husbands demand that their wives quit barbershop singing activities.

American women are faced with constraints to their serious leisure quilting in the form of time and space, and they also resist such constraints as has been addressed in the literature. However, this research demonstrates that the negotiations women make to continue to quilt *and* to continue to spend time and share space with their families go beyond the concepts of constraint and resistance. The accommodations women make to accomplish both are knowingly chosen. They do not substitute leisure for family time, but instead make room for both. Women in this study do not fully resist the posed constraints from family activities, but instead integrate quilting into carpooling, or watching television with family in the evenings. They have found ways to make this work.

Previous research demonstrates that those devoted to running marathons (Baldwin et al. 1999; Goff et al. 1997) and doing dog sports competitions (Gillespie et al. 2002) have accomplished personal goals, traveled extensively, and received awards from competitions, but support, admiration, and respect from family members are not always tangible. Serious leisure quilters argue that their quilting efforts save the family time and money, for as quilters construct homemade gifts, family members benefit from receiving them, or they benefit from gifting them to friends. In this way, then, family members have something to curl up with, or to point to that speaks of the quilter's accomplishments. Making claims to the finished cultural product is how family and friends benefit from the activity – they can see tangible proof of the serious leisure efforts. Because it relates to the production of a cultural object, is resistance more likely to occur in quilting rather than in other serious leisure activities?

## NOTES

1. Both women and men engage in quilting activities solely and partially for capital. The majority of women in this study, however, engage in quilting as a form of non-economic cultural production.
2. In comparison, the *Quilting in America Survey* (Leman Publications 2006) reports that 83 percent of "dedicated quilters" have their own quilt rooms. Defined by the *Quilting in America Survey*, the dedicated quilter annually spends an average of $2,304US on quilting purchases, is approximately fifty-nine years old, well-educated, and affluent (Leman Publications 2006). I posit, then, that the dedicated quilters of the *Quilting in America Survey* do not necessarily represent the experiences of the quilters in this study.

# 6 COMING OUT OF THE CLOSET: QUILTING IS FOR SELF AND FOR OTHERS

> I have a friend who says, "You know, a quilt never hurt anybody, you know, it just never hurt anybody"

> Heather

Women in this study quilt first for themselves, and second for others as they fulfill family needs in gendered ways (e.g., to give homemade gifts that cement ties to family and friends, to provide a material representation of important family events). Even though women quilt for personally fulfilling reasons, and do carework for themselves, they are also simultaneously doing carework for others as they accept and reproduce traditional notions of gender within families. Leisure quilting practices are embedded in women's lives, recording extraordinary events for each quilter.

While raising six girls and working outside the home part time, my mother had little time to work on large or complex craft projects, despite her enjoyment of these activities. During her pregnancies, and mostly while spending time away from the family in the maternity ward of the hospital, she finished an intricate needlepoint project that is the basis for the face of a clock that hangs in my parents' living room. Very often she tells us, "When I die, that clock goes in the grave with me, strapped to my chest" (fieldnotes 2000).

This clock represents great effort by my mother to complete a creative project in between giving birth to six children. The clock represents her creative efforts and is uniquely hers, unlike a Halloween costume or clothing that she sewed for her children when they were young. She has something to measure this period in her life by, and she has not outgrown it in the way that children outgrow their clothes, or in the way that children grow up and leave the family home. In taking the clock with her when she dies, symbolically she will have with her forever evidence for herself of her creative efforts, linked with memories of all of her children. Similar to midlife quilters in this study, since her children have grown and moved out of the house, my mother has also increased her quilting activities, turned a former bedroom into a quilt room, and established a fabric stash.

Like my mother and her embroidery clock, women use quilts in similar ways. Quilts mark time for women by bookmarking life events, and maintaining memories symbolically. Quilters process, store, and retrieve in quilts things they want to remember about their everyday lives, whether or not anyone else believes they are important. Such memories include who the quilt was made for, the occasion it

FIG. 6.1. Mom's embroidery clock. Personal photograph.

represents, and the people with whom these women shared time during the quilting process. Yet, quilts are also life bookmarks of non-obvious things, such as what was occurring in women's lives at the time quilts were made. Women, therefore, bookmark their lives with quilts.

As many artists organize portfolios of their work to document the breadth and depth of their talent, women's finished quilts mark the carework completed for self and others. Individually, women simply remember quilts and the process of making them in their heads, and some actually assemble scrapbooks or photo albums to document their quilting activities. Collectively, quilt guilds and groups record quilts made by individual members through guild photo albums, and also demonstrate the group's creative work in local and regional quilt shows. Study participants found it important to remember their quilting efforts, with a majority of women keeping some type of quilting record, either mental, written, or photographed, or a combination of the three. Such quilt records reveal important aspects of the meaning of quilting in women's lives.

Quilts and the quilting process have important symbolic meaning to their makers, marking women's significant personal and family life events. As markers of history and women's lives, quilts reveal important meaning-making processes in the social institutions of gender, family, and culture. As "[m]onuments resolve in stone the contradictions of the nations that erect them" (Schwartz 1996a: 395), quilts establish through fabric the identity of women as quilters, the development and continuity of

FIG. 6.2. Mom's embroidery clock, close-up. Personal photograph.

gendered familial, personal, and cultural traditions, as well as a way in which to mark time within women's non-economic cultural production activities. For women who quilt, quilts act as vehicles of memory, bookmarking their lives. Similar to family photo albums and the recent craze of scrapbooking (Dickerson 2000; Kelly and Brown 2005), when women make, handle, and view quilts, they are able to remember and honor the women who made quilts in their pasts, or friends, family members, personal and historical events. Quilts evoke memories specific to their makers, locally to friends and family, and more broadly to the non-quilting public, who nowadays are fascinated by and appreciative of quilts.

Collective-memory scholars address the complexity of memory on many levels, ranging from local to global (e.g., Halbwachs 1941, 1992; Olick 1999; Schwartz 1996a, 1996b; Zerubavel 1996). Collective memory is "a reconstruction of the past [which] adapts the image of ancient facts to the beliefs and spiritual needs of the present" (Halbwachs 1941: 7). Quilts and the quilting process contribute to both the individual memory of women quilters and collective memory generally. Women quilters reach back through history to make connections to unknown women artists who constructed quilts before them, and they leave messages embedded in their quilts for quilters and non-quilters in generations to come. Quilting serves women at the personal, familial, and historical levels as they create a social fabric through the creation of cultural objects made out of fabric. Yet, outsiders to quilting are also able to connect personal, familial, and historical memories to quilts.

Halbwachs (1992) offers a useful way in which to think about memory. He suggests that we remember events by placing them within a network of social markers, such as holidays, gift exchanges, and family events:

> What makes recent memories hang together is not that they are contiguous in time: it is rather that they are part of a totality of thoughts common to a group, the group of people with whom we have a relation at this moment, or with whom we have had a relation on the preceding day or days. To recall them it is hence sufficient that we place ourselves in the perspective of the group, that we adopt its interests and follow the slant of its reflections ... Based on such memories, the family group is accustomed to retrieving or reconstructing all its other memories following a logic of its own. (Halbwachs 1992: 52)

Quilts guide women in organizing their family and leisure time, and, once completed, quilts mark a specific time period through memory. From simply looking at an image of a quilt, or describing a quilt that they have made, women can recall the process of making that quilt. They discuss the intention of the quilt and the artistic processes surrounding it, and they detail what they were experiencing in their personal lives at the time that the quilt was constructed. Quilters rarely focus on the number of quilts they have made, the order in which they made quilts, or how long it took to make any given quilt from start to finish, although these aspects of the quilting process often interest outsiders to the activity.

Creating and preserving memories through quilting is highlighted by the common practice of keeping mementos of the quilt process and product. When women discuss their quilting with other quilters, there are more elements of the creative process that they are willing to share – some women revisit their quilts, and the relationships surrounding those quilts. In revisiting their quilts, women keep the memory of the cultural process alive as well as the levels of memory they and others have attached to quilts. The quilt itself, or the memory of the quilt, becomes an object that is intentionally woven into others' lives.

Women in this study often gave finished quilts to family and friends, and recalled important relationships when speaking about specific quilts. Such quilts provide evidence of women's close personal relationships with other quilters, friends, and family members. Yet, in recalling quilts, women also reference their artistic skills and take great satisfaction in self-identifying as quilters, even if that role might incur ridicule.

## QUILTING AS CAREWORK FOR SELF

Quilting is important to women on a personal level, for quilters garner personal, physical, emotional, and artistic fulfillment from participating in the activity. The actual physical act of quilting benefits women emotionally, because while they engage in quilting, they enjoy the flow of the activity. As discussed in Chapter 3, quilting leaves them with a calmness and focus not achieved through other requisite, everyday activities such as childcare, laundry, meal preparation, or housework, and it is something they wish to do regularly. Some women used quilting to develop identities that were not directly tied to their identities and roles in their families. Women make quilts that reflect and give voice to their lives, and to revive the aesthetic in their lives. Quilters demonstrate the meaning embedded in their artistic lives, discussing quilts and quilting experiences that document the development of a quilting identity, as well as a means of self-expression.

Quilting, similar to many other artistic processes, offers numerous possibilities for self-expression. Many women find that quilts are an appropriate way in which to express themselves personally, spiritually, and artistically. Linda explains that being able to do with quilts virtually anything one can imagine is quilting's most attractive feature: "There are no rules. It is just the matter of your own imagination deciding on whatever message you want to convey with an idea. Everybody brings their ideas into it and so there are many ways that the quilts can express individuality and personality." Linda's comments indicate that through making quilts, women are able to find and use their personal and artistic voices.

Women are deeply committed to their quilting activities, and as an activity, quilting holds an important and meaningful place in their lives. Feeling connected to other quilters is important, and assists women in developing their artistic voices through their quilting endeavors. Linda comments on the family-like ties that a common interest in quilting engenders: "It's like growing up in the same neighborhood and when you find out that someone is a quilter, it helps bring a bond with that person."

Women also describe their quilting experiences as a serious commitment in their lives. Kelly recalls that when she first got really involved in quilting, it encompassed her life: "When you get into a new area of learning about something that you didn't know anything about before, it just permeates your life." Michelle echoes this sentiment, as she views quilting as an essential component to her life. Here she draws on historical notions of quilting and women's lives to define why and how she values quilting: "It's preserving an art form and cherishing these women that just did this on a regular basis without any pat on the back or just provided something for their family. I think it's just saying you had a worthwhile thing going there. I hope it never disappears." Michelle's quilting is based heavily in family tradition, and she wants to be remembered as one of the quilters in the family. In many ways, quilting represents the continued valuation of women's work, and ensuring women's creative traditions through generations.

Melinda discusses reflexively her time spent quilting in comparison to the unpaid work she does for her family as a stay-at-home mom.

> I need to have my own little photo album of my own stuff. And the reason that I do is because I'm a stay-at-home mom, basically. And I keep thinking one of these years I'm going to look back and I'm going to say look at what all I did while I stayed at home, it was worth it.

Melinda's comments suggest that women's work in the home is continually devalued, even by those engaged in it. Additionally, Melinda makes an effort to validate her work at home, and to justify that it was "worth it."

Chelsea realizes that her children may or may not take up quilting themselves. Since she enjoys introducing people to the process of quilting, Chelsea passes on her quilting knowledge to other interested audiences, mainly by teaching a local quilting class. Although the classes she teaches do not pay well, and take up valuable personal quilting time, she continues to devote time to teaching others how to quilt. Chelsea explains why she continues to teach other women to quilt:

> I was at one of the guild meetings and everybody got up and said their name and how they began quilting. And about every other woman said my class. And then they said it has been so great. That is such a wow to have been able to be the person who got somebody going and feeling confident with something that allowed them to be creative.

Through her teaching, Chelsea has established a community of women who have learned to quilt under her guidance, thus helping to create a local community of quilters, and has developed a sense of worth.

Loretta explains how quilting is just a part of who she is now, how quilting is a part of her identity that she hopes to pass on through her quilts to her grandchildren: "I would like for my kids, my grandkids to be able to pick up a quilt and see my stitching and see my color selection and know something about my personality. They would know that I was either funny or silly or serious, they would know it." Quilting provides Loretta a creative outlet that also allows her to make connections to her family and friends.

Sandy finds quilting to be satisfying because she is constantly leaving a tactile record of significant events in her and her family's life through her finished quilts: "I just want to make more and more quilts and have them stack up. I want to be able to document them and let people know what was happening in the world at the time. Different quilts remind me of different times in my life." Sandy likes quilts in part because they represent her as a creative person. Through her quilts, she is knowingly documenting her personal experiences. She is relying on her quilts to outlast her and to become legacies to future generations, including future generations of quilters.

After moving to a new city, Heather soon lost her good friend Kris, who died in a car accident. Kris was a quilter and her friends gathered to finish her last quilt-in-progress as a way of dealing with her death:

> Kris had picked out the pattern and had pretty much gotten her fabrics together and all of that was in the car with her when she died and some of the fabric has little bits of her blood on it and [we] sort of in a very cooperative consensus way had designed her quilt and that was sort of the way we dealt with grieving for Kris, was to finish a quilt that she had started.

As Heather was new to the city, she was also relatively new to the group of friends, but she found that this grieving process allowed her to join a new community of quilters:

> I ended up quilting with that group of ladies for probably four years, a lot of the original people kind of fell by the wayside after a while because I think finishing that quilt was, that was sort of the task, and once that was done, it wasn't so much that quilting was important to these ladies, it was really making that quilt for their friend that was important, and hanging out and just sort of having what was referred to as the stitch and bitch. Everybody would come over and bring beer or wine and chocolate. It was just a way to spend time more than anything.

Heather's experience demonstrates how women were engaging in carework for themselves through their collective quilting efforts in completing Kris' quilt. The creative healing process of finishing a friend's quilt and spending time together during grieving took precedence over what would happen to the quilt once finished, or anyone's specific quilting skills.

Quilting can also get one through tough times, as was the case with Karla's breast cancer. Karla told me that she worked on two quilts during her treatment, one that she had been working on for a long time to give to a very close friend, and one that she ended up selling. Here she discusses the quilt that she sold: "When I was recovering from the mastectomy and doing chemotherapy I quilted a white-on-white [quilt] and I sold it. I didn't want to keep it so I sold it. I don't know why, I just didn't want that reminder I guess. I have enough reminders of that time." Karla sent the other quilt to her friend, and "when she got the quilt in the mail she threatened anybody that touched it. If their hands were dirty she would kill them." During Karla's treatment and recovery, her quilt friends were a huge source of support for her. Throughout her interview Karla continually tells stories about being in the hospital, mentioning which of her quilting friends is present, and how she even talked about family quilts with her surgeon. For Karla, quilting is an activity that brings her joy in both good and bad times in her life.

## QUILTING AS CAREWORK FOR OTHERS

Quilts made within the framework of the traditional family, or those quilts gifted to family members, summon family-related memories. Through quilting, women make meaning in their own lives, preserve and transmit quilting heritage, and secure historical markers that represent them, their life events, and their families. These quilts may represent a quilter's individual life memories, but they also incorporate family and friends in more obvious ways.

Midlife women most often learn to quilt from taking a class as was mentioned earlier, and many women were brought into quilting by an interested friend or relative. Learning how to quilt, then, is linked to a larger community of quilters, the relationships formed through the quilting experience, and the family-linking role of quilts in women's lives. Recall from Chapter 3 that women in this study give three reasons for learning to quilt: quilting heritage, skipped generation of quilters, and new quilters. Through these different ways of learning to quilt, family is heavily present as a connecting force of quilting. For regardless of whether or not women have quilting in their family trees, quilters cite family as a reason for quilting. Women either want to carry on a long tradition of quilting, pick up a dropped tradition, or begin a tradition. Women reach backward through their family tree to re-establish connections with once-forgotten quilters, or use the family tree to defend their establishment of new quilting traditions that they hope will grow into family memories. This strong connection to family as a justification for quilting speaks to the gendered nature of this form of leisure.

Hannah notes that both her grandmothers quilted, but she didn't grow up with quilting surrounding her as one might suspect: "Neither one of my grandmothers made quilts or quilted when the grandchildren were there." Hannah's earliest quilting memories instead consist of quilts being made for her, rather than learning how to quilt from her grandmothers:

> When my sister and I were seven and eight, we were spending one of our summers with my grandmother. She took us into one of her bedrooms one day and started getting all these wrapped packages down from the closet, spread them out on the bed, and they were quilt tops. She said, "Now, we're going to go through these and I want you each to pick out the six tops you like and I'm going to pin your names on them and those are going to be your quilt tops. When you grow up and get married that will be part of your wedding trousseau."

These quilts were made with a specific purpose – to help prepare Hannah and her sister for marriage. These finished quilts would play an important and expected role of traditional femininity as prescribed by Hannah's grandmother.

While Cassie was preparing for her wedding, she struggled to find an appropriate and meaningful gift to give to her husband to mark this significant event in both of their lives. Cassie's mother and grandmother quilt, as does her husband's mother. Cassie decided to use their quilting commonalities to link the women in her now husband's life symbolically in making a quilt for him: "As a sign of unity between our families, I bought all the fabric and sent a quarter of it to my mom, to his mom, and my grandmother, and kept one for me. They pieced parts of the top; I arranged the four pieces and quilted it. I put everyone's initials on it. I love it." This marriage quilt currently holds a significant yet everyday place of importance in Cassie's life and home. Although the quilt is not hers as she gave it to her husband on behalf of the women in the newly joined family tree, it does have a permanent place on the couch and it serves as a daily reinforcement of her marriage and the common interests bonding her to the women in her and her husband's family.

In addition to celebrations and accomplishments, quilts also commemorate sorrow, and quilting can be used as a therapeutic strategy for women, to help one overcome difficult times. Such rough times in a quilter's life can include illness, death, endings, or working through other particularly painful situations. Leslie discusses the personal comfort she gained from assembling and using her divorce quilt: "I made a quilt specifically to commemorate my divorce. I needed something to crawl into, to comfort myself, and to be able to hide away. I knew it had to be pink, like a womb, so that I could heal while I was snuggled in it." To cope with the pain surrounding the dissolution of her marriage, Leslie, who is in her fifties, decided to engage in quilting, which provided her a positive and creative outlet. Through assembling her divorce quilt, she was also constructing a daily memorial of her life circumstances which include her marriage and divorce. Leslie sleeps under this quilt regularly, curls up on the couch with it, and is reminded of her ability to survive negative events and to move on through life in a way that suits her. Leslie shared with me the haiku poem that she wrote about the quilt:

> Haiku Quilt #607
> Wounded. Comfort sought.
> Reentering my self's womb
> Healing can begin.

When looking at the quilt, which looks like a normal quilt, one would not necessarily speculate that this is Leslie's way of dealing with her divorce. But, importantly, we must understand that there is some type of "back story" to quilts.

Certainly, some quilts present more obvious meaning than others, and the NAMES quilt provides us with one such example. Imogene is in her eighties, and her son died of AIDS in the 1990s. Before he died, he asked Imogene to make him a panel for the NAMES quilt. Here she shares her experience in celebrating her son's life, and memorializing the loss of her son:

> My work with the AIDS panel was so hard because I didn't know anybody that was doing one, and I still don't know anybody and I'll bet you there are some quilters in our group who have made an AIDS quilt but have never said anything and I would like to get with those people. Before my son died, the last time he came down here, he said to me, "Mom, you've got to make me a panel for the quilt." And I said, "Okay. I've got the material that you chose for your quilt." Because when he moved I said, "Well someday I'm going to make you a quilt. So look at this material and see which one you like." So he chose it, and my daughter helped me make it, six feet by three feet. I mean I think it's a very important thing because it just makes kids think.

> *And so you did this, you and your daughter did this.*

> Yes, I did. Before that I saw in the newspaper that they were having something, and I called the woman and talked to her and she came out to see me and she wasn't a quilter, but she was a mother of another victim and so her son was very active in getting the quilt going. I think he died in 1990. But she was very nice, very helpful, as much as she could and when I had it finished she took it for me.

*Have you ever seen yours on display?*

No, but I have a friend who was a friend of my son's and she went to Washington D.C. when it was there. She told them the number that it was and they sent her the exact bus stop and everything to get off at and she said it was just wonderful and she was so glad that she went. That was in 1995, because my son said, "I'm going to go, you know." He was such fun.

*Well you tell a lot of good stories about him. And I think it's really great that he was involved in picking out the fabric, I think that's rare.*

I do too.

Imogene experiences layers of meaning when thinking about the NAMES quilt, as she is a creator of a piece of the larger quilt and social statement. Like many other women quilters, Imogene's quilting is focused on gifts for her children. Unfortunately, though, her life circumstances resulted in burying a child to an international health epidemic, and creating a NAMES quilt panel that honored her son's life.

Imogene still intends to complete her lifetime goal of making a quilt for each of her remaining children and including a piece of blue fabric with cranes on it that was used for her son's NAMES quilt panel to connect the children's quilts together: "I've got to make five quilts. I've got the tulip appliqué and of course I worked on that while I was waiting for my son to die, and my daughter really wants it. There isn't any of the blue crane fabric in that, but the others, I will see that it gets in." Those aware of Imogene's intended meaning of the blue crane fabric will be able to understand and appreciate her quilts in a different way than the outside onlooker might. Additionally, a viewer of the NAMES quilt understands its international importance, but perhaps not the meaning of the blue crane fabric. Thus, the quilt serves both the individual and collective construction of meaning.

Sarah also documented explicitly her personal life through her quilting. The frog quilt began documenting personal sorrow, but turned into a bookmark of a joyful life event. Until she met her husband-to-be and married, she was frustrated about her dating life and decided to express that frustration by making a quilt: "I had been collecting frog fabrics for about two years and it was supposed to be a statement because it had to do with the fact that I was single and had dated all these people, but they were all frogs. So I collected frog fabrics and came up with this quilt idea." From simply looking at the quilt and having no other information about the quilt or its maker, one might think that Sarah is a huge fan of frogs. However, in discussing this quilt-in-progress, Sarah indicated that this quilt is instead a symbol of her dissatisfying dating life during her twenties and thirties. She sees it as akin to the fairy tale *The Little Princess*. Before she recently married, Sarah was frustrated with her romantic life. Convinced she was going to be stuck with frogs rather than princes the rest of her life, she decided to express her frustration about dating by making a quilt composed entirely of frogs.

Right before she married, Sarah bought the remaining frog fabric she needed to complete the quilt. When telling a fabric store salesperson about her quilt, she declared, "That's the last frog fabric now." To commemorate her wedding, Sarah plans to make a quilted wall hanging, using fabric she bought while on her honeymoon: "I'm going to use my fabric that I bought on our honeymoon in Las Vegas. Then I'll put our names and the date we got married underneath it, and then have a little wall memory quilt." Sarah's quilts undoubtedly explicitly tell stories, but it is clear by these two quilt examples that they implicitly tell stories on a more personal, less publicly understood level.

Rachel (early seventies) participated in the quilt exchange program sponsored by the Atlanta Historical Center for the 1996 Summer Olympic Games held in Atlanta, GA. She was one of many women who made quilts to be given to each participating country. This tradition was started by Georgia quilters and has been continued in successive Olympic Games (The Quiltmakers of Georgia 1996). This quilt has multiple levels of meaning for Rachel, some more obvious and some less obvious. Completing this quilt meant Rachel would finally quit smoking, which was a personal and familial goal: "This quilt was finished in June of 1995. The reason I know that is because my husband had bugged me for years to stop smoking, and I said, 'When this quilt is done I will stop.' I sent it June 9th, and June 10th I quit smoking." When discussing this quilt, Rachel reveals the less obvious personal and familial meanings embedded in its stitches. This quilt holds meaning for Rachel far beyond its surface characteristics, as it marks in her life when she was finally able to stop smoking. It also evokes the ties she has with her family, for they had been encouraging her to quit smoking for some time. Yet, Rachel's Olympic quilt has additional meaning for her, as she believes she has contributed importantly to global events, and is part of the beginning of a new tradition, merging quilting with the Olympic Games. As is true for most quilts, quilts hold deep meanings created and attached to the quilt during the quilting process. Often these are not easily available to viewers (and sometimes recipients of finished quilts), who may be unaware of the story of its creation.

Understanding the current and past memories attached to quilts helps us view quilts not just in a historical or familial sense, as we may be accustomed, but also helps us conceptualize quilts as life bookmarks, personally meaningful creative objects that assist people in marking time and recording important life events. Additionally, the meanings quilts carry with them assist us in defining who we are, and who our ancestors were. Quilts act as material artifacts and represent both present and past memories of women who quilt. A quilt made today, for example, reminds one of the creator of that specific quilt, as well as the quilters who came before her. The subjective meanings of quilts and quilt making enable women to honor and remember past quilters and to ensure the legacy of quilting within a family.

Memories concerning historical family quilts made by ancestors were highly valued and remembered, with women tracing their quilting heritage through female ancestors. For example, Heather attributes both her mathematical ability and her quilting ability to a quilt she slept under for years when she visited her grandmother:

> It was a school house pattern and at night I would sit and look at all of the different black and white fabrics that were the roofs of the school houses, none of them were the same, or very few of them were the same, and the blue and whites that were in the windows, most of those were different as well, they would be two different patterns on one, the same pattern on the next one and it was just, that's what I did, was I sat and tried to figure out the logic of the person who did it, and there really wasn't any logic, but it kept me interested for a long time.

Heather continues to discuss the personal connection she has with quilts she has made after becoming interested in quilting from her grandmother: "That's what I want for my quilts – for there to be layers on layers on layers of information that you can access so that as you live with the quilt, it's like a person, you get to know it better and there is more to learn than just what's on the surface." Similar to Heather, most women are interested in the lives of their quilts. They see a finished quilt as an object that continues to have meaning. When possible, quilters will visit finished quilts gifted to others, as they hope to see their quilts used well, and for the intended purpose of a loved one curled up in quilt they have made.

The terrorist attack on 9/11/2001 has been memorialized and commemorated through quilting, and I participated in this quilting tradition as well. I was working as a graduate teaching assistant in fall semester 2001 at the University of Georgia when the terrorist attacks in New York, Washington, DC, and Pennsylvania occurred. A few days after the 9/11 bombings, I faced four discussion groups of twenty-five undergraduate students. Not really feeling up to discussing the topics on the syllabus and knowing that the students desperately wanted to talk about what was happening, I decided that I could use my personal/professional expertise as a quilter/scholar of quilting to help the students process what was happening. I knew from my research that spending time at a creative activity and keeping one's hands busy is therapeutic, meditative, and often helps one deal with one's problems. Quilts serve as memorials of women's lives and I felt that this medium could certainly be used successfully in a college classroom. In deciding to suggest to the students that we use quilting to begin our discussions about 9/11, I raided my personal stash of fabric and brought fabric, markers, glue, paints, etc. to the discussion sessions.

I organized the students into groups of two to five people, and we first talked about what we were going to do in merging quilting and memorializing the lives lost during the terrorist attacks. We first discussed the role of quilting and how quilts can serve as memorials of women's and men's lives, and also of major events, both positive and negative. I asked students to consider their feelings and others' feelings in their small groups, and to, together, come up with an idea for a commemorative quilt block. I told them I would put their quilt blocks together to form a 9/11 memorial. I gave the students the majority of the fifty-minute class period to create their quilt block.

Students collectively came up with a variety of blocks, and some turned in descriptions of their completed blocks. After collecting the quilt blocks from students, I then assembled them into two quilts which in essence "bookmark" students' immediate responses to 9/11 (see Plates 13 and 14 for "Black Quilt" and "Red Quilt"). The quilts were hung up for display for the fall semester of 2001 on campus, and students reported to me that the quilting activity was comforting and meaningful to them.

I have included some of the students' quilt block descriptions below to demonstrate how this quilting process allowed students to reflect upon the events and to come up with their responses, their ways to deal with the attacks.

## BLACK QUILT

My quilt block's meaning has two levels. One, it is an attempt to calm the emotional distress that the terrorist attacks caused for me. Two, it is a call to action: peace starts with the individual looking at herself and going on to create change worldwide.

In our block we wanted to show the unity of the nation after the terrorist attacks, September 11, 2001. We chose to cut out two people holding hands. Each person has another arm extended for all the other U.S. citizens.

The star is in the middle because it represents what we are focused on. It represents whatever goal we are working for at the time. The people are underneath. It is like the network and organization it takes to reach our goal. Women must organize themselves in the same fashion as a building is built, strength comes from the different parts interlocking. The red represents the life force of women, and the bright yellow signifies our impact on the world.

Unity was the one word we felt summed up our feelings about what has resulted from the terrorist attacks. Unity between countries and between Americans in our nations. We wanted the word to speak for itself. We made it strong, simple and free from the images (flags, peace signs) that have a tendency to become cliches and lose their meanings.

## RED QUILT

We wanted to show everyone how America will never forget this tragedy that has befallen on every American. The day "911," September 11, 2001 will be a day never forgotten, and we will never forget the suffering and pain shared by each and every American. We cried for the victims, their families, and our great nation that had its precious freedom compromised. September 11, 2001 will be a day that we will never forget.

We chose to portray the skyline of New York City with the World Trade Center towers outlined to make them stand out. We chose the quote "United We Stand,

Divided We Fall" because it basically describes what most Americans are feeling right now. The towers stood tall and were what anyone looking at the sky saw first in New York City. Now they have crumbled and fallen and we have the choice to give in to fear or to stand together as proud and patriotic Americans. "United we stand, divided we fall," how relevant this quote is at this time. We must stand together and fight terrorism.

Unite all Americans ... every race, every age, every gender.

We as a nation will stand together in times of crisis; as one. We will prevail and stand united. Our people are of different colors because we as Americans are diverse. And we all support one another and our nation and flag.

M does not want her man to go to war! She wants peace. J and C believe that prayer is the way to achieve that peace (M, too).

Examined as a whole, these quilt blocks depict varied and raw emotional responses to the 9/11 terrorist attacks, and range from the global to the local, much like the quilts made by study participants, that commemorate perhaps more ordinary, but, nonetheless, important life events.

## BOOKMARKING LIFE THROUGH QUILTING

Quilts have a potential historical value that will be viewable and interpretable beyond the life of a quilter.[1] Women generally want the quilts they have made to become a part of the lives of those important to them, as family heirlooms. When admiring historical family quilts, one can recall women's important creative and work culture in the home, the family, and the community. This recollection through quilts serves quilters and non-quilters alike. Delineating women's accomplishments in this way reveals that collective-memory processes have been gendered, highlighting men's public accomplishments, yet giving little to no attention to women and the important contributions they have made toward society.

And yet, women's lives may not be as visible or as publicly well known as men's lives. For example, men's historical contributions to society range from something as grand as war monuments, or something as everyday as city, street, or building names. Men memorialized in the former are recognized for their military valor, and men in the latter may have been city founders, or, in today's times, purchased naming rights for a building to be named after them. Women, just as men, have made fabulous contributions to society, though not perhaps as noticeable or as publicly memorialized. Certainly, war monuments have become more inclusive and note women's supportive efforts during wartime (e.g., the Vietnam War Memorial in Washington, DC), but these and other public forms of recognition consider women in comparison to men and their measured efforts, and do not necessarily recognize women's efforts in their own light.

Quilts and other elements of women's domestic culture (e.g., embroidery, knitting, lace-making, crocheting) can reveal a great deal about women's lives. From simply observing quilts as the majority of quilt scholars do, we have gained technical information about historical forms of quilting, including dating quilts through investigating the fabric, patterns, and techniques used, centering on the surface of the quilt. We need to continue examining quilting and quilts, and add to this research on the quilting process the meaning imbued in quilts, as well as looking at quilts from quilters' perspectives. For when asking a quilter about the story behind her quilt, we can learn remarkable and sometimes hidden things about women's lives, as demonstrated in the frog quilt, the Olympic quilt, and the divorce quilt.

As illustrated by these quilt stories, there is important hidden meaning in cultural objects. As a cultural product, a quilt has layers of meaning, which are understood and appreciated both at multiple levels and by multiple audiences. Quilts in this study were made primarily for the maker or were given as gifts. These quilts were not intentionally part of the economic marketplace, although women bought new fabric and equipment to make said quilts. That is, women made quilts as gifts for important others in their lives rather than to sell quilts to others for profit. As the women in this study practiced quilting as amateurs, they were not constrained, as professional artists are, by artistic reputation, market trends, production costs, or pressure to sell their quilts. They therefore were not constrained by economic success, and whether a quilt was successful depended upon the quilter's vision, if the recipient of the finished quilt liked it, how the relationship between creator and receiver was going at the time, and the like. Thus, non-economic and private, or subjective measures indicated a quilt's success or failure, and not simply economic success or traditionally defined artistic reputation.

Quilters, similar to many professional artists, keep records of their finished quilts. They remember the process and purpose surrounding making quilts for others, with some women keeping portfolios or photo albums to document their creative endeavors. Study participants found it important to remember their quilting efforts, with a majority of women keeping some type of quilting record. Some quilters kept very detailed records, including planning the quilt, fabric swatches, and what they named the quilt. For example, Heather kept an extensive quilt journal:

> This is my journal as well. No, it has nothing to do with quilting, although it all has to do with quilting. I mean, it's really what's going on in my life. For every quilt I leave two pages. It's a reference for me, to be able to look back at a quilt. I understand stuff that I didn't understand or didn't see when I was making it. I have tons of disjointed journals everywhere, and this way, I know that I will have this quilting book the rest of my life, it's pretty personal.

Such quilt records like Heather's reveal important aspects of the meaning of quilting in women's lives. Heather can look back at her records to see both what was happening in her quilt process, and in her life. Quilts, therefore, establish the personally and artistically fulfilling importance of quilting for women. They also provide evidence of women's close personal relationships with other quilters, friends, and family members.

Quilts serve as vehicles of memory for both quilters and non-quilters on personal, familial, and historical levels. Collectively, onlookers reminisce about ordinary women in historical eras who lived difficult lives (e.g., the Colonial U.S.), or about the greater meaning present in the quilt, such as when viewing the AIDS quilt (Jones and Dawson 2000; Lewis and Fraser 1996). The meaning and use of quilts have changed and expanded, no longer simply a household item to keep the family warm. Quilts do keep us warm, and we also use them to make important connections with family and friends, decorate our homes, express ourselves, compete for artistic recognition, and establish a collection. As quilts are no longer necessary home items, they do contain special meaning for those living in more modern times who own them in a variety of forms and ways.

The creative process of quilting remains important and meaningful in women's lives specifically, and to our cultural history generally. Women view quilting as a way to speak to other quilters, to care for their families and friends, and to leave behind material objects that perpetuate women's perspectives on their lives. In making quilts, women leave historical markers, revealing that they had enough control over their lives to devote time to a pleasurable activity. Today, on some level women realize that their everyday mundane efforts (e.g., washing dishes, preparing meals) will not usually be remembered or memorialized in the ways that family members treasure finished quilts as cultural objects. Finished quilts serve women as memory markers, and help them to recall what was happening in their lives as they made certain quilts.

## SELF, SPACE AND SANITY

While obtaining my master's degree in sociology, I lived alone in a one-bedroom apartment. My computer and my workspace were in my bedroom. Waking up to the computer every morning was not an encouraging way for me to begin my day, especially when faced with composing and revising my thesis. I vowed if possible in living spaces after this one to have only my bed in the bedroom. At that point in my life, I was focused solely on taking classes and writing my thesis. Wanting to succeed in graduate school, I was an earnest and compliant student, with my nose to the grindstone and little time for activities beyond the necessary reading and writing related to my thesis.

After my youngest sister, Stacey, was killed in a car accident in spring 1996, I had a difficult time managing my grief while simultaneously trying to complete my thesis. Her death at sixteen was certainly unexpected, definitely a tragedy, and something that I will never get over. At the time, many people advised me to get involved in new activities, take an art class, even learn how to kickbox. All these recommendations were good ideas, certainly, but they were not familiar to me. Familiarity was something that I desperately craved in my lonely path of learning to live without my sister.

One day I dragged my sewing machine from the closet and unpacked it, as I had no specific public space in my apartment for sewing and/or quilting. I had been carrying my sewing machine with me since my parents gave it to me when I left for college in 1989. I shared apartments and houses with others while in college, and there was never enough room to have a sewing machine sitting out. I did not have room in this apartment either to set up my machine, but I decided to forfeit the kitchen table to provide a permanent space for my sewing machine.

When I got back into sewing, I was not interested in making anything specifically. I just needed to have a creative outlet like sewing because in the past it had been a comforting activity for me. I knew I enjoyed doing it, and I also knew that I was good at it, as it is the only creative activity I have done throughout my life. Spending time at this creative outlet was exactly what I needed, and I began sewing furiously. I made clothes and gifts for my friends and their children and started making clothes for myself again. Having the sewing machine up permanently proved useful and necessary to me at that point in my life. I especially found peace in doing something that I enjoyed, and I found pleasure in giving gifts that I had made myself to those meaningful in my life. Others around me commented that my actions did not make sense to them. In my immediate grieving period they felt that I should be seeking comfort in other ways, such as taking it easy, taking care of myself, and letting people take care of me and do nice things for me. I did enjoy it when people did take care of me, and did nice things for me, but it was not enough. I needed to do something proactive, to take care of myself in my own way, so that I could endure this particularly tough period in my life. I needed the emotional benefits from engaging in something creatively challenging, and something that I could do with my hands. It made me feel like I was doing something positive for myself, and I was. In making gifts for others, I felt that I was reaffirming important relationships with other people in my life.

While engaged in this research, I realized the importance of a permanent sewing space. I had seen other women's quilting spaces via my research pursuits, and thought that I would benefit on many levels from having a specific and permanent space for my sewing equipment. Making a sewing room for myself has definitely made a positive difference in my life. Currently, I own a one-and-a-half-story house, with the half story serving as my quilt room. Making this creative space has given me a way to make much needed personal time for myself. I have always enjoyed making gifts for other people, and the processes of sewing and quilting. In addition to the small quilts that I make for friends' children, in the last few years I have also finished three bed-sized quilts for myself. This is something that I have wanted to do for a long time, but it has been difficult to find the time to do this. With the room already set up, the quilt-in-progress is ready when I am. I simply walk into the room and get creatively engaged immediately. Having the room does not dictate that I spend all my creative time in it, though. I use the rest of the house as it suits me: I work in the quilt room when sewing or dealing directly with fabric, I cut fabric at the kitchen table, and do hand quilting in the evenings in front of the television.

I am able to sew and quilt whenever I feel like it. Making gifts for others gives me great pleasure, for I think about them and our relationship as I work on the item. Sewing and quilting have provided me activities I feel completely confident and comfortable doing. It can certainly be frustrating and challenging, but, just like academia, it provides me with an acceptable mix of challenge and satisfaction. This research has provided me the opportunity to become embedded within the community of women quilters. I share regularly with quilters and non-quilters alike my quilting identity, and have used it as a measure of many things. Most valuable, though, is the supportive and understanding community that embraces women's non-economic cultural production.

## NOTE

1. The recent establishment of the International Quilt Study Center at the University of Nebraska-Lincoln, with a 2,000-plus collection of quilts, many of them rare antiques made by anonymous women artists, provides evidence of the growing historical value of quilts through its institutionalization (International Quilt Study Center 2006; "Nebraska Holds Executive Session" 2003: 16).

# 7 PIECING IT ALL TOGETHER

Quilting, understood as a form of gendered leisure, reveals much about the modern family, and the contemporary U.S. woman's everyday struggles in finding time, space, and a quilting room of one's own (Woolf 1929). The family shapes midlife women's leisure experiences especially when they are done for fun, and not for money. Even though these women are not earning money for their efforts by choice, they are indeed cultural producers in their own right and need to be viewed as such. This allows outsiders to better understand how these women practice quilting with intensity, and how their quilting at midlife can result in tension at home.

Why do these women choose quilting and not some other leisure activity as they reach midlife? Quilting appealed to them for gendered familial, creative, and personal reasons. As they provided familial reasons, they drew upon their family histories to point out foremothers who were quilters and who left evidence of their handiwork through family heirlooms, and noted how quilting traditions were culturally transmitted, or not, in the case of the skipped generations of quilters. Others wanted to have quilting traditions present in their families and fall under the category of "new quilters" where they envisioned being viewed as quilting foremothers for generations of quilters to come. And finally, some wanted to explore their creative selves through the leisure activity of quilting.

Women cited quilting as a creative activity that allowed them to express themselves, and as they developed into self-identified quilters, they broadened their skills and their confidence in their quilting. Quilting also fits into the rest of their lives in ways that other activities might not: quilting is considered a highly feminine activity, and falls in line with these women's lives. Described earlier as traditional women with spouses and children, these women have *chosen* to spend great amounts of time and attention on family needs. Their identities are tied to such feminine and domestic activities, and they even practice quilting in gendered ways. Thus, quilting (and gifting finished quilts) allowed women to "do gender" appropriately and traditionally as they gifted finished quilts to family and friends, fulfilling aptly their feminine family roles and engaging in gendered carework duties. For some women, quilting is an activity that fulfills feminine familial gendered expectations, at least for a time.

However, once women become self-identified quilters and heavily involved in the activity, quilting can cause family tension in terms of time, attention, and monies spent on the equipment and process of quilting. This seemingly unexpected tension is actually very much in line with research regarding leisure activities and family members. For regardless of newly chosen activity (e.g., dog shows, running, skiing, traveling, gardening, golf, scrapbooking, gambling), spouses and children can feel ignored or left out, as I did when I was five years old and my mom quilted with her friends for an entire afternoon.

With quilting, family and friends initially respond quite positively. Who wouldn't want a quilter in the family? And who wouldn't happily accept a finished quilt as a gift, made especially for them? Yet, as women become more involved in quilting, their total time and attention are divided. For spouses and children who are accustomed to great amounts of time and attention spent on them, this sudden change can be quite upsetting. As women develop creatively at midlife, their interests and needs change from being entirely family-focused to allowing some time and attention to their selves. This shift in perspective alone can be alarming to family members, and would be so whether the newly acquired activity were quilting or something else entirely different.

I speculate that similar responses can be found to the leisure activity of scrapbooking, which is oft cited as the "new quilting." Avid scrapbookers often meet together to work on their own pages, purchase and stockpile new equipment and supplies, and gift others with finished products that are deeply meaningful and sentimental, often designed to cement family and kin relationships (Dickerson 2000; Kelly and Brown 2005). Perhaps scrapbookers and other crafters have their own stashes, hidden from family and friends (Stalp and Winge 2006). Additionally, quilting happens in the home where there are other, family-centered needs, and when those needs are not met, the activity on the receiving end of the woman's time and attention is quite noticeable. One of the central tensions revealed here is that family and friends do not value the process of quilting as much as the product, while quilters value both, and, at times, probably value the process over the product of quilting.

To avoid potential family disruptions, women learn how to integrate quilting into their already established lives. Because they derive great pleasure from family involvement and also from quilting, women fold their newly developed creative lives into family events and processes. Women regularly engage in carework for others throughout the life course, and quilting allows them to continue to do this. Quilters choose family-friendly projects that can be broken down into more transportable projects: they quilt while attending children's extracurricular activities, plan a stop at a quilt shop while on family vacation, and the like. In these ways, women are able to quilt and spend time with family, both of which they value highly. Women regularly engage in carework for others throughout the life course, and quilting allows them to continue to do this. Women in this study quilt in gendered ways, and quilting itself becomes another form of carework for quilters and their families.

## WHAT'S SO IMPORTANT ABOUT QUILTING?

Quilters take part in a complex form of cultural creation, preservation, and transmission. Currently, women are quite engaged in quilting activities. Once women discover that they enjoy quilting, they spend a great deal of time not only quilting, but also shopping for fabric and equipment, meeting with other quilters in small and large group settings, taking classes from other quilters, and attending quilt exhibits and shows. Activities surrounding quilting provide a space in which women interact inter- and intra-generationally, learning women's lives generally. In these spaces women learn about the physical mechanics of quilting and pass along their knowledge to other women. They leave clues about their lives in the quilts they make: the patterns, fabrics, and time available to them to spend quilting, and evidence of their artistic vision and intricate sewing skills. The clues women leave in their quilts and how they talk about them differ from how art critics usually discuss quilts. A particular quilt may have deeply personal meaning to its maker, but this dimension may be overlooked by others – consider Sarah's frog quilt, which, on the surface, is probably about frogs, but when looking "behind the quilt" if you will, to the maker's intent, there is potential to uncover a rich and complex meaning attached to that quilt.

Similar to other cultural objects, quilts mean different things to different people (for an example of a quilt with quite diverse and complicated responses, see the NAMES quilt). Quilters value quilting on many important levels, yet they do not expect non-quilters to be interested in, or value, quilting in the same ways that they do. Many quilters claim it is difficult to articulate why they quilt in a way that makes sense to non-quilters. To the contrary, the struggle to articulate why they do what they do is not present when communicating with other quilters. In fact, some women have been quilting for so long that it has become a fundamental part of their lives that they talk about quilting as a passion. While non-quilters who admire quilts often focus solely or primarily on the product – the finished quilt – quilters give far more emphasis to the *process* of quilting. The production of a quilt is often as important as, or even more important than, the finished quilt itself.

Many aspects of contemporary social life can be thought of as stripping women's distinctive identities, and particularly the creative potential of women. The unpaid and invisible work that women do in households (e.g., preparing meals, doing laundry, supervising children's homework, contributing to the comfort and well-being of family members) is rarely regarded or rewarded as "real" work. Doing this work has an element of depersonalization. Women who engage in this invisible work may feel trapped in a lose/lose situation: good and faithful performance is unrewarded and poor performance is stigmatized. Women are performing a type of alienated labor that can result in a diminishing of identity and one's sense of self. In private lives, women's unwaged and emotional labor – their carework – is frequently appropriated and undervalued within the family (Williams 2000). Inequitable divisions of domestic labor not only assign women a "second shift" of labor at home in comparison to men (Hochschild 1989), but they also produce a "leisure gap" where men have, on the average, one month more of leisure per year in comparison to their wives (Mattingly and Bianchi 2003).

Since leisure in contemporary life is a major mechanism through which people seek self-renewal that allows them to perform work in other social roles and opportunities to express a "true" or "genuine" self, women have fewer opportunities for this type of leisure experience than do men. Women engaged in quilting at the serious leisure levels actually build layers of distinctive identities which become central to their lives. Quilting becomes a subjective career for women to seek expression of a genuine self through leisure activity, and it gives women a collective voice as creators of culture. As a process, quilting provides a respite from the demands of everyday lives of contemporary women, and it also provides a mechanism for women to see themselves as part of a larger culture, a community of culture creators with a past and a future.

## LEISURE, CAREWORK AND THE FAMILY

Society does not acknowledge regularly the value of unpaid work that occurs in the home (Oakley 1974a, 1974b; Williams 2000). As quilting occurs in the home and is done primarily by women, it often suffers from a similar consideration. Thus, outsiders to quilting often consider it to be an obliterated, old-fashioned, even unnecessary form of housework. Because there is little value placed on what occurs in the home, those who do value it can sometimes also feel devalued. When women quilt, they do participate in a somewhat old-fashioned and antiquated way of providing physical warmth, visual beauty, and care to family and friends, but, importantly, this is an activity that they value. The amount of time that women spend at quilting, or how many quilts they have made is not what matters to them. The enjoyment in the creative process is what is important to quilters.

Carework through quilting is complicated, as are many of the roles that women hold in contemporary society. For example, we consider women to be good mothers (whether engaged in paid work or not) when they appear to be unselfish caretakers. As Hays (1996: 167) suggests, "The image of an appropriate mother is one of an unselfish nurturer." This role is extended into what it means to be a woman. Women fulfill this role when they make homemade gifts for their children, spouses, extended kin, and others through quilting. But the time and effort that go into the making of quilts (e.g., the process) is still seen as wasted time, or time taken away from being a good mother, spouse, or friend. Yet, through constructing and gifting quilts, women can fulfill the role of unselfish nurturer by expressing their care for others not just as quilters, but as appropriately gendered female spouses, mothers, and friends too. In the eyes of women who produce quilts, quilting as a caring act is deeply intertwined with gendered notions of family and motherhood. I speculate that in the eyes of those being cared for, quilting is sometimes viewed with suspicion, as it is not as efficient or as noticeable on a daily level as other forms of carework. Quilters in this study affirmed this speculation, but as I did not have access to non-quilting outsiders in any systematic way, I can only speculate at this point.

As occurs with family dynamics and work life (Crosby 1991; Hochschild 1997), and mothers who support their family's sports activities (Chafetz and Kotarba 1995; Thompson 1999), women quilters challenge and embrace contemporary family dynamics as they simultaneously carve out time to quilt and incorporate the family. Rather than women resenting their families for the energy and time that goes into managing family and work responsibilities, they instead use their quilting activities as a strategy to achieve both family and work (Collins 1991). They both embrace their families and they continue to quilt. Instead of taking time away from the family, women's quilting efforts actually contribute to the healthy maintenance of their families. As women find time through quilting to care for themselves, they nurture themselves and their families, and simultaneously engage in carework for self and family. Perhaps midlife women feel they need to justify quilting in these ways in order to pursue a chosen leisure activity.

## DEVELOPING A MIDLIFE IDENTITY THROUGH QUILTING

As women in this study developed identities as quilters and began to frame subjective careers around quilting, they began to see themselves as cultural workers on a personal, and, in some cases, a societal level. Quilters are cultural producers connected to past and future, and the quilts that they make can influence others in multiple ways for generations to come. Additionally, these women can engage in creation and design, and have their skills recognized locally and within broader contexts.

Most women do not enter quilting as a "quest" in which to discover and develop their artistic identities. Instead, they become interested in quilting for a variety of reasons, ranging from being able to do something creative on their own, to commemorating family ties through making quilts as family gifts. Some women come from families where quilting has been a long-standing tradition among women. Most others who learn as adults are inspired by friends, media, or public displays of quilts. Perhaps most intriguing of all, some decide to "recover" family traditions of quilting that were lost in past generations, when quilting was regarded as quaint and antimodern. Once they learn and enjoy quilting, women find deeper layers of meaning the longer they pursue it. They begin to "see quilts everywhere" and relate many other life activities to quilting. Children's activities and family vacations inspire quilts (and stopping to shop for fabric), through a complicated mix of visual and emotional phenomena.

When women get hooked on quilting they begin to self-identify as quilters and the serious identity work begins. Women discover that through quilting they can develop subjective careers in their seemingly constrictive feminine carework roles as wives and mothers, and purposefully construct and maintain their selves. In this process of developing a subjective career, the self becomes identified and developed in the context of the work that women do. Quilting for women blends traditional and modern feminine roles. After some passage of time, women come to see themselves as cultural workers, doing important and meaningful work, even if others do not always acknowledge this. The sense of oneself as a cultural worker is most evident when women contribute to such projects as Olympic quilts or the AIDS quilt where their quilts will clearly have impact over time and beyond their local communities, or when they enter quilts into local or national competitions. In addition, women who treasure quilts made by their female kin of prior generations envision the quilts that they make will be used, admired, and interpreted by friends and descendants.

Being viewed as creative actors by subsequent generations also assists quilters as they develop a sense of themselves as contributors to culture.

Many aspects of contemporary social life for women strip away their distinctive identities and their creative potential. Processes of identity development and individuation allow women to construct distinctive identities. Women use quilting as an avenue through which they develop and maintain their creative selves, and express their individual identities as women, as historical actors, and as cultural producers. Quilting then becomes a way in which to challenge the heretofore undervalued feminized activities in society, the subordination of women, and the invisibility of women's contributions to culture through their unpaid creative work.

Holyfield (1995: 171) notes in her research on adventure-seekers (e.g., white-water rafters) that people make important meaning out of their lives through leisure activities in which they choose to become involved: "Modern society … represses 'aesthetic experience,' devaluing the emotional and thus turning meaningful things into objects, forcing us to seek escape (e.g., adventure)." Similarly, quilters seek to revive the aesthetic in their lives by participating in quilting activities, which they find invigorating. Through quilting, women make individual and collective meaning in their lives, preserve and transmit a chosen cultural heritage, and forge historical markers that represent them as women and as cultural producers. The process of quilting is likely less dangerous than outdoor adventure pursuits such as white-water rafting, but both types of leisure pursuits are daring in their own ways and can provide the necessary aesthetic experience to escape from everyday life.

## QUILTING AND OTHER CREATIVE PROCESSES AND PRODUCTS

Is quilting distinctive from other kinds of creative activities that women do? Could this study have been carried out with another unpaid creative form, such as knitting or weaving? Many of women's traditional creative activities do share similarities with quilting. Those most similar to quilting are elaborations of women's everyday domestic roles and result in long-term, tangible, and functional cultural products. Additionally, some of these activities, at least those which can be pursued individually and collectively, will share more characteristics with quilting. Quilting, however, possesses some important differences, both in the meaning-making process, and in how quilts are considered as finished products in a society's collective past, present, and future.

First, from a leisure standpoint, quilting is both a process and a product. People who want to relax from everyday stress turn to a variety of activities, including exercise and sports, surfing the internet, movie-watching, going out to eat, and spending time with family and friends. Highlighted in these activities is the experience of relaxation, as they define it. When people engage in these activities, they have a sense of doing something besides paid work that brings them relaxation and rejuvenation. Yet, besides the transitory feeling of relaxation, engaging in many leisure pursuits at this level does not produce a lasting, finished product. This makes quilting different from many other leisure activities.

Quilting produces a product for others to enjoy. Decorative cake baking and gourmet cooking are somewhat similar to quilting as traditional feminine activities and as creative processes. The products of these efforts are appreciated, but are soon consumed by family and friends. Memories of women's creative efforts in these activities may be strong, and though the event may be recorded visually, in people's memories, or in a scrapbook, journal, or cookbook, there is not the lasting, tangible product that the quilting process produces. This product of a finished quilt can be interpreted by others at later dates, even beyond the lifetime of the quilter. It extends as an element of her identity across time and place.

So, in addition to being a relaxing process and producing a product for others' enjoyment, the quilting process produces an enduring product – a quilt that is typically given away as a gift. Activities similar to quilting are knitting, crocheting, scrapbooking, weaving, stained glass, cross stitching, and even woodworking (traditionally considered to be a man's activity). Different from these activities, quilts often have a story to tell. They bookmark quilters' lives (e.g., living memories of the relaxing process for the quilter, recording visually the event or person for which it was made), and exist as living memorials of the women who constructed the quilts. Finished products are often used as everyday home decoration items (e.g., a cross-stitched sampler, a quilted wall hanging, a stained glass window decoration), as well as artifacts used to celebrate special events (e.g., a woven tablecloth, a wedding scrapbook, a knitted or crocheted baptismal gown, an anniversary quilt). Because there are tangible products remaining from the creative process of these types of cultural activities, they can be used both in everyday life as well as for special occasions, as symbolic markers of important social ties and connections with the past. However, quilts often outlive their makers and also become treasured heirlooms, which are subject to "reading" and interpretation in future generations. In this way, quilts keep alive something of the effort and creative vision of their makers.

Finally, quilts and the quilting process possess tactile elements that encourage a range of emotional outlets. The quilting process is both exciting and soothing to women, and quilts themselves can be physically and emotionally comforting and disconcerting to quilters and non-quilters alike, as viewers of the AIDS quilt report after seeing it (Lewis and Fraser 1996). Similarly, recall Leslie's divorce quilt that she made specifically for herself to crawl into and heal. Women also derive pleasure from imagining the comfort that others (and themselves) will derive from use of the quilts that they make. They imagine grandchildren curling up for a nap, warmed by a quilt they have made especially for them. Women's caretaking efforts are thus extended beyond their immediate surroundings, and the quilts women make can provide care for others even when the makers are not physically present.

Quilting and quilts are unique in that they bring together components of leisure, memory, and aesthetics in instrumental objects. A quilt can have multiple dimensions of meaning embedded in it for the creator, as well as for those who come in contact with it. Beyond the immediate relationship between the creator and receiver, a quilt has a public audience as well. The arts and antiques worlds in the last thirty years or so have begun to recognize the quilt as an artistic and financially valuable medium. Historically, quilts have had the ability to carry women's political messages (e.g., the AIDS quilt, the Olympics quilt, and quilts made for disaster survivors). With political voice, private and public memory, and commemoration, quilts can travel through time in both public and private ways that other cultural objects cannot. Quilts carry the identities of their makers into the fabric of culture.

Quilts as finished cultural products currently occupy more than one place in society (e.g., craft, art, leisure, work, family heirloom, utilitarian object), which makes both classification and study complicated and difficult. Regardless of whether or not the quilting processes result in relaxation, treasured family heirlooms, the means to a paycheck, or all these outcomes, they can provide rejuvenation from everyday stressors, and they can be enjoyed in non-competitive and non-economic ways. Women in this study did not seek out quilting specifically to rebuild their creative identities, but those at midlife found themselves re-examining their lives, happened upon quilting and "took to it." They had friends or family who got them interested and involved, some relied upon continual or disrupted family connections to quilting, and some began a family connection to quilting. Quilting is one of many ways in which women can connect with other women on personal and societal levels, develop a creative self in which women find themselves not just as family caretakers, but as subjects of their own lives as well.

## QUILTING AS GENDERED NON-ECONOMIC CULTURAL PRODUCTION

Quilting as a form of non-economic cultural production encourages women to reju-venate themselves in appropriately gendered ways so that they can go about the rest of their everyday lives. For example, on an episode of the television talk show *Oprah*, a young mother was encouraged to reinstate time for quilting in her life to remedy her depression, giving missing meaning to her life, and most importantly, to take some time for herself every day (*The Oprah Winfrey Show* 2000). Making time for quilting in this example would also enable this young mother to continue to engage in carework for her family by making them homemade quilts. The popular press also reports that Hollywood actresses in growing numbers are turning to forms of non-economic cultural production, specifically knitting and other forms of needlework on movie sets for personal reasons: relaxation, self-renewal, and to make gifts for family and friends (*People Magazine* 2001). Knitting and now crocheting are publicly visible, with best-selling books *Stitch 'n Bitch*, *Stitch 'n Bitch Nation*, and *Stitch 'n Bitch Crochet* by Stoller (2004a, 2004b, 2006). Without the pressures to succeed or fail in the economic market as professional artists have, non-economic cultural producers such as leisure quilters are more free to enjoy the process and the product than they would be if they pursued these activities as paid work.

As women developed an identity as quilters, they balanced personal and family needs in seeking time and space to quilt. Women primarily produced quilts for personal non-economic reasons, such as creative expression or stress relief. None of the women depended entirely on her quilting efforts to support her family financially.

They instead engaged in quilting to fulfill personal, emotional, and artistic needs. The creative activity provided them the peace that they were seeking, and acted as a haven from the rest of their everyday lives. For some, part of the benefit of quilting was the opportunity to spend time with other women, exchanging not only information about quilting, but also thoughts about a variety of issues relevant to contemporary women's lives. After engaging in quilting and escaping from their life stressors, they were better able to engage with the complex and trying systems in which they already existed, mainly within the family and the economy. For quilters, their intimate, connected quilting communities are supportive to their creative selves in ways that their families, non-quilting friends, and paid-work lives are not.

Thus, quilting is an essential part of these women's identities, and for many women becomes a subjective career. They self-identify as quilters, and state that quilting encourages self-expression, provides a way to establish a conscious legacy of themselves, as well as fulfilling other society-level needs. As a feminized activity, the process of quilting is not always understood or supported by non-quilters, such as family and friends. Thus, women rely upon one another to garner support and encouragement from other quilters for their quilting activities. Gifting quilts to others also reveals the importance of the process and products of quilting. When women give quilts as gifts to others, they say that symbolically they are giving/gifting a part of themselves. If quilters feel that their gifts (their selves) are being mistreated or treated well, they feel it deeply. Most recognize that these deep feelings are fully appreciated primarily within the community of quilters.

Women use very complex strategies to gain time and other resources needed to quilt. Establishing a fabric stash and finding space for both the stash and a permanent quilt space in the home represent a challenge to the inequitable distribution of opportunities for leisure between women and men. Thus, to these women legitimation for quilting is a form of respect, represented by having time alone, engaging in freely chosen leisure, and enhancing their creative interests. Establishing and hiding the fabric stash and negotiating for space in the home to quilt and store materials, for example, exhibit women's difficulties generally in marking time for themselves in homes that operate under patriarchal norms that subordinate women's leisure interests to those of others. When financially and spatially able, women seek to obtain "a room of their own" for quilting, and for themselves. Attaining such a space represents a validation of one's self and one's self-worth.

Through quilting, women work out complex balances between personal and family needs. Women want to quilt, but they also want to involve the family in their everyday lives as much as is possible. Quilters find ways to value both the family and their quilting passions. They realize the tension that exists between the sometimes competing components of their lives. For example, they complain about it, give in to family demands, and cause disruption in their family as they find and devote adequate resources to continue quilting. To accommodate the family, some break down quilting into smaller tasks, which can be carried along on family outings or combined with other family activities. Others struggle to find private, uninterrupted time and treasure days when family members are otherwise occupied to be able to immerse themselves in their quilting projects. They continually negotiate and renegotiate their everyday lives, determined to include their families into their quilting, and their quilting activities into family life.

Women also simultaneously do carework for themselves and for others through quilting. Women do the work of the family, or carework, when they are making quilts for other people. How they remember their quilts is significant for them and for the relationships they have with people in their lives. How many quilts one makes is not particularly important, for values are not measured in metrics or economic terms. For whom the quilts are made and what they represent to the quilters are what is salient for the women of this study. Quilting practices are embedded in women's lives, recording extraordinary events. Sarah's frog quilt, which represents her social commentary on her dating experiences, Emma's anger quilt, which helps her through difficult times, and the quilt that Karla made and sold while taking treatment for breast cancer are examples of how women can use quilts to mark important life events that might not seem as important as international events such as the Olympics. The stories quilters have shared indicate that the creative meaning imbued in quilts is to them, at least, more important than the surface appearance of a quilt.

Women used quilting to develop identities that were not directly tied to their identities or their roles within the family. In seeking out other women outside of the family from whom to learn quilting techniques as adults, midlife quilters learn to quilt and practice quilting in gendered ways: women make quilts that reflect and give voice to their lives, and make quilts as gifts for family members and close friends. By engaging in these creative acts, women exhibit carework for those close to them, maintaining family ties, and passing on memories of themselves as skilled quilters and caretakers.

Self-identified quilters often become self-conscious cultural producers, creating visual and tactile objects that document important aspects of their lives that are often not commemorated in public, commercialized forms of contemporary culture (e.g., war monuments as studied by Schwartz and Bayma 1999; Wagner-Pacifici and Schwartz 1991). By engaging in quilting, women both re-enact and transform gender relations in families, challenging stratified social relations that grant more time, attention, and resources to others' leisure pursuits than their own. As quilters communicate with others about quilting activities and using quilts in gift exchanges that cement kin and friendship ties, women build communities of local knowledge and innovate and transmit a culture that is distinctively feminized and that successfully integrates tradition and modernity.

I have analyzed quilting as a meaning-laden form of non-economic gendered cultural production among midlife U.S. women. As a gendered activity, quilting provides a case in which to examine the complex role unpaid creative work plays in contemporary women's lives. Quilting may appear to be a simple pastime, but for many women it represents important and multidimensional work. When women quilt, they preserve the gendered nature of cultural transmission, as well as the gendered culture in which quilting activities exist. Through quilting, women reach back into history and connect with their quilting foremothers, the women who quilted before them and passed on the tradition of quilting in which they now engage. Women also quilt as individuals, embedded within their own homes and families. Women reveal how the creative activity of quilting challenges power imbalances and family dynamics within the home. Such analysis of women's everyday activity teaches us much about women's position within society and culture, and holds the potential for great sociological yield.

The meaning-laden process of quilting and the finished products from that process are part of women's gendered cultural production. Quilts were made primarily as gifts, and were not intentionally part of the economic marketplace. Although they bought new fabric and equipment to make quilts, women were not constrained by market trends, production costs, or pressure to sell their quilts. Much of the current cultural production research fails to notice women's contributions to cultural production, under-conceptualizing the importance of process in meaning-making activities, while over-emphasizing direct connections to the economic sphere. Additionally, as it is currently studied and conceptualized by sociologists of culture and sociologists of gender, the cultural production research overlooks many unpaid forms of cultural production altogether, quilting being one of them.

Although 15 percent of U.S. households participate in quilting, this activity is thought by many to be a harmless, traditional, even quaint or silly feminized activity (Leman Publications 2006). Most contemporary U.S. midlife women who quilt for leisure purposes bring in little if any money to the family economy from their quilting efforts. Furthermore, no obvious or clear outlets exist that legitimate this activity as for other leisure pursuits with professional or commercial venues (e.g., professional golf). Because of these and other factors, quilting is thought to be a traditional pursuit, one that is unimportant and therefore non-threatening to regular, traditional family life.

As of late, quilting has transformed from a necessary home activity to a non-essential one that resembles leisure more than work. Thus, for American women in traditional heterosexual relationships and with families, serious leisure quilting takes up their already limited time and space in the household (Stalp 2006b). Women quilters challenge traditional family dynamics when they take leisure time for themselves, yet they simultaneously embody feminine characteristics by engaging in what we consider a feminine and traditional activity. Sometimes both quilters and their families feel that valuable time and space should be devoted to family needs, not women's individual creative needs. However, women negotiate these tensions between family and quilting demands by finding the time and space in their lives to accomplish both.

Certainly, quilting is a meaning-laden form of culture production among contemporary American women. As a feminized cultural activity, quilting provides a successful case in which to examine the complex role non-economic culture production plays in contemporary women's lives. This research expands the production of culture theoretical tradition in the sociology of culture by analyzing feminized processes of non-economic culture creation in privatized, women-dominated sites that have rarely been analyzed. In doing so, my research highlights the significant relationship between cultural object and culture creator, and demonstrates that women are legitimate cultural creators in their own right.

# REFERENCES

Abrahams, Ethel Ewert, and Rachel K. Pannabecker. 2000. "'Better Choose Me': Addictions to Tobacco, Collecting, and Quilting, 1880–1920." *Uncoverings* 21: 79–104.

Acker, Joan. 1992. "Gendering Organizational Theory." Pages 248–260 in *Gendering Organizational Analysis*. Edited by Albert J. Mills and Peta Tancred. Newbury Park, CA: Sage.

Adams County Ohio Quilt Sampler Project. 2006. http://www.appalachiandiscovery.com/

Adler, Patricia A., Steven J. Kless, and Peter Adler. 1992. "Socialization to Gender Roles: Popularity Among Elementary School Boys and Girls." *Sociology of Education* 65: 169–187.

The Alliance for American Quilts. 2006. http://www.quiltalliance.org/index1.html

The American Quilt Study Group. 2006. http://www.h-net.org/~aqsg/ Accessed 7/15/2006.

American Quilter's Society. 2006. http://www.americanquilter.com/ Accessed 7/15/2006.

The American Sewing Guild. 2000. "Twenty Years of Creativity…" www.asg.org/store/about.asp Accessed 10/1/2000.

Amott, Teresa, and Julie Matthaei. 1996. *Race, Gender and Work: A Multi-Cultural Economic History of Women in the United States*. Boston, MA: South End Press.

Anderson, Laura, and Karen Gold. 1998. "Creative Connections: The Healing Power of Women's Art and Craft Work." *Women and Therapy* 21 (4): 15–36.

Aptheker, Bettina. 1989. *Tapestries of Life*. Amherst, MA: The University of Massachusetts Press.

Ardery, Julia. S. 1998. *The Temptation: Edgar Tolson and the Genesis of Twentieth-Century Art*. Chapel Hill, NC: The University of North Carolina Press.

Avni, Noga. 1991. "Battered Wives: The Home as a Total Institution." *Violence and Victims* 6 (2): 137–149.

Baca Zinn, Maxine. 1979. "Field Research in Minority Communities: Ethical, Methodological, and Political Observations by an Insider." *Social Problems* 27 (2): 209–219.

Baldwin, J.H., G.D. Ellis, and B.M. Baldwin. 1999. "Marital Satisfaction: An Examination of Its Relationship to Spouse Support and Congruence of Commitment Among Runners." *Leisure Sciences* 21: 117–131.

Baldwin, Cheryl K., and Patricia A. Norris. 1999. "Exploring the Dimensions of Serious Leisure: 'Love Me – Love My Dog!'" *Journal of Leisure Research* 31 (1): 1–17.

Barkley Brown, Elsa. 1988. "African-American Women's Quilting: A Framework for Conceptualizing and Teaching African-American Women's History." Pages 9–18 in *Black Women in America: Social Sciences Perspectives*. Edited by Micheline R. Malson, Elisabeth Medimbe-Boyi, Jean F. O'Barr, and Mary Wyer. Chicago, IL: The University of Chicago Press.

Barn Quilts of Grundy County, IA. 2006. www.grundycountyia.com Accessed 7/15/2006.

Barn Quilts of Pocahontas County, IA. 2006. http://www.iowaartists.org/quilts/ Accessed 7/15/2006.

Barn Quilts of Sac County, IA. 2006. http://www.barnquilts.com/ Accessed 7/15/2006.

Barreras, Vivian, and Denise D. Bielby. 2001. "Places, Faces, and Other Familiar Things: The Cultural

Experience of Telenovela Viewing among Latinos in the United States." *The Journal of Popular Culture* 34 (4): 1–18.

Bartram, Sherry A. 2001. "Serious Leisure Careers Among Whitewater Kayakers: A Feminist Perspective." *World Leisure* 2: 4–11.

Bassett, Lynne, and Jack Larkin. 1998. *Northern Comfort: New England's Early Quilts 1789–1850*. Nashville, TN: Rutledge Hill Press.

Bateson, Mary Catherine. 1990. *Composing a Life*. New York: Plume.

Beardsley, John, William Arnett, Pauljane Arnett, and Jane Livingston. 2002. *The Quilts of Gee's Bend*. Atlanta, GA: Tinwood Books.

Beaudoin-Ross, Jacqueline. 1979–1980. "An Early Eighteenth-Century Pieced Quilt in Montreal." *Canadian Art Review* 6 (2).

Becker, Howard. 1963. *Outsiders: Studies in the Sociology of Deviance*. New York: The Free Press.

Becker, Howard. 1982. *Art Worlds*. Berkeley, CA: The University of California Press.

Belk, Russell W. 2001. *Collecting in a Consumer Society*. London: Routledge.

Benberry, Cuesta. 1993. "The Threads of African-American Quilters are Woven Into History." *American Visions* October/November: 14–18.

Beoku-Betts, Josephine. 1994. "When Black is Not Enough: Doing Field Research Among Gullah Women." *NWSA Journal* 6 (3): 413–433.

Berenson, Kathryn. 1996. *Quilts of Provence*. New York: Henry Holt and Company.

Blumer, Herbert. 1969. *Symbolic Interactionism: Perspective and Method*. Berkeley, CA: The University of California Press.

Brackett, Kim Pettigrew. 2000. "Facework Strategies among Romance Fiction Readers." *The Social Science Journal* 37 (3): 347–360.

Brackman, Barbara. 1993. *Encyclopedia of Pieced Quilt Patterns*. Paducah, KY: American Quilter's Society.

Brackman, Barbara. 1997. *Patterns of Progress*. Los Angeles, CA: Autry Museum of Western Heritage.

The British Quilt Study Group. 2006. http://www.quilt.co.uk Accessed 7/15/2006.

Burman, Barbara. 1999. *The Culture of Sewing: Gender, Consumption, and Home Dressmaking*. Oxford: Berg Publishers.

Butsch, Richard. 1984. "The Commodification of Leisure: The Case of the Model Airplane Hobby and Industry." *Qualitative Sociology* 7 (3): 217–235.

Callahan, Nancy. 1987. *The Freedom Quilting Bee*. Tuscaloosa, AL: The University of Alabama Press.

Cerny, Catherine. 1991. "A Quilt Guild: Its Role in the Elaboration of Female Identity." *Uncoverings* 12: 32–49.

Cerny, Catherine. 1997a. "Quilted Apparel and Gender Identity: An American Case Study." Pages 106–120 in *Dress and Gender: Making and Meaning*. Edited by Ruth Barnes and Joanne B. Eicher. Oxford: Berg Publishers.

Cerny, Catherine. 1997b. "Quilt Ownership and Sentimental Attachments: The Structure of Memory." *Uncoverings* 18: 95–119.

Cerny, Catherine A., Joanne B. Eicher, and Marilyn R. DeLong. 1993. "Quiltmaking and the Modern Guild: A Cultural Idiom." *Clothing and Textiles Research Journal* 12 (1): 16–25.

Chafetz, Janet Saltzman, and Joseph A. Kotarba. 1995. "Son Worshippers: The Role of Little League Mothers in Recreating Gender." *Studies in Symbolic Interaction* 18: 217–241.

Channer, Catherine, and Anne Buck. 1991. *In The Cause of English Lace*. Carlton: Ruth Bean.

Cheek, Cheryl, and Kathleen W. Piercy. 2004. "Quilting as Age Identity Expression in Traditional Women." *International Journal on Aging and Human Development* 59 (4): 321–337.

Colby, Averil. 1971. *Quilting*. New York: Charles Scribner's Sons.

Collins, Patricia Hill. 1991. *Black Feminist Thought*. New York: Routledge.

Collis, Marion. 1999. "Marital Conflict and Men's Leisure: How Women Negotiate Male Power in a Small Mining Community." *Journal of Sociology* 35 (1): 60–76.

Coser, Lewis. 1974. *Greedy Institutions: Patterns of Undivided Commitment*. New York: The Free Press.

Cox, Meg. 2007. *The Quilter's Catalog: A Comprehensive Resource Guide*. New York: Workman Publishing Company.

Crosby, Faye. 1991. *Juggling: The Unexpected Advantages of Balancing Career and Home for Women and their Families*. New York: The Free Press.

Crothers, Pat. 1993. "Gender Misapprehensions: The 'Separate Spheres' Ideology, Quilters, and Role Adaptation, 1850–1890." *Uncoverings* 14: 41–61.

Csikszentmihalyi, Mihaly. 1990. *Flow: The Psychology of Optimal Experience*. New York: HarperPerennial.

Csikszentmihalyi, Mihaly. 1996. *Creativity: Flow and the Psychology of Discovery and Invention*. New York: HarperPerennial.

Csikszentmihalyi, Mihaly, and Eugene Rochberg-Halton. 1995. *The Meaning of Things: Domestic Symbols and the Self*. Cambridge: Cambridge University Press.

Curran, Geoffrey M. 1996. "From 'Swinging Hard' to 'Rocking Out': Classification of Style and the Creation of Identity in the World of Drumming." *Symbolic Interaction* 19 (1): 37–60.

Delaney-Mech, Susan, M.D. 2000. *Rx for Quilters: Stitcher-Friendly Advice for Every Body*. Lafayette, CA: C & T Publishing, Inc.

DeVault, Marjorie L. 1991. *Feeding the Family: The Social Organization of Caring as Gendered Work*. Chicago, IL: The University of Chicago Press.

DeVault, Marjorie L. 1999. *Liberating Method: Feminism and Social Research*. Philadelphia, PA: Temple University Press.

Di Leonardo, Micaela. 1987. "The Female World of Cards and Holidays: Women, Families, and the Work of Kinship." *Signs* 12 (3): 440–453.

Dickerson, Anne E. 2000. "The Power and Flow of Occupation Illustrated Through Scrapbooking." *Occupational Therapy in Health Care* 12 (2/3): 127–140.

Doyle, Amanda. 1998. "The Fabric of Their Lives: Quilters Negotiating Time and Space." *Women's Studies Journal* 14 (1): 107–129.

Dunn, Margaret M., and Ann R. Morris. 1992. "Narrative Quilts and Quilted Narratives: The Art of Faith Ringgold and Alice Walker." *Explorations in Ethnic Studies* 15 (1): 27–32.

Eikmeier, Barbara J. 2001. "A Style Emerges: Korean Culture in Contemporary Quilts." *Uncoverings* 22: 87–116.

Elsley, Judy. 1995. "Making Cultural Connections in Quilt Scholarship." *Uncoverings* 16: 229–243.

Emerson, Robert M., Rachel I. Fretz, and Linda L. Shaw. 1995. *Writing Ethnographic Fieldnotes*. Chicago, IL: The University of Chicago Press.

Enarson, Elaine. 2000. "'We Will Make Meaning Out of This': Women's Cultural Responses to the Red River Valley Flood." *International Journal of Mass Emergencies and Disasters* 18 (1): 39–62.

Ethridge, F. Maurice, and Jerome L. Neapolitan 1985. "Amateur Craft-Artists: Marginal Leisure Roles in a Marginal Art World." *Sociological Spectrum* 5: 53–76.

Evetts, Julia. 1996. *Gender and Career in Science and Engineering*. London: Taylor & Francis Publishers.

Ferriss, Lucy. 1999. "Writing in No-Time." Pages 55–63 in *Sleeping With One Eye Open: Women Writers and the Art of Survival*. Edited by Marilyn Kallet and Judith Ortiz Cofer. Athens, GA: The University of Georgia Press.

Fieldnotes. 1997, 1999, 2000.

Fine, Gary Alan. 1996. *Kitchens: The Culture of Restaurant Work*. Berkeley, CA: The University of California Press.

Fine, Gary Alan. 1998. *Morel Tales: The Culture of Mushrooming*. Cambridge, MA: Harvard University Press.

Fogle, Melinda. 2002. "Joining the Pezzimist Party: Pez Convention as Rite of Passage and Communal Bonding." *The Journal of Popular Culture* 36 (2): 236–249.

Fonow, Mary Margaret, and Judith A. Cook. 1991. *Beyond Methodology: Feminist Scholarship as Lived Research*. Bloomington, IN: Indiana University Press.

Forrest, John, and Deborah Blincoe. 1995. *The Natural History of the Traditional Quilt*. Austin, TX: The University of Texas Press.

Foster, Joan. 2002. *Game Tekstiler*. Oslo, Norway: N.W. Damm & Son.

Freeman, Roland L. 1996. *A Communion of Spirits: African-American Quilters, Preservers, and their Stories*. Nashville, TN: Rutledge Hill Press.

Freysinger, Valeria J., and D. Flannery. 1992. "Women's Leisure: Affiliation, Self-Determination, Empowerment, and Resistance?" *Loisir et Société/Society and Leisure* 15: 303–322.

Friedlich, Karla. 1991. "Quilts of Conscience: Quilts are Made for More than Warmth." *The Clarion* 16 (1): 47–54.

Fry, Gladys-Marie. 1990. *Stitched from the Soul: Slave Quilts from the Ante-Bellum South*. New York: Dutton Studio Books.

Gabbert, Lisa. 2000. "'Petting the Fabric': Medium and the Creative Process." *Uncoverings* 21: 137–153.

Geertz, Clifford. 1973. *The Interpretation of Cultures: Selected Essays*. New York: Basic Books.

Geertz, Clifford. 1983. *Local Knowledge: Further Essays in Interpretive Anthropology*. New York: Basic Books.

Gervais, Sandy. 1995. *Living the Life of a Fabric-aholic*. Algona, IA: Midlife Printing.

Gillespie, Dair L., Ann Leffler, and Elinor Lerner. 2002. "If it Weren't for My Hobby, I'd Have a Life: Dog Sports, Serious Leisure, and Boundary Negotiations." *Leisure Studies* 21: 285–304.

Glaser, Barney G., and Anselm L. Strauss. 1967. *The Discovery of Grounded Theory*. New York: Aldine de Gruyter.

Gluck, Sherna Berger, and Daphne Patai. 1991. *Women's Words: The Feminist Practice of Oral History*. New York: Routledge.

Goff, Stephen J., Daniel S. Fick, and Robert A. Oppliger. 1997. "The Moderating Effects of Spouse Support on the Relation Between Serious Leisure and Spouses' Perceived Leisure-Family Conflict." *Journal of Leisure Research* 29 (1): 47–60.

Goffman, Erving. 1959. *The Presentation of Self in Everyday Life*. New York: Anchor Books.

Goffman, Erving. 1961. *Asylums: Essays on the Social Situation of Mental Patients and Other Inmates*. Garden City, NY: Anchor Books.

Goffman, Erving. 1963. *Stigma: Notes on the Management of Spoiled Identity*. Englewood Cliffs, NJ: Prentice-Hall, Inc.

Goffman, Erving. 1976. *Gender Advertisements*. New York: Harper & Row.

Green, Eileen, Sandra Hebron, and Diana Woodward. 1987. "Women, Leisure, and Social Control." Pages 75–92 in *Women, Violence and Social Control*. Edited by Jalna Hanmer and Mary Maynard. Atlantic Highlands, NJ: Humanities Press International, Inc.

Green, Eileen, Sandra Hebron, and Diana Woodward. 1990. *Women's Leisure, What Leisure?* London: Macmillan.

Griswold, Wendy. 2004. *Cultures and Societies in a Changing World*. Thousand Oaks, CA: Pine Forge Press.

Gunn, Virginia. 1984. "Crazy Quilts and Outline Quilts: Popular Responses to the Decorative Art/Art Needlework Movement, 1876–1893." *Uncoverings* 5: 131–152.

Gunn, Virginia. 1992. "From Myth to Maturity: The Evolution of Quilt Scholarship." *Uncoverings* 13: 192–205.

Halbwachs, Maurice. 1941[1992]. *On Collective Memory*. Edited and Translated by Lewis A. Coser. Chicago, IL: The University of Chicago Press.

Halbwachs, Maurice. 1992[1941]. *La Topographie Legendaire Des Evangiles en Saint-Terre (The Legendary Topography of the Gospels in the Holy Land)*. Paris: Presses Universitaires de France.

Hanson, Marin, and Janneken Smucker. 2003. "Quilts as Manifestations of Cross-Cultural Contact: East-West and Amish-'English' Examples." *Uncoverings* 24: 99–129.

Harding, Sandra. 1987. *Feminism and Methodology*. Bloomington, IN: Indiana University Press.

Harre, Ron. 1979. *Social Being: A Theory for Social Psychology*. Totowa, NJ: Rowman and Littlefield.

Harrington, C. Lee, and Denise D. Bielby. 1995. *Soap Fans: Pursuing Pleasure and Making Meaning in Everyday Life*. Philadelphia, PA: Temple University Press.

Harris, Mary. 1997. *Common Threads: Women, Mathematics and Work*. Stoke-on-Trent: Trentham Books Limited.

Hawley, Jana M. 2005. "The Commercialization of Old Order Amish Quilts: Enduring and Changing Cultural Meanings." *Clothing and Textile Research Journal* 23 (2): 102–114.

Hays, Sharon. 1996. *The Cultural Contradictions of Motherhood*. New Haven, CT: Yale University Press.

Herda, Phyllis S. 2000. "Creating a New Tradition: Quilting in Tonga." *Uncoverings* 21: 57–78.

Herridge, Kristi L., Susan M. Shaw, and Roger C. Mannell. 2003. "An Exploration of Women's Leisure within Heterosexual Romantic Relationships." *Journal of Leisure Research* 35 (3): 274–291.

Hertz, Rosanna (Ed.). 1997. *Reflexivity and Voice*. Thousand Oaks, CA: Sage.

Hochschild, Arlie Russell. 1989. *The Second Shift*. New York: Avon Books.

Hochschild, Arlie Russell. 1997. *The Time Bind: When Work Becomes Home and Home Becomes Work*. New York: Metropolitan Books.

Holstein, Jonathan. 1991. *Abstract Design in American Quilts: A Biography of an Exhibition*. Louisville, KY: The Kentucky Quilt Project.

Holyfield, Lori. 1995. "Generating Excitement: Organizational and Social Psychological Dynamics of Adventure." Unpublished Ph.D. Dissertation, The University of Georgia.

Holyfield, Lori, and Lilian Jonas. 2003. "From River God to Research Grunt: Identity, Emotions, and the River Guide." *Symbolic Interaction* 26 (2): 285–306.

Hurston, Zora Neale. 1995[1942]. *Dust Tracks on a Road*. New York: HarperCollins.

Ice, Joyce Ann. 1984. "Quilting and the Pattern of Relationships in Community Life." Unpublished Ph.D. Dissertation, The University of Texas at Austin.

International Quilt Study Center. 2006. http://quiltstudy.unl.edu//CEN_main.html

Janesick, Valerie. 1994. "The Dance of Qualitative Research Design: Metaphor, Methodolatry, and Meaning." Pages 209–219 in *Handbook of Qualitative Research*. Edited by Norman K. Denzin and Yvonne S. Lincoln. Thousand Oaks, CA: Sage.

Janesick, Valerie. 2000. "The Choreography of Qualitative Research Design." Pages 379–400 in *Handbook of Qualitative Research, Second Edition*. Edited by Norman K. Denzin and Yvonne S. Lincoln. Thousand Oaks, CA: SAGE.

Jenkins, Susan, and Linda Seward. 1991. *The American Quilt Story*. New York: Wings Books.

Johnson, Joyce Starr, and Laurel E. Wilson. 2005. "'It Says You Really Care': Motivational Factors of Contemporary Female Handcrafters." *Clothing and Textiles Research Journal* 23 (2): 115–130.

Jones, Cleve, and Jeff Dawson. 2000. *Stitching a Revolution*. New York: HarperCollins.

Kallet, Marilyn, and Judith Ortiz Cofer (Eds). 1999. *Sleeping With One Eye Open: Women Writers and the Art of Survival*. Athens, GA: The University of Georgia Press.

Kelly, Nuala. 1987. "Women Knitters Cast Off." Pages 169–183 in *Gender in Irish History*. Edited by Chris Curtin, Pauline Jackson, and Barbara O'Connor. Galway: Galway University Press.

Kelly, Ryan E., and Charles M. Brown. 2005. "Cutting Up with the Girls: A Sociological Study of a Women's Scrapbooking Club." Paper Presented at The Eastern Sociological Society Annual Meetings, March 17, 2005, Washington, DC.

Kendall, Diana. 2002. *The Power of Good Deeds: Privileged Women and the Social Reproduction of the Upper Class*. New York: Rowman and Littlefield.

King, Faye Lynn. 2001. "Social Dynamics of Quilting." *World Leisure* 2: 26–29.

Kotre, John. 1984. *Outliving the Self: Generativity and the Interpretation of Lives*. Baltimore, MD: The Johns Hopkins University Press.

Krenske, Leigh, and Jim McKay. 2000. "'Hard and Heavy': Gender and Power in a Heavy Metal Music Subculture." *Gender, Place and Culture* 7 (3): 287–304.

Krouse, Mary Elizabeth. 1993. "Gift Giving and Social Transformation: The AIDS Memorial Quilt as Social Movement Culture." Unpublished Ph.D. Dissertation, The Ohio State University.

Lang, Gladys Engel, and Kurt Lang. 1988. "Recognition and Renown: The Survival of Artistic Reputation." *American Journal of Sociology* 98: 79–109.

Lang, Gladys Engel, and Kurt Lang. 1990. *Etched in Memory: The Building and Survival of Artistic Reputation*. Chapel Hill, NC: The University of North Carolina Press.

Lang, Gladys Engel, and Kurt Lang. 1993. "The Rescue of Reputation: Re-Examining the Fate of American Women Etchers." *Current Research on Occupations and Professions* 8: 33–54.

Langellier, Kristin M. 1992. "Show-and-Tell as a Performance Event: Oppositional Practice in Contemporary Quiltmaking Culture." *Uncoverings* 13: 127–147.

Larson, Reed W., Sally A. Gillman, and Maryse H. Richards. 1997. "Divergent Experiences of Family Leisure: Fathers, Mothers, and Young Adolescents." *Journal of Leisure Research* 29 (1): 78–97.

Laureau, Annette. 1989. *Home Advantage*. London: The Falmer Press.

Leman Publications, Inc. 2003. *Quilting in America Survey*. Golden, CO.

Leman Publications, Inc. 2006. *Quilting in America Survey*. Golden, CO.

Lenz, Heather. 1998. "Learning to Quilt with Grandma Mary Sibley: Gift Labor, Traditional

Quiltmaking, and Contemporary Art." *Uncoverings* 19: 109–136.

Lewis, Jacqueline, and Michael R. Fraser. 1996. "Patches of Grief and Rage: Visitor Responses to the NAMES Project AIDS Memorial Quilt." *Qualitative Sociology* 19 (4): 433–451.

Liddell, Jill, and Yuko Watanabe. 1991. *Japanese Quilts*. London: Cassell.

Lincoln, Yvonne S., and Egon G. Guba. 1985. *Naturalistic Inquiry*. Beverly Hills, CA: SAGE.

Lipsett, Linda Otto. 1985. *Remember Me: Women and their Friendship Quilts*. San Francisco, CA: The Quilt Digest Press.

Long, Elizabeth. 2003. *Book Clubs: Women and the Uses of Reading in Everyday Life*. Chicago, IL: University of Chicago Press.

Lucal, Betsy. 1999. "What It Means to be Gendered Me: Life on the Boundaries of a Dichotomous Gender System." *Gender & Society* 13 (6): 781–797.

Lydon, Susan Gordon. 1997. *The Knitting Sutra: Craft as a Spiritual Practice*. New York: HarperCollins.

Lynch, Annette, Marybeth C. Stalp, and M. Elise Radina. 2007. "Growing Old and Dressing (Dis)gracefully." In *Dress Sense*. Edited by Donald Clay Johnson and Helen Bradley Foster. Oxford: Berg Publishers.

Lyons, Mary E. 1993. *Stitching Stars: The Story Quilts of Harriet Powers*. New York: Aladdin Paperbacks.

Lyons, Nick. 1999. *My Secret Fishing Life*. New York: Atlantic Monthly Press.

Macdonald, Anne L. 1988. *No Idle Hands: The Social History of American Knitting*. New York: Ballantine Books.

McMorris, Penny, and Michael Kile. 1996. *The Art Quilt*. Lincolnwood, IL: The Quilt Digest Press.

Madson, John. 1996. "Why Men Hunt." Pages 130–135 in *A Hunter's Heart: Honest Essays on Blood Sport*. Edited by David Petersen. New York: Henry Holt and Company.

Mainardi, Patricia. 1975. *Quilts: The Great American Art*. San Pedro, CA: Miles & Weir, Ltd.

Major, Wayne F. 2001. "The Benefits and Costs of Serious Running." *World Leisure* 2: 12–25.

Marks, S.R., T.L. Huston, E.M. Johnson, and S.M. MacDermid. 2001. "Role Balance Among White Married Couples." *Journal of Marriage and Family* 63: 1,083–1,098.

Mattingly, Marybeth, and Suzanne M. Bianchi. 2003. "Gender Differences in the Quantity and Quality of Free Time: The U.S. Experience." *Social Forces* 81 (3): 999–1,031.

Mavor, Carol. 1997. "Collecting Loss." *Cultural Studies* 11 (1): 111–137.

Mead, George Herbert. 1934. *Mind, Self and Society*. Chicago, IL: The University of Chicago Press.

Miller, Jean Baker, and Irene Pierce Stiver. 1997. *The Healing Connection: How Women Form Relationships in Therapy and in Life*. Boston, MA: Beacon Press.

Mishler, Elliott G. 1999. *Storylines: Craftartists' Narratives of Identity*. Cambridge, MA: Harvard University Press.

Mueller, Mary-Rose. 1995. "Significant Symbols, Symbolic Boundaries, and Quilts in the Time of AIDS." *Research in the Sociology of Health Care* 12: 3–23.

Myers, Lisa R. 2001. *The Joy of Knitting: Texture, Color, Design, and the Global Knitting Circle*. Philadelphia, PA: Running Press.

National Quilting Association. 2006. http://www.nqaquilts.org/ Accessed 7/15/2006.

Neapolitan, Jerry. 1985a. "The Art/Craft Object: Its Styles and Conventions." *Sociological Spectrum* 5: 231–243.

Neapolitan, Jerry. 1985b. "Craft Media Workers: Success in Sales Generated Income." *Sociological Focus* 18 (4): 313–324.

Neapolitan, Jerry. 1986. "Art, Craft, and Art/Craft Segments Among Craft Media Workers." *Work and Occupations* 13 (2): 203–216.

"Nebraska Holds Executive Session." 2003. *Quilter's Newsletter Magazine* October: 16.

Nelson, Nancy J., Karen L. LaBat, and Gloria M. Williams. 2002. "Contemporary Irish Artists: Exploring Experiences of Gender, Culture, and Artistic Medium." *Clothing and Textiles Research Journal* 20 (1): 15–25.

Nelson, Nancy J., Karen L. LaBat, and Gloria M. Williams. 2005. "More than 'Just a Little Hobby': Women and Textile Art in Ireland." *Women's Studies International Forum* 28 (4): 328–342.

Not Barn Yesterday: A Clothesline of Quilts in Appalachia. 2006. http://www.clinchpowell.net/quilts.html Accessed 7/15/2006.

Notman, Malkah Topin. 1980. "Changing Roles for Women at Mid-Life." Pages 85–109 in *Mid-Life: Developmental and Clinical Issues*. New York: Brunner/Mazel Publishers.

Oakley, Ann. 1974a. *The Sociology of Housework*. New York: Pantheon Books.

Oakley, Ann. 1974b. *Woman's Work: The Housewife, Past and Present*. New York: Vintage Books.

Oakley, Ann. 1987. "Interviewing Women: A Contradiction in Terms." Pages 30–61 in *Doing Feminist Research*. Edited by H. Roberts. London: Routledge & Kegan Paul.

Ohio Quilt Barns. 2006. http://www.ohiobarns.com/otherbarns/quilt/quiltbarns.html Accessed 7/15/2006.

Olsen, Tillie. 1978. *Silences*. London: Virago Press.

Olick, Jeffrey. 1999. "Collective Memory: The Two Cultures." *Sociological Theory* 17 (3): 333–348.

*The Oprah Winfrey Show*. 2000. "Lifestyle Makeovers." July 31.

Ostrander, Susan A. 1986. *Women of the Upper Class*. Philadelphia, PA: Temple University Press.

Palliser, Mrs. Bury. 1984/1911. *History of Lace*. New York: Dover Publications.

Parker, Rozsika. 1984. *The Subversive Stitch: Embroidery and the Making of the Feminine*. London: The Women's Press.

Parker, Rozsika, and Griselda Pollock. 1981. *Old Mistresses: Women, Art, and Ideology*. New York: Pantheon Books.

Patchwork Jewels of Monroe County. 2006. http://www.monroecountyohio.net/ Accessed 7/15/2006.

*People Magazine*. 2001. "Victorian Secret." September 10: 25.

Pershing, Linda. 1993. "'She Really Wanted to Be Her Own Woman': Scandalous Sunbonnet Sue." Pages 98–125 in *Feminist Messages: Coding in Women's Folk Culture*. Edited by Joan Newlon Radner. Urbana, IL: The University of Illinois Press.

Peterson, Karin E. 2003. "Discourse and Display: The Modern Eye, Entrepreneurship, and the Cultural Transformation of the Patchwork Quilt." *Sociological Perspectives* 46 (4): 461–490.

Peterson, Richard A. 1997. *The Fabrication of Authenticity: Country Music*. Chicago, IL: The University of Chicago Press.

Proeller, Marie. 1998. "The Top 10 Quilts." *Country Living Magazine* October 21(10):76–80.

Przybysz, Jane. 1987. "Competing Cultural Values at The Great American Quilt Festival." *Uncoverings* 8: 107–127.

Przybysz, Jane. 1989. "The Body En(w)rapped: Contemporary Quilted Garments." *Uncoverings* 10: 102–122.

The Quilt Index. 2006. http://www.quiltindex.org/since_kentucky.php Accessed 8/24/06.

Quilt National. 2006. http://www.quiltnational.com/ Accessed 7/15/2006.

*Quilt Treasures of Great Britain*. 1995. Nashville, TN: Rutledge Hill Press.

The Quilter Community. 2007. "A Cooperative Project to Comfort Victims of Hurricane Katrina." http://www.thequiltercommunity.com/Wc680d7e8c15ba.htm Accessed 2/14/07.

Quilter's News Network. 2006. http://www.quiltersnewsnetwork.com/ Accessed 8/24/06.

"The Quiltmakers of Gee's Bend." 2004. Alabama Public Television.

The Quiltmakers of Georgia. 1996. *The Olympic Quilts: America's Welcome to the World*. Birmingham, AL: Oxmoor House, Inc.

Radner, Joan Newlon (Ed.).1993. *Feminist Messages: Coding in Women's Folk Culture*. Urbana, IL: The University of Illinois Press.

Radway, Janice. 1991. *Reading the Romance*. Chapel Hill, NC: University of North Carolina Press.

Rake, Valerie Sanders. 2000. "'In the Old Days, They Used Scraps': Gender, Leisure, Commodification, and the Mythology of Quiltmaking, Wayne County, Ohio, 1915–1995." Unpublished Ph.D. Dissertation, The Ohio State University.

Reinharz, Shulamit. 1992. *Feminist Methods in Social Research*. New York: Oxford University Press.

Rhoades, Ruth. 1997. "Feed Sacks in Georgia: Their Manufacture, Marketing, and Consumer Use." *Uncoverings* 18: 121–152.

Richardson, Laurel. 1997. *Fields of Play: Constructing An Academic Life*. New Brunswick, NJ: Rutgers University Press.

Rolfe, Margaret. 1988. "Quilting: Its Absence in Australia." *Uncoverings* 9: 87–104.

Romero, Mary, and Abigail J. Stewart (Eds). 1999. *Women's Untold Stories: Breaking Silence, Talking Back, Voicing Complexity*. New York: Routledge.

Rothbart, Davy. 2004. *Found: The Best Lost, Tossed, and Forgotten Items From Around the World*. New York: Simon & Schuster.

Rubin, Herbert J., and Irene S. Rubin. 1995. *Qualitative Interviewing: The Art of Hearing Data*. Thousand Oaks, CA: SAGE.

Ruyak, Jacqueline. 2002. "Tokyo: Largest Quilt Festival Ever?" *Fiberarts* 29 (1): 13.

Ryer, John. 1997. *A Husband's Guide to Quilt Appreciation*. Ventura, CA: Calico Press.

Schofield-Tomschin, Sherry, and Mary A. Littrell. 2001. "Textile Handcraft Guild Participation: A Conduit to Successful Aging." *Clothing and Textile Research Journal* 19 (2): 41–51.

Schwartz, Barry. 1967. "The Social Psychology of the Gift." *American Journal of Sociology* 73 (1): 1–11.

Schwartz, Barry. 1996a. "Rereading the Gettysburg Address: Social Change and Collective Memory." *Qualitative Sociology* 19 (3): 395–422.

Schwartz, Barry. 1996b. "Memory as a Cultural System: Abraham Lincoln in World War Two." *American Sociological Review* 61 (5): 908–927.

Schwartz, Barry, and Todd Bayma. 1999. "Commemoration and the Politics of Recognition: The Korean War Veterans Memorial." *American Behavioral Scientist* 42 (6): 946–967.

Shapiro, Patricia Gottlieb. 1996. *My Turn: Women's Search for Self after the Children Leave*. Princeton, NJ: Peterson's.

Shaw, Susan M. 1994. "Gender, Leisure and Constraint: Towards a Framework for the Analysis of Women's Leisure." *Journal of Leisure Research* 26 (1): 8–23.

Shaw, Susan M. 1997. "Controversies and Contradictions in Family Leisure: An Analysis of Conflicting Paradigms." *Journal of Leisure Research* 29 (1): 98–113.

Siegenthaler, Kim L., and Irma O'Dell. 2001. "Older Golfers: Serious Leisure and Successful Aging." *World Leisure* 1: 47–54.

Sinha, Anita. 1979. "Control in Craft Work: The Case of Production Potters." *Qualitative Sociology* 2 (2): 3–25.

Smith, Dorothy E. 1987. *The Everyday World as Problematic: A Feminist Sociology*. Boston, MA: Northeastern University Press.

Spain, Daphne. 1992. *Gendered Spaces*. Chapel Hill, NC: The University of North Carolina Press.

Stalp, Marybeth C. 1998. "Not a Dying Art: Commodified Worlds Within U.S. Quiltmaking." Paper Presented at the American Sociological Association Annual Meetings, San Francisco, CA, August 1998.

Stalp, Marybeth C. 1999. "The Tissue Issue: 'Quilted' Northern Toilet Paper and Sites of Resistance." Paper Presented at the Southern Sociological Society, April, 1999.

Stalp, Marybeth C. 2001. "Women, Quilting, and Cultural Production: The Preservation of Self in Everyday Life." Unpublished Ph.D. Dissertation, Athens, GA: The University of Georgia.

Stalp, Marybeth C. 2006a. "Negotiating Time and Space for Serious Leisure: Quilting in the Modern U.S. Home." *Journal of Leisure Research* 38 (1): 104–132.

Stalp, Marybeth C. 2006b. "Hiding the (Fabric) Stash: Fabric Collecting, Hoarding and Hiding Strategies of Contemporary U.S. Quilters." *Textile: Journal of Cloth & Culture* 4 (1): 100–121.

Stalp, Marybeth C. 2006c. "Creating an Artistic Self: Amateur Quilters and Subjective Careers." *Sociological Focus* 39 (3): 193–216.

Stalp, Marybeth C., and Theresa M. Winge. 2006. "Mine's Bigger than Yours: Tales from the Material Culture Stash." Paper Presented at the Midwest Popular Culture Association/American Culture Association Annual Meetings, Indianapolis, IN, October 2006.

Stalp, Marybeth C., Elise Radina, and Annette Lynch. 2008. "'We Do It Cuz It's Fun': Creating Women's Leisure Space through Red Hat Society Membership." *Sociological Perspectives* 51, in press.

Stebbins, Robert A. 1970. "Career: The Subjective Approach." *The Sociological Quarterly* 11 (1): 32–49.

Stebbins, Robert A. 1971. "The Subjective Career as a Basis for Reducing Role Conflict." *Pacific Sociological Review* 14 (4): 383–402.

Stebbins, Robert A. 1979. *Amateurs: On the Margin Between Work and Leisure*. Beverly Hills, CA: Sage.

Stebbins, Robert A. 1996. *The Barbershop Singer: Inside the Social World of a Musical Hobby*. Toronto: The University of Toronto Press.

Stoller, Debbie. 2004a. *Stitch 'n Bitch: The Knitter's Handbook*. New York: Workman Publishing Company.

Stoller, Debbie. 2004b. *Stitch 'n Bitch Nation*. New York: Workman Publishing Company.

Stoller, Debbie. 2006. *Stitch 'n Bitch Crochet: The Happy Hooker*. New York: Workman Publishing Company.

Stone, Gregory. 1981. "Appearance." Pages 101–113 in *Social Psychology Through Symbolic Interaction*. Edited by Gregory P. Stone and Harvey A. Farberman. New York: John Wiley & Sons.

Thompson, Shona M. 1999. *Mother's Taxi: Sport and Women's Labor*. Albany, NY: SUNY Press.

Thorne, Barrie. 1997. *Gender Play: Girls and Boys in School*. New Brunswick, NJ: Rutgers University Press.

Tobin, Jacqueline L., and Raymond G. Dobard. 1999. *Hidden in Plain View: A Secret Story of Quilts and the Underground Railroad*. New York: Doubleday.

Todd, Sharon Leidy. 1997. "Means or Ends? An Expanded Model of Competitiveness Based on Quiltmakers' Perceptions of Success and Constraints to Continued Progress." Unpublished Ph.D. Dissertation, Pennsylvania State University.

Tokyo Great International Quilt Festival. 2006. http://www.nhk-ed.co.jp/eng/quilt-2.html

Torsney, Cheryl B., and Judy Elsley. 1994. *Quilt Culture: Tracing the Pattern*. Columbia, MO: The University of Missouri Press.

Tuchman, Gayle. 1984. "Fame and Misfortune: Edging Women Out of the Great Literary Tradition." *American Journal of Sociology* 90 (1): 72–96.

Tuchman, Gayle, and Nina Fortin. 1980. "Edging Women Out: Some Suggestions About the Structure of Opportunities and the Victorian Novel." *Signs* 6 (2): 308–325.

"United in Memory: 9/11 Victims Memorial Quilt." 2003. Promotional Brochure for National Sewing Weekend. Beaver Dam, WI: Nancy's Notions.

Valentine, Fawn. 2000. *West Virginia Quilts and Quiltmakers: Echoes from the Hills*. Athens, OH: Ohio University Press.

Von Gwinner, Schupe. 1988. *The History of the Patchwork Quilt: Origins, Traditions and Symbols of a Textile Art*. West Chester, PA: Schiffer Publishing Ltd.

Wagner-Pacifici, Robin, and Barry Schwartz. 1991. "The Vietnam Veterans Memorial: Commemorating a Difficult Past." *American Journal of Sociology* 97 (2): 376–420.

Walker, A.J. 1996. "Couples Watching Television: Gender, Power, and the Remote Control." *Journal of Marriage and Family* 58 (4): 813–823.

Wearing, Betsy. 1998. *Leisure and Feminist Theory*. Thousand Oaks, CA: Sage.

Weidlich, Lorre Marie. 1986. "Quilting Transformed: An Anthropological Approach to the Quilt Revival." Unpublished Ph.D. Dissertation, The University of Texas.

West, Candace, and Don H. Zimmerman. 1987. "Doing Gender." *Gender & Society* 1 (2): 125–151.

Wettre, Asa. 1995. *Old Swedish Quilts*. Loveland, CO: Interweave Press.

Williams, Joan. 2000. *Unbending Gender: Why Family and Work Conflict and What to Do About It*. New York: Oxford University Press.

Williams, Mary Rose. 1990. "A Reconceptualization of Protest Rhetoric: Characteristics of Quilts as Protest." Unpublished Ph.D. Dissertation, The University of Oregon.

Williams, Mary Rose. 1994. "A Reconceptualization of Protest Rhetoric: Women's Quilts as Rhetorical Forms." *Women's Studies in Communication* 17 (2): 20–44.

Wolf, Diane L. 1996. *Feminist Dilemmas in Fieldwork*. Boulder, CO: Westview Press.

Woolf, Virginia. 1929. *A Room of One's Own*. San Diego, CA: Harcourt Brace & Company.

Wooten, David B. 2000. "Qualitative Steps Toward an Expanded Model of Anxiety in Gift-Giving." *Journal of Consumer Research* 27 (June): 84–95.

Zerubavel, Eviatar. 1996. "Social Memories: Steps to a Sociology of the Past." *Qualitative Sociology* 19 (3): 283–300.

Zolberg, Vera L., and Joni Maya Cherbo (Eds). 1997. *Outsider Art: Contesting Boundaries in Contemporary Culture*. Cambridge: Cambridge University Press.

# INDEX

Abrahams, Ethel Ewert, 77
Acker, Joan, 22
Adams County Ohio Quilt Sampler Project, 18
Adler, Patricia A., 5
Alliance for American Quilts, The, 12
American Quilt Study Group, The, 12
American Quilter's Society, 10
American Sewing Guild, The, 10
Amish quilts, 2–4, 23, 61
Amott, Teresa, 54
Anderson, Laura, 63
Aptheker, Bettina, 20, 30
Ardery, Julia. S., 20
Avni, Noga, 93

Baca Zinn, Maxine, 27, 31, 33, 37
Baldwin, J.H., 99, 108
Baldwin, Cheryl K., 108
Barkley Brown, Elsa, 23
barn quilt, 18–19
Barn Quilts of Grundy County, IA, 18
Barn Quilts of Pocahontas County, IA, 18
Barn Quilts of Sac County, IA, 18
Barreras, Vivian, 108
Bartram, Sherry A., 77
Bassett, Lynne, 7
Bateson, Mary Catherine, 20
Beardsley, John, 13–14, 18
Beaudoin-Ross, Jacqueline, 7
Becker, Howard, 13, 20, 59, 89
Belk, Russell W., 77
Benberry, Cuesta, 8, 23
Beoku-Betts, Josephine, 22, 31, 37
Berenson, Kathryn, 6
Blumer, Herbert, 27
Brackett, Kim Pettigrew, 77, 108
Brackman, Barbara, 7, 9, 20, 30

British Quilt Study Group, The, 12
Burman, Barbara, 9, 22
Butsch, Richard, 21

Callahan, Nancy, 18
Cerny, Catherine, 8, 17, 23
Chafetz, Janet Saltzman, 22, 104, 132
Channer, Catherine, 10
Cheek, Cheryl, 58
childcare, 22, 63, 115
children
    gifting quilts to, 43, 55–6, 132
    leaving home, 5, 58–60, 104–6
    rearing, 6, 13, 22, 60, 95
    teaching to quilt and, 51
Colby, Averil, 6–7
collecting
    fabric and, 13, 40, 51, 77–93, 120
    quilts and, 12–13, 77
collective memory, 17, 113, 124
collectors, 1–2, 12, 77–8, 83–4, 91–3
Collins, Patricia Hill, 7, 30, 133
Collis, Marion, 97, 108
community
    academic, 12, 35
    quilting, 57, 70, 116–17, 128, 132, 137
Coser, Lewis, 89
Cox, Meg, 12
Crosby, Faye, 58, 132
Crothers, Pat, 8
Csikszentmihalyi, Mihaly, 61, 64, 77
cultural production, 50
    gendered, 5–6, 20–1, 27, 29, 139
    non-economic, 20–1, 136–40
Curran, Geoffrey M., 20

Delaney-Mech, Susan, M.D., 63

DeVault, Marjorie L., 20, 22
deviance, 25, 78, 82, 87, 90–2
Di Leonardo, Micaela, 22
Dickerson, Anne E., 113, 130
Doyle, Amanda, 23, 78, 96
Dunn, Margaret M., 23

Eikmeier, Barbara J., 23
Elsley, Judy, 23, 79
Emerson, Robert M., 31
Enarson, Elaine, 18
Ethridge, F. Maurice, 21
Evetts, Julia, 58–9

fabric
    hoarding and, 25, 78, 86, 88, 90–1, 93
    shopping and, 61, 84
    stash and, 25, 40, 77–93, 105, 111, 137
family
    constraints and, 97, 107
    duties and, 20, 91, 98
    heterosexual families, 44, 89, 107, 139
    grandchildren, 51, 74, 82, 103, 135
    see also childcare, children, spouses
feminine
    stereotypes, 50, 108
    see also traditional
feminist methodology, see methods
feminized activities, 22–5 passim, 37, 65, 91–2, 134, 137–9
Ferriss, Lucy, 20–1
fieldwork, see methods
Fine, Gary Alan, 20–1
Fogle, Melinda, 77
Fonow, Mary Margaret, 30
Forrest, John, 23
Foster, Joan, 7
Freeman, Roland L., 7–8, 23
Freysinger, Valeria J., 104
Friedlich, Karla, 8
Fry, Gladys-Marie, 7–8, 23

Gabbert, Lisa, 78
Geertz, Clifford, 27–9, 36

gendered
    assumptions and, 24, 27, 40
    leisure and, 6, 129
Gervais, Sandy, 79
gifting quilts
    as carework, 25, 35, 43, 117–23, 138
    as gendered tradition, 43, 47, 92, 129, 132–3
    as way to establish ties, 43, 47, 70–1, 96–7, 111, 127
    family and, 51, 55–8
    historically, 7
    personal enjoyment via, 4
    reason to quilt, 5, 108
    responses, 72
    unintended uses, 1, 71–4, 137
Gillespie, Dair L., 77, 99, 108
Glaser, Barney G., 35
Gluck, Sherna Berger, 30
Goff, Stephen J., 77, 99, 108
Goffman, Erving, 5, 49, 89, 93
greedy institution, 89–90
Green, Eileen, 58, 89, 104
Griswold, Wendy, 74
guilds, 10, 54, 60–1, 64, 112, 116
    fieldwork and, 31–2, 36, 44–5
guilt, 25, 62, 77–8, 87–99 passim, 103
Gunn, Virginia, 8, 17

Halbwachs, Maurice, 113–14
Hanson, Marin, 23
Harding, Sandra, 30
Harre, Ron, 27
Harrington, C. Lee, 108
Harris, Mary, 22
Hawley, Jana M., 23
Hays, Sharon, 132
heirlooms, 5, 55, 58, 124, 129, 135–6
Herda, Phyllis S., 23
heritage
    cultural, 7, 134
    quilting, 50–5, 117–18, 121
Herridge, Kristi L., 58, 104
Hertz, Rosanna, 27, 33
heterosexual families, see family

Hochschild, Arlie Russell, 22, 58, 70, 89, 131–2
Holstein, Jonathan, 12–13
Holyfield, Lori, 59, 134
Hurston, Zora Neale, 30

Ice, Joyce Ann, 23
identity
    as a quilter, 29, 49, 61–71 passim, 86–9
        passim, 133–4
    development, 5–6, 23,
    marginalized, 24, 49
    subjective careers and, 58–9
International Quilt Study Center, 7, 12, 128
interviews, *see* methods

Janesick, Valerie, 33, 35
Jenkins, Susan, 7
Johnson, Joyce Starr, 58
Jones, Cleve, 17, 126

Kallet, Marilyn, 20
Kelly, Nuala, 9
Kelly, Ryan E., 113, 130
Kendall, Diana, 58
King, Faye Lynn, 58
Kotre, John, 57
Krenske, Leigh, 20
Krouse, Mary Elizabeth, 23

Lang, Gladys Engel, 22
Langellier, Kristin M., 23
Larson, Reed W., 104
Laureau, Annette, 33
Leman Publications, Inc, 10, 24, 59, 109, 139
Lenz, Heather, 50
Lewis, Jacqueline, 23, 126, 135
Liddell, Jill, 6
Lincoln, Yvonne S., 33
Lipsett, Linda Otto, 7, 18
Long, Elizabeth, 22
Lucal, Betsy, 5
Lydon, Susan Gordon, 79
Lynch, Annette, 48
Lyons, Nick, 17, 67

Macdonald, Anne L, 9–10, 79
Madson, John, 67
Mainardi, Patricia, 79
Major, Wayne F., 77, 99
Marks, S.R., 104
Mattingly, Marybeth, 58, 70, 89, 104, 131
Mavor, Carol, 77
McMorris, Penny, 13
Mead, George Herbert, 27
methods
    feminist methodology, 27, 30–3
    fieldwork, 6, 24, 33, 40, 44
    interviews, 6, 27, 31–6, 41
    purposive snowball sampling, 31–2
    qualitative research, 24, 27–8, 31, 35
Miller, Jean Baker, 57
Mishler, Elliott G., 20
Mueller, Mary-Rose, 23
Myers, Lisa R., 79

NAMES Project AIDS Memorial Quilt, 14,
    119–21, 124, 131
National Quilting Association, 10
Neapolitan, Jerry, 21
needlework, 53, 91, 136
Nelson, Nancy J., 9, 23
Not Barn Yesterday: A Clothesline of Quilts in
    Appalachia, 18
Notman, Malkah Topin, 57

Oakley, Ann, 22, 32, 132
Ohio Quilt Barns, 18
Olick, Jeffrey, 113
Olsen, Tillie, 20–2
*Oprah Winfrey Show, The*, 136
Ostrander, Susan A., 58

Palliser, Mrs. Bury, 10
Parker, Rozsika, 79, 107
patchwork, 6–7, 10, 14, 18, 56
Patchwork Jewels of Monroe County, 18
*People Magazine*, 136
Pershing, Linda, 46
Peterson, Karin E., 12–13, 20

Peterson, Richard A., 20
Proeller, Marie, 13
Przybysz, Jane, 23
purposive snowball, *see* methods

qualitative research, *see* methods
Quilt Index, The, 12
Quilt National, 10
*Quilt Treasures of Great Britain*, 7, 12
Quilter Community, The, 7, 12
Quilter's News Network, 10, 12
Quiltmakers of Gee's Bend, The, 4, 13–4, 18
Quiltmakers of Georgia, The, 121

Radner, Joan Newlon, 79
Radway, Janice, 22, 77, 108
Rake, Valerie Sanders, 23
Reinharz, Shulamit, 20, 27, 30–1, 33
Rhoades, Ruth, 9
Richardson, Laurel, 20
Rolfe, Margaret, 23
Romero, Mary, 20
Rothbart, Davy, 78
Rubin, Herbert J., 32
Ruyak, Jacqueline, 11
Ryer, John, 79

Schofield-Tomschin, Sherry, 23, 64
Schwartz, Barry, 72, 112–13, 138
second shift, 70, 89, 131
Shapiro, Patricia Gottlieb, 58
Shaw, Susan M., 31, 97
Siegenthaler, Kim L., 77
Sinha, Anita, 21
Smith, Dorothy E., 33
snowball sampling, *see* methods
Spain, Daphne, 95
spouses
  interviews and, 41
  leisure, 70, 77–8,
  retirement and, 58–9
  time and, 57, 129–30
  quilting space and, 80, 101, 106
Stalp, Marybeth C., 8–9, 40, 48, 58, 61, 67, 83, 89, 96–7, 107, 130, 139

stash, *see* fabric
Stebbins, Robert A., 9, 20, 59, 96–7, 107–8
Stoller, Debbie, 79, 136
Stone, Gregory, 63, 112
subjective careers, 25, 49, 58–71 passim, 132–3, 137

textile, 12, 14, 17, 23–4
Thompson, Shona M., 22, 104, 132
Thorne, Barrie, 5
Tobin, Jacqueline L., 18
Todd, Sharon Leidy, 23
Tokyo Great International Quilt Festival, 11
Torsney, Cheryl B., 79
traditional
  activities
    families, 25, 58, 89–90, 95, 97
    femininity, 8, 58, 108, 118
  quilts, 1–2, 7, 10–11, 23
Tuchman, Gayle, 22

United in Memory: 9/11 Victims Memorial Quilt, 17–18, 122–4
University of Georgia, 122
University of Nebraska, 12, 128

Valentine, Fawn, 9
Von Gwinner, Schupe, 6–7

Wagner-Pacifici, Robin, 138
Walker, A.J., 104
Wearing, Betsy, 58
Weidlich, Lorre Marie, 23
West, Candace, 5
Wettre, Asa, 7
Williams, Joan, 46, 131–2
Williams, Mary Rose, 8
Wolf, Diane L., 33
Woolf, Virginia, 129
Wooten, David B., 72

Zerubavel, Eviatar, 113
Zolberg, Vera L., 13, 20, 28, 78